Sunset

Discovery Trips in
Europe

By the Editors of Sunset Books and Sunset Magazine

Fira, on island of Thera, Greece

LANE PUBLISHING CO. ▪ MENLO PARK, CALIFORNIA

Book Editor
Cornelia Fogle

Design
Joe di Chiarro

Maps
Eureka Cartography
  John Parsons
  Mark Williams
Vernon Koski
Ells Marugg

Illustrations
Rik Olson

Alsatian couple, Eguisheim, France

Cover: Ruins of Urquhart Castle overlook Loch Ness, south of Inverness, Scotland (see page 18). Design by Susan Bryant. Photography by Darrow M. Watt.

Editor, Sunset Books: Elizabeth L. Hogan

First printing January 1989

Copyright © 1989, 1980, 1972, 1967, Lane Publishing Co., Menlo Park, CA 94025. Fourth edition. World rights reserved. No part of this publication may be reproduced by any mechanical, photographic, or electronic process, or in the form of a phonographic recording, nor may it be stored in a retrieval system, transmitted, or otherwise copied for public or private use without prior written permission from the publisher. Library of Congress Catalog Card Number: 88-51142. ISBN 0-376-06174-X. Lithographed in the United States.

Discover Europe's Special Places

Europe holds few secrets anymore. Yet each trip can yield newly discovered destinations and experiences that create special memories. In this book, we present a lively selection of ideas to whet your travel appetite and enhance your next European adventure.

Most of the excursions suggested on these pages lure you away from cities and into the surrounding countryside, to places with rich traditional or scenic appeal. Many offer opportunities to wander off the usual tourist route in pursuit of your favorite hobby or special interest. If your time is limited, there are trips to enjoy in one eventful day. Many take advantage of public transportation. Other excursions will be most enjoyed if you travel independently by car.

Our thanks go to the many national tourist organizations and individuals who assisted in the preparation of this guide. Special appreciation goes to the Netherlands Board of Tourism, especially Gerrie Davidson and Willem Schouten; KLM Royal Dutch Airlines, especially Karen Kozel; the Scandinavian Tourist Board, especially Jens Michael Wilhelmsborg; Scandinavian Airlines System; the Danish Tourist Board, especially Bo Biilmann; the Italian Government Tourist Office, especially Agostino Petti and Nicoló R. Fougier; and the Swiss National Tourist Office, especially Joe Lustenberger.

CONTENTS

EUROPE'S SPECIAL PLEASURES

Whether you're planning your first or your twenty-first trip to Europe, wonderful adventures await you. Each region and season has its special pleasures, and we hope *Discovery Trips in Europe* will offer fresh ideas to enhance your journey.

Many of the excursions in this book can be fitted into a flexible itinerary on short notice and can be enjoyed in a few hours. Others cover a larger area and require more time and planning. Often several excursions can be combined into a loop trip.

Discovery is the essence of travel. Whether you seek stimulation or relaxation on your trip abroad, you'll enrich your experience by including new activities along with familiar ones.

Be adventuresome. Range outside the large cities to discover the real Europe off the main routes. Take time to explore charming country byways that follow the contours of the land. As you sharpen your senses, you'll revel in small delights—the patterns of cultivated fields, the shapes of mountains cleanly etched against the sky, the local ways of staking grapevines or of stacking freshly cut hay to dry in the sun.

Be a participant, not merely a spectator. Take a hike in the hills, rent a bicycle, ride a local bus, or explore inland waterways by boat. Stay a few days with a farm family, or enjoy the hospitality of castle hotels or country inns. Allow time to explore village markets, to pause at a seaside fish auction, or to linger at a sidewalk cafe. Pursue your favorite leisure-time interests—music, art, sports activities, handicrafts—in a foreign locale.

Travel is an experience of the senses, a blending of vivid impressions you recall long after photographs have been put away. It provides an incomparable opportunity to broaden your horizons in human as well as geographic terms. Often the most fascinating discoveries are those you make about yourself.

As you plan your explorations, remember that your trip is more than just an itinerary—it's a means of indulging your dreams, of capturing your fantasies, and of enjoying serendipitous pleasures along the way.

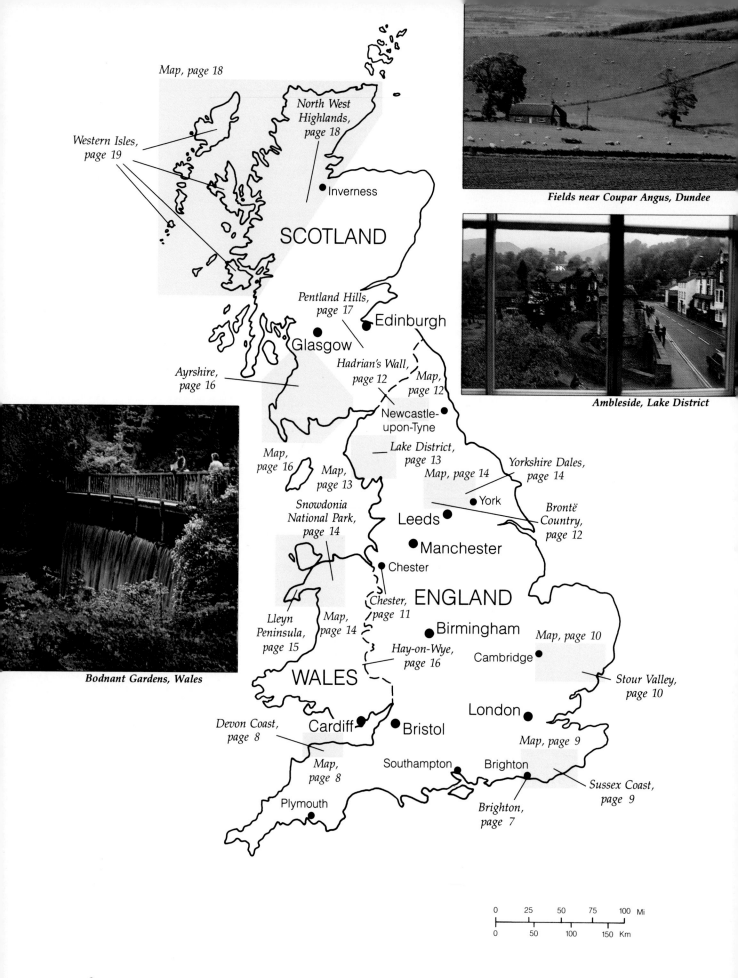

Fields near Coupar Angus, Dundee

Ambleside, Lake District

Bodnant Gardens, Wales

Map, page 18

*Western Isles,
page 19*

*North West
Highlands,
page 18*

• Inverness

SCOTLAND

*Pentland Hills,
page 17*

● Glasgow   Edinburgh

*Ayrshire,
page 16*

*Hadrian's Wall,
page 12*

*Map,
page 12*

Newcastle-
upon-Tyne •

*Map,
page 16*

*Map,
page 13*

*Lake District,
page 13*

Map, page 14

*Yorkshire Dales,
page 14*

• York

*Snowdonia
National Park,
page 14*

Leeds
●

*Brontë
Country,
page 12*

● Manchester

Chester •

*Chester,
page 11*

ENGLAND

*Lleyn
Peninsula,
page 15*

*Map,
page 14*

● Birmingham

Map, page 10

*Hay-on-Wye,
page 16*

Cambridge •

WALES

*Stour Valley,
page 10*

London
●

*Devon Coast,
page 8*

Cardiff
●

● Bristol

Map, page 9

*Map,
page 8*

Southampton •

Brighton
●

*Sussex Coast,
page 9*

• Plymouth

*Brighton,
page 7*

| 0 | 25 | 50 | 75 | 100 | Mi |
| 0 | 50 | 100 | 150 | | Km |

BRITAIN

England ▪ Wales ▪ Scotland

Intriguing variety whets the explorer's travel appetite in Britain. Here you'll find historic towns and captivating villages, dramatic coastlines and pastoral countryside, lonely moors and windswept isles.

You can hike along the coast or into wooded hills, stroll through exceptional gardens, ride narrow-gauge steam trains or cruise on scenic waterways, follow in the footsteps of the Romans, venture to lonely Atlantic islands, or seek out a landscape associated with a favorite writer or painter.

EXUBERANT BRIGHTON

See map page 9

A lively town of delightful architectural contrasts, Brighton is one of England's oldest and best-known seaside resorts. It began as a simple fishing village but became fashionable in the 18th century when the Prince of Wales (later George IV) spent much of his time there and built the riotously extravagant Royal Pavilion.

Many elegant Regency houses remain, most notably in and around Lewes Crescent. They contrast with the informal district known as The Lanes, a delightful maze of narrow pedestrian streets lined with one-time fishermen's cottages; now restored, they contain antique stores, a variety of shops, and restaurants.

Completed in 1822, the magical Royal Pavilion is an oriental fantasy complete with domes and minarets. Its exterior architecture is reminiscent of Moghul India, while Chinese themes prevail in the opulent interior decoration. The pavilion contains some of the original furnishings.

Brighton's Marina is Europe's largest yacht harbor. Visitors can arrange for deep-sea fishing excursions or harbor sightseeing trips. You can enjoy bracing sea air on a stroll along the seafront promenade, watch dolphins at the Palace Pier aquarium, visit local museums, or ride the local railway to an open-air swimming pool.

▦ **TOURING TIPS** Frequent trains depart from London's Victoria Station for Brighton, covering the 53 miles in less than an hour. Information centers are located at Marlborough House, 54 Old Steine (open daily from March to mid-September, daily except Sunday the rest of the year), and at the Brighton seafront. Larger stores are open Monday through Saturday; shops close early Wednesday in the St. James Street area, and early Thursday on London and Western roads. The Royal Pavilion is open daily except December 25 and 26; hours are 10 A.M. to 6 P.M. from June to September, 10 to 5 the rest of the year.

Devon hikers follow clifftop path high above Bristol Channel. Trail begins in Lynton and heads west to Valley of the Rocks.

Along the seacoast. Another favorite route is the cliff path above the sea from Lynton west to the Valley of the Rocks, and beyond to Combe Martin. The countryside here typifies the varied charm of the north Devon coast: rugged cliffs and headlands punctuated by beaches, and high rolling hills where you'll find the area's famed strawberry fields.

West along the path is Ilfracombe, once a bathing resort for wealthy Victorians. Here you can enjoy numerous beaches in coves (including two reached by tunnels through rocks), a promenade, and public gardens for strolling. Local commercial fishermen and visiting yachters mingle around the harbor.

Superb coastal views await hikers on the zigzag Torrs Walk path west of town; it leads to Lee, a tiny village known for its fuchsias. A more rugged path continues around Lee Bay to Bull Point, where a lighthouse guides boats around the coast into the Bristol Channel.

■ **TOURING TIPS** You can reach north Devon by train from London, departing from either Paddington or Waterloo station and changing trains at Exeter for Barnstaple. Local buses connect the region's larger towns. Coastal inns, frequented by fishermen, offer seafood fresh from the channel. In many of these, you can sample hard cider made from local apples as well as regular pub fare. You may prefer to indulge in a Devon cream tea—a pot of tea accompanied by scones, butter, jam, and farm-fresh clotted cream.

HIKING THE DEVON COAST

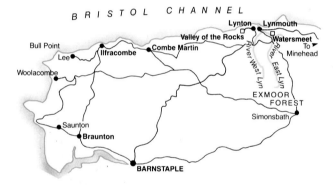

A favorite destination for English family vacations, the north Devon coast offers rugged scenery and inviting villages without the crowds that often take over popular port towns. Much of this seacoast belongs to the National Trust and is preserved for its great scenic beauty.

Hikers enjoy footpaths—overlooking the Bristol Channel, along wooded river valleys, and through meadows and moorland dotted with grazing sheep.

River valleys. A funicular railway links the towns of Lynton and Lynmouth. From Lynton, high on a cliff overlooking the Bristol Channel, you descend some 400 feet to Lynmouth, where the rivers East Lyn and West Lyn meet and pour into the sea. Attractive cottages flank the small harbor, in which fishing boats anchor each evening.

From Lynmouth, it's a pleasant walk upstream along wooded riverbanks—up the East Lyn through a rock-strewn valley to Watersmeet, and along the West Lyn to Glen Lyn. To sample the lonely moorland, head southeast into Somerset's Exmoor Forest.

ENGLISH GARDENS

Spring is the time to see England at its blooming best, but you'll find public and private gardens to browse in whenever you visit. Most are open daily between March and October; many admit visitors year round.

In London, flower lovers will head for Hyde Park, Holland Park, and Kensington Gardens. The big Chelsea Flower Show takes place the third week of May on the grounds of the Royal Hospital in Chelsea.

Other fine gardens near London include the Royal Botanic Gardens at Kew and the gardens at Hampton Court Palace, both west of London along the River Thames; and the Wisley Garden of the Royal Horticultural Society at Wisley in Surrey, south of London.

Among the outstanding gardens in the countryside are Bodnant Garden at Tal-y-Cafn, in the Vale of Conway, Wales (see page 15); Hidcote Manor Garden, northeast of Chipping Campden in Gloucestershire; the Sissinghurst Castle gardens, near the village of Sissinghurst, Kent; the Exbury Gardens at Exbury, Hampshire; and the Savill Garden at Windsor Great Park, Berkshire.

Several publications, available at British bookshops and tourist information centers, provide full details on the gardens and when to visit them.

THE HISTORIC SUSSEX COAST

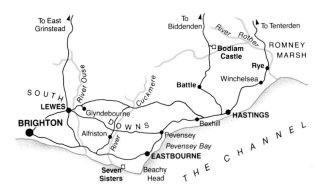

Throughout history, invaders have entered Britain from its southeast coast. Romans landed here in A.D. 43, followed in the 5th and 6th centuries by Anglo-Saxon tribesmen. Hastings and other seaport towns—known as the Cinque Ports—were established to repel Danish invaders. In 1066, William of Normandy and his troops landed at Pevensey Bay and went on to conquer Saxon troops in the famous battle north of Hastings.

Today you can visit these historic sites and relax in holiday resorts that dot the East Sussex seacoast. Inland are the rolling green hills of the South Downs.

Rye. Built on a hill above the River Rother, historic Rye was an important seaport in medieval times. The sea began to recede in the 16th century, and the town now overlooks flat and misty Romney Marsh. Formerly a haunt of smugglers, the marsh now attracts bird-watchers, who come to see its migratory waterfowl and seabirds.

Steep cobbled streets climb the slopes of the town. On a stroll you'll find fascinating old buildings bordering Mermaid Street, Church Square, Watchbell Street, and High Street. Town landmarks include St. Mary's Church, built in 1120, with its remarkable clock; the 18th-century Lamb House, once the home of novelist Henry James; and Ypres Tower, now a museum.

The town's most famous building is the renowned Mermaid Inn, built in 1420. Once a rendezvous for smugglers, the inn still accommodates travelers.

Winchelsea. Another fortified seaport in medieval days, this peaceful village occupies a hilltop southwest of Rye. You'll enjoy a short stroll around the orderly little town, with its old church, tree-shaded churchyard, and white houses adorned with climbing roses and wisteria.

Hastings. Originally the chief member of the Cinque Ports, Hastings has been a fishing village since Roman times. At the east end of town, you'll see the hilltop ruins of a castle built by William the Conqueror after his victory. Below, fishermen pull their boats onto the shore to unload their catch. Nearby, you can stroll through the narrow streets of the old fishermen's quarter.

After 18th-century doctors discovered the benefits of sea air, Hastings became a popular coastal resort. Sam-ple this fresh air for yourself on a promenade stroll or an energetic walk along the cliffs east of town. You can also visit the amusement arcades and a seafront pavilion. Don't miss the Hastings Embroidery, a modern Bayeux-style tapestry depicting scenes from British history from 1066 to the present.

At the town of Battle, north of Hastings, an abbey stands on the site where William triumphed over King Harold in the Battle of Hastings. A village grew up outside the abbey; many of its buildings date from the 13th and 14th centuries.

Bodiam Castle, 11 miles north of Hastings, is a romantic ruin of a moated castle, built in 1385 for protection against French raids. From Easter through October, visitors are welcome daily between 10 A.M. and 6 P.M. (or sunset); in winter, the castle is closed on Sunday.

Pevensey. Nearly 2000 years ago, boats carrying Roman soldiers sailed into Pevensey Bay. Later, in 1066, William of Normandy landed on this shore.

Huge 4th-century Roman walls enclose the ruins of medieval Pevensey Castle, which was built on the site of an earlier Roman fortress.

In the village outside the castle walls, take a look at the fine old buildings bordering High Street. Distinctive village buildings include the stone courthouse, museum, and jail. As with other towns along this coast, the retreating sea stranded Pevensey some distance inland.

Eastbourne. One of the most popular resorts on Britain's south coast, Eastbourne enjoys an attractive setting beside the high, white cliffs of Beachy Head. The town has a 3-mile seafront with traditional amusements, flower gardens, a pier, and a bandstand.

Stroll around the older section of town to enjoy its many fine buildings. One, known as Pilgrims, dates from the early 12th century and has underground passages linking it to St. Mary's Church and to the Lamb Inn, both built in the same era.

South Downs Way. Hikers and pony trekkers enjoy superb, well-marked paths along the coast, including the South Downs Way. This long-distance footpath extends from Beachy Head, southwest of Eastbourne, some 80 miles west to Brighton and beyond. Mounds and earthworks along the track mark sites of Stone Age forts.

A branch of the South Downs Way runs west from Beachy Head along the chalk cliffs called the Seven Sisters. Walkers can enjoy an exhilarating clifftop hike.

Inland at Lewes, a historic town on the River Ouse, you can visit Barbican House museum and the house given by Henry VIII to his fourth wife, Anne of Cleves, when he divorced her. Glyndebourne has a summer opera season from late May to August. Once a smugglers' hideout, Alfriston has interesting old buildings.

■ **TOURING TIPS** Trains for Rye, Hastings, and Battle depart from Charing Cross and Waterloo East stations; trains bound for Lewes, Eastbourne, and Pevensey leave from Victoria Station. National Express buses depart from London's Victoria Coach Station for Lewes, Hastings, and Battle (summer only). You'll find tourist information centers in Rye, Hastings, and Eastbourne. Many shops close early on Tuesday in Rye; Wednesday in Hastings, Battle, and Eastbourne; and Thursday in Pevensey.

BYWAYS IN SLEEPY SUFFOLK

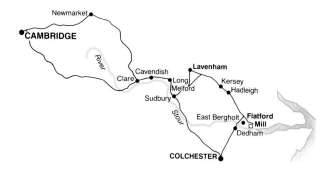

Travelers who explore English country byways delight in serendipitous discoveries—delightful stone villages, impressive churches, half-timbered inns, roadside craft shops, thatched cottages with country gardens. One of the loveliest regions is uncrowded East Anglia; its pastoral landscape was immortalized in the paintings of John Constable, who grew up in the Stour Valley on the border of Suffolk and Essex.

The English wool boom of the 14th, 15th, and 16th centuries heaped prosperity on many towns and villages in Suffolk, as it did elsewhere in the country. Wealthy merchants and traders spent money freely on splendid houses and great parish churches. Many East Anglian villages preserve a rich legacy of handsome old buildings, each with its church tower or spire rising prominently above the countryside. You'll come upon them as you drive along country roads.

The Stour Valley. Some of Suffolk's most delightful villages are sprinkled through the quiet Stour Valley. The meandering river marks the boundary between the counties of Suffolk, north of the river, and Essex, to the south. From Cambridge, follow the road southeast through the rolling Gog Magog Hills.

You'll come upon such delightful hamlets as Clare, where old houses display the East Anglian craft of pargeting, a technique that decorates exterior walls with raised ornamental plasterwork. At Cavendish, attractive thatched cottages face a wide village green.

Dignified houses and attractive shops line Long Melford's wide thoroughfare. This Suffolk town has a lovely church, half-timbered buildings, and two impressive mansions, Kentwell Hall and the Tudor brick Melford Hall.

Sudbury, a sturdy country market town, was the birthplace of painter Thomas Gainsborough. Though he gained his primary fame painting portraits of the aristocracy, he also re-created scenes of the countryside around his native town. The Gainsborough family home is now a museum.

Ornamental plasterwork, called pargeting, adorns exterior walls of many East Anglian houses. In Suffolk village of Clare, pargeting decorates façade of this house built in 1473.

Other Suffolk villages. North of the Stour valley, you'll enjoy a visit to Lavenham, where the town's wool-trading ancestors built a magnificent Perpendicular-style church. However, the attractive town is best known for its wealth of black-and-white, timber-framed cottages and venerable inns.

Timbered and pastel-tinted cottages line the main street of Kersey, one of Suffolk's prettiest villages. Its church sits high above on a hill. At its base, a shallow, tree-shaded stream flows across the village's main road; watch for ducks as you splash through the water. The wool town of Kersey gave its name to a coarse cloth; nearby Lindsey contributed its name to linsey-woolsey, a fabric that clothed many American colonists.

In Hadleigh, town houses and mansions from the Tudor, Elizabethan, and Jacobean periods mix with smaller houses and cottages built in half-timbered style.

Constable country. The lush valley near the mouth of the Stour is known as Constable country, a region much painted by landscape artist John Constable. Born in East Bergholt in 1776, he roamed these meadows, heaths, and woodlands as a youth.

Near Dedham you can visit two places closely associated with Constable: Flatford Mill, which was once operated by the Constable family; and Willy Lott's cottage, the subject of one of Constable's best-known paintings, which looks much as it did in the artist's day.

Cross the wooden bridge and follow the towpath into a rural world of trees, meadows, and winding river.

■ **TOURING TIPS** You can travel to Cambridge by train from London's Liverpool Street or King's Cross stations. Buses serve some of the larger Suffolk towns, but you'll see the region best by car. Attractions are generally open daily from April to October, weekends only in winter.

ANCIENT CHESTER

See map page 6

One of Britain's oldest cities, Chester is the historical jewel of northwest England and Britain's only remaining completely walled city. Records of the town cover more than 1,900 years. Since that early era, rivers have silted up and defensive points on ancient walls now overlook meadows instead of the harbor.

Chester's captivating narrow streets and pedestrian thoroughfares maintain the original Roman pattern. Medieval buildings border many streets, making this town near the Welsh border a fascinating place to explore on foot. Chester is also Britain's premier shopping city outside London.

The most noteworthy survivor of the centuries is the 2-mile loop of 12-foot-high Roman and medieval walls that surrounds a portion of present-day Chester. Whatever the weather, take a walk along the top for intriguing glimpses into the remains of a 7,000-seat Roman amphitheater, ancient churchyards and cloistered gardens dating from the 9th century, Elizabethan row houses, 19th-century canals and ornate clock towers, and modern commercial districts. You'll also have wide-ranging views of lush green countryside and the River Dee.

Within the walls, parts of Northgate and Eastgate are reserved for pedestrians. Here and on Bridge and Watergate streets are The Rows—half-timbered, covered galleries with shops one level above the street. From April through September the town crier, dressed as a Victorian city bellman, cries the news and nonsense of the day at noon and 3 P.M.

Other streets also show great diversity of architectural styles: Grosvenor Street's Falcon Inn boasts a 16th-century facade and 13th-century cellars; nearby are fine restored 18th- and 19th-century buildings.

■ **TOURING TIPS** You can reach Chester by train from London's Euston Station in about 3 hours; it is 18 miles south of Liverpool and only 5 miles from the Welsh border. Stop at the visitor center, on Vicar's Lane across from the Roman amphitheater, for suggestions on planning your visit. The Chester Heritage Center on Bridge Street publishes inexpensive walking-tour booklets.

LONDON'S VILLAGES

Several of the once-rural villages absorbed during London's outward spread still retain much of their village character. There's something in the atmosphere, in their church steeples and graveyards, in the curving streets and narrow courtyards, in the contrast between urban and rural, that captures the imagination. An afternoon in one of these villages should end with a stop at one of its neighborhood pubs, where you absorb the flavor of small-town intimacy by chatting with the locals.

Hampstead is only a few minutes from Piccadilly Circus on the underground, yet the city seems distant as you stroll streets of the old village at the top of the hill and stride over the open expanse of Hampstead Heath. Hampstead has always been a favorite retreat for members of the literary and art worlds. In the 18th century it was also a spa.

On the other side of the heath is Highgate, where you admire gracious 18th-century houses and take refreshment at an inn beneath cherry trees. Older than Hampstead, Highgate existed long before wealthy refugees from the plague settled there in 1665. Stroll along the delightful Georgian residential streets of the old village. The hillside cemetery contains the tombs of Karl Marx and other famous people.

Other suburban villages also offer the charm of an earlier era. Kew, with its Royal Botanic Garden, has a village green lined by mellow old houses. Across the Thames from Kew is charming Strand-on-the-Green, and other pleasant Thames-side villages are found at Twickenham and Chiswick. In south London, Dulwich has a fine art gallery.

Hadrian's Wall snakes across lonely countryside of northern England at Walltown Crags, near Greenhead.

several miles westward to Steel Rigg. Another fine stretch of wall can be found at Walltown Crags.

South of the wall, Roman infantry and cavalry were garrisoned in 17 large forts. Excavated settlements and fortresses at Corbridge, Chesters, Housesteads, and Vindolanda, and museums near Carvoran (Walltown Crags) and Vindolanda offer insights into the surprisingly sophisticated life led during the Roman occupation.

■ **TOURING TIPS** **For a self-guided tour of the district, you'll want to purchase a guidebook with detailed maps and comments on specific attractions. The Tourist Information Centre in Hexham can help in finding local accommodations; it is open weekdays from 9 to 6 and Sundays from 1 to 5 from mid-May to mid-September, 9 to 5 weekdays the rest of the year. Another information center is located at Once Brewed Inn, near the Vindolanda site. Picnickers will find a pleasant lakeside site at Cawfields, north of Haltwhistle.**

ALONG HADRIAN'S WALL

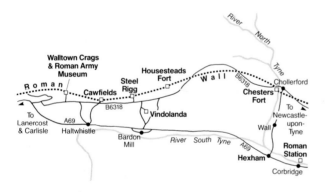

In the far north of England, Hadrian's Wall snakes across the rolling green hills of Northumberland and Cumbria. Often veiled by low-hanging mist and chilled by a stiff northwest wind, the wild and lonely countryside still retains the mood of the frontier. Sites of the main Roman outposts are never far from Route B6318, which parallels the wall along most of its way. Main arteries lead from Highway A69 to key points.

Built by order of Emperor Hadrian between A.D. 120 and 128, the wall traversed the narrow neck of Britain and gave protection against the wild tribes roaming lands to the north.

Primarily constructed of local stone, the wall averaged 15 feet in height and 7½ to 9 feet in thickness. The route can be walked its entire length, but the finest sections lie between Lancrost and Chollerford. From Housesteads, best preserved of the Roman forts, energetic walkers can stride along the top of the wall for

BRONTË COUNTRY

See map page 14

Travelers exploring the Yorkshire Dales may enjoy a detour to the small moorland village of Haworth, rich in memories of the Brontë sisters.

The three daughters of the local parson—Charlotte, Emily, and Anne—spent much of their brief lives in the parsonage in Haworth, with writing as their only emotional outlet. Their novels captured the wild beauty of the bleak Yorkshire countryside and brought literary recognition to their village.

If you approach from the north, the harsh reality of the Industrial Revolution confronts you at Keighley. Woolen mills rise starkly against the sky with tired, smoke-blackened houses clustered nearby.

As you climb Haworth's steep main street, note the stone blocks, set like steps to keep horses' hooves from slipping.

Facing the grim churchyard is the stone parsonage where the girls and their brother Branwell began writing as a childish game during long winters. The parsonage appears much as it was when the Brontës knew it. An adjoining museum contains handwritten manuscripts, letters, and first editions.

The lonely moorlands the Brontës knew so well became the setting for their best novels—Charlotte's *Jane Eyre*, Emily's *Wuthering Heights*, Anne's *The Tenant of Wildfell Hall*. If the day is pleasant, button your coat against the wind and follow the sisters' favorite walk across the moor to the Brontë's waterfall, about 1¼ miles from the paved road, where a small creek tumbles down the valley. Often you'll have the path to yourself, with only sheep for company. The dirt walk ends at a ruined farmhouse called Withens, the model for Wuthering Heights.

■ **TOURING TIPS** **To reach Haworth, drive west from Ilkley to Addingham, then turn south for Keighley. Follow road signs toward Halifax until you come to the Haworth turnoff. Wear sturdy shoes to the waterfall; the route is relatively level but uneven.**

WORDSWORTH'S LAKE DISTRICT

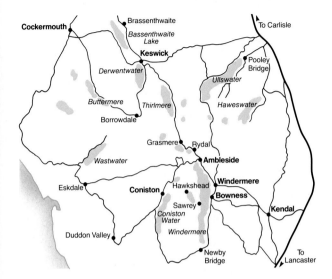

England's Lake District is closely associated with the poet William Wordsworth, who described this countryside as "the loveliest spot that man has ever known." It is a land of soft green hills spotted with lonely farms, old gray villages built of native limestone, sharp peaks and deep glens and waterfalls, more than a dozen large lakes, and a multitude of tiny tarns and ponds.

Born in Cockermouth in 1770, Wordsworth traveled widely but always returned to his favorite region. In the late 18th and early 19th centuries, he was joined in the Lake District by Samuel Taylor Coleridge, Robert Southey, and other poets. Their works—emotional, subjective, yearning for the past—ushered in the period of English Romanticism.

Roads through the Lake District are congested in summer, but there's little traffic in spring and fall.

The southern lakes.   The old town of Kendal is the gateway to Wordsworth's scenic countryside. Lake District National Park protects the heart of the region, which includes England's highest peak, Scafell Pike (3,210 feet), and its largest lake, Windermere, along with many smaller lakes and tarns, including Coniston, Grasmere, Rydal, and Esthwaite Water.

Many travelers stop at the lakeside town of Windermere or neighboring Bowness, or at Ambleside at the head of the lake. From mid-May to mid-September, lake cruises provide a look at Windermere's upper reaches and its wooded west shore.

You can visit several museums and sites associated with Wordsworth. In Grasmere, you can stop at the Wordsworth museum and also at tiny Dove Cottage, the poet's home for nine years. His final home at Rydal Mount, where he lived for 37 years until his death in 1850, is also open to the public.

In April you can see "Dora's field," full of the famous daffodils, and the "old grey stone" overlooking Rydal Water, where Wordsworth loved to sit. He is buried in Grasmere churchyard.

A museum in Keswick has some manuscripts of Wordsworth and Coleridge. In the market town of Cockermouth, Wordsworth's birthplace also is open to visitors.

Among other writers who settled in the Lake District was Beatrix Potter, author and illustrator of *The Tale of Peter Rabbit* and other children's stories. Her home and its grounds at Hill Top in Near Sawrey are open to the public.

Other attractions.   Beyond Wordsworth's countryside you can enjoy many additional activities. Families come to Keswick, the area's major resort, for boating on Derwentwater or Bassenthwaite Lake, and for mountain hikes or walks on the gentler fells nearby. Rock climbing is popular on Cumbria's crags. You can rent rowboats and powerboats at many lakeside resorts.

To the northeast you'll find Ullswater and several smaller lakes. The western lakes of Wastwater and Ennerdale and the delightful valleys of Eskdale and Dunnerdale have their own charm.

■ **TOURING TIPS**   You can reach the Lake District by road or rail via Kendal; buses travel between the region's main towns. However, you'll see the Lake District best by leisurely driving, stopping where and when you like. Country hotels, inns, and guest houses are clustered in the towns of Windermere, Bowness, and Ambleside—all bordering Windermere—and at Keswick, which overlooks Derwentwater. However, you'll find comfortable accommodations throughout the area. Tourist offices are open year round in Kendal, Windermere, and Keswick; many others are open in summer only. Inquire for help in obtaining accommodations or for information on Lake District attractions and events.

HORSE RACING AT NEWMARKET

Newmarket, northeast of Cambridge, has been the headquarters of British horse racing since the 17th century. On race days, this horse-crazy town is swamped by enthusiastic crowds. At other times, Newmarket is a staid country town; outdoor markets take place each Tuesday and Saturday.

Landmarks include the Jockey Club, originally built in 1722, and the historic Rutland Arms Hotel. In the National Horse Racing Museum, 90 High Street, you can learn more about the sport; the museum is closed each Monday except on Bank Holidays and during August.

Most of Britain's valuable racing thoroughbreds are bred and trained here. Often you'll see jockeys and stableboys around the rambling stables, and elegant racehorses and their riders enjoying a practice trot on the rolling heath encircling the town.

Many stud farms are located in the nearby countryside near Newmarket. In autumn and early winter, the annual bloodstock sales take place at Newmarket's stables.

SAMPLING THE YORKSHIRE DALES

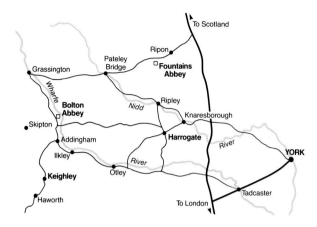

Not for every traveler is the solitude of Yorkshire's moors and dales, but those who seek out its hidden pleasures will be well rewarded. It has a wild grandeur all its own.

From high in the Pennine Mountains, rivers flow and tumble through the green hills, down pastoral valleys known as the Yorkshire Dales. Ruins of ancient abbeys, burned in the 16th century by troops of King Henry VIII, still stand as reminders of the awesome wealth and power of the medieval church.

A loop trip west from York offers a fine sampling of the Yorkshire Dales National Park. You'll follow the River Wharfe upstream to Grassington, then return to the city of York by a different route. You can detour to visit the Brönte museum in Haworth (see page 12).

The ruins of Bolton Abbey, overlooking the River Wharfe in a green and lovely setting, have fascinated many painters. English families also come here to enjoy the spacious grounds near the river. Built in 1151, the monastery once sheltered 200 people before it was surrendered to the king's forces.

Follow the path up Wharfedale into Bolton Woods, through some of the country's loveliest river scenery. A mile above the abbey, the Wharfe funnels into a narrow chasm of rushing white water, called The Strid. A path leads along the river.

Beyond Bolton Woods the road climbs into the grassy dales, crisscrossed by dry-stone walls and public paths. Sheep and cattle graze in solitude, and abandoned stone buildings are lonely mementos of former habitation.

From Pateley Bridge you can return to York through Nidderdale (the valley of the River Nidd) or you can head northeast toward Ripon. Here you can stop at the ruins of Fountains Abbey, another 12th-century monastery sacked by the king's troops during the dissolution of the monasteries in 1539–40.

■ **TOURING TIPS** Ilkley, Skipton, and Harrogate are the usual centers for touring the Yorkshire Dales. Tourist offices in these towns or in York can help you arrange accommodations in inns or bed-and-breakfast houses. Regional buses connect major towns, but check for specific information in York before starting out.

GREAT LITTLE TRAINS OF WALES

Are you a rail buff? No visit to Wales is complete without a ride on at least one of the narrow-gauge steam railways that chug through some of the region's prettiest countryside. Passengers delight in trips through wooded valleys, beside lakes, and even up the slopes of Snowdon, the highest mountain in Wales.

In the 19th century, many of these small trains hauled slate, coal, and farm produce from remote communities to seaports. But the slate trade declined, passengers gravitated to buses and automobiles, and the little trains seemed destined for oblivion. Fortunately, hundreds of railway enthusiasts volunteered long hours to restore the trains.

The railways transport holiday travelers through the scenic countryside on weekdays or weekends from Easter through September or October (daily in summer and during holiday periods). Inquire locally for a list of steam trains and current schedules.

A RUGGED CORNER OF WALES

The Welsh love their country with a fierce devotion. Pushed into Britain's wild western mountains during ancient battles with the Saxons, they defended their land passionately against all invaders, retreating to impregnable mountain strongholds.

In many ways, Wales remains a remote country-within-a-country. The pace of life reflects a calmer, simpler era. Though part of Britain, it has kept a unique identity, clinging to an ancient Celtic language and to many traditions. Place names, with their complicated spellings, may puzzle you, but you'll be relieved to know that everyone speaks English—with a charming lilt.

From the seaside resort of Llandudno, you can head inland, up the Vale of Conway, to Snowdonia National Park.

Conway. The daily life of a modern town goes on inside the medieval walls of Conway (Conwy in Welsh). A well-preserved castle dominates this fortress town, built in the 1280s by Edward I as a frontier post on the west bank of the River Conway. Immense circular towers rise above the thick curtain of a wall surrounding the town.

To appreciate Conway's special appeal, explore the castle and walk along the town walls and across Thomas Telford's famous suspension bridge. Discover old buildings and inns and unexpected touches of greenery. Along the ancient riverside quay, you'll mingle with anglers and yachters.

Vale of Conway. Traveling 20 miles inland up the scenic Vale of Conway to Betws-y-Coed, a crossroads town at the foot of Snowdon, you'll discover several inviting places to stop.

Near Tal-y-Cafn, the spectacular displays of Bodnant Gardens slope down the eastern bank of the River Conway with Snowdonia's peaks as a backdrop. One of Britain's finest gardens, Bodnant is open from April through October. Seasonal exhibits of azaleas, magnolias, rhododendrons, and roses enhance its landscaped ponds, formal terraces, and rock gardens.

At Llanrwst, a three-arch stone bridge spans the river.

Snowdonia National Park. Once a natural barrier against invaders, the high rugged mountains of Snowdonia are today a favorite destination for those who love the outdoors. Snowdon, at 3,560 feet, is the highest mountain in Wales. You can tour parts of Snowdonia National Park by car or mountain railway, picnic under the trees, or explore on foot. Nature trails leave from Beddgelert, Betws-y-Coed, Capel Curig, Maentwrog, and Pen-y-Gwryd.

Mountaineering, fishing, and pony trekking are other favorite activities. Look for mountain climbers near Llanberis Pass. In the town of Llanberis you can see Welsh textile designers at work at the Seion Weaving Centre.

The Snowdon Mountain Railway, a rack-and-pinion railway built in 1896, takes passengers from Llanberis on a 7-mile round trip to the summit of Snowdon. The railway climbs more than 3,000 feet in less than 5 miles. Allow about 2½ hours for the round trip.

■ **TOURING TIPS** From English border towns, trains travel west to Llandudno and along the north coast; local buses depart from main towns, following roundabout routes through the countryside. You can obtain information about Snowdonia National Park and nearby attractions at tourist information centers in the region.

Conway Castle, built in the 1280s, guarded mouth of river valley. From lofty viewpoint, you gaze over walls and towers.

LLEYN PENINSULA—A WORLD APART

See map page 14

The "Land's End" of northern Wales, the Lleyn Peninsula thrusts westward into the sea. Its gorse-covered slopes and breezy headlands seem a world apart, and you'll delight in the old-world atmosphere of its small towns and villages. One of its main attractions is historic Caernarvon Castle.

Churches along the peninsula's northern coast mark the route taken by ancient pilgrims to the old island of Bardsey, just off the peninsula's tip. Narrow lanes wander down to long, sandy beaches and secluded bays—smugglers' coves at one time—embraced by sheer cliffs. Massive stone ramparts more than 2,000 years old rise above wild heather near Llanaelhaearn, site of a large Iron Age stronghold.

The main holiday centers are along the protected south coast—Criccieth, Pwllheli, Abersoch, and Aberdaron. Criccieth has a medieval hilltop castle. Pwllheli bustles with summer activity, particularly on Wednesday when there's a market in the town square. Yachters anchor in sheltered harbors at Pwllheli and Abersoch.

Facing a river estuary just south of Lleyn Peninsula is whimsical Portmeirion, an architectural fantasy of Italianate buildings and landscaped subtropical gardens. Farther south is battle-scarred Harlech Castle, built in the 13th century by English invaders.

■ **TOURING TIPS** Welsh towns take on a festive air on market day, when farmers come to town to sell their produce. In Porthmadog at the mouth of the River Glaslyn, rail fans can board the narrow-gauge Festiniog Railway, built in 1836, for a trip into the hills above the Vale of Festiniog.

GOLFING IN SCOTLAND

What better way for a serious golfer to spend a holiday than by playing some of the most famous golf courses in the world?

Visiting golfers are welcome at the Old Course at St. Andrews, and at Turnberry, Troon, Gleneagles, Carnoustie, Nairn, Muirfield, Royal Dornoch, and elsewhere throughout Scotland—and at challenging golf courses in England and Wales. Add your name to the visitors' book and test your golfing skills against the course and the fabled Scottish weather.

Tee times are often hard to get, unless you're a single, but there's an easy way to beat this problem: Take one of the golfing tours available. You can build your own itinerary and travel independently by car, or you can join a group of fellow golfers. Costs include land transportation, accommodations, some meals, and greens and booking fees. Some tours offer special activities for non-golfers as well.

To learn more about golfing holidays, see your travel agent or contact the British Tourist Authority (address on page 128).

BROWSING FOR BOOKS IN WALES

See map page 6

Bibliophiles head for the Welsh border town of Hay-on-Wye, cradled in the valley of the River Wye between the Black Mountains and the Brecon Beacons. The self-proclaimed secondhand book capital of the world, this small town is a treasure house of previously owned and out-of-print works.

The first bookshop was opened in an old fire station in 1962 by Richard Booth, who has since added several stores. Many other booksellers have set up shop in Hay-on-Wye as well, and you'll find hundreds of thousands of volumes now cramming the shelves of more than a dozen bookstores.

Scholars, students, collectors, and bibliophiles seek books on every conceivable subject—from military history and modern poetry to science fiction and horticulture. You can find books on American Indians, natural history, French literature, golf, medieval architecture, astronomy, humor, geography, Shakespeare, Roman roads, children's literature, and photography, along with collectors' Bibles, fiction of all types, and rare first editions of beloved classics. Other shops stock maps and prints.

Open seven days a week year round, Hay-on-Wye stores will ship purchases to your home and handle mail orders.

A holiday in the border district offers many outdoor activities. Near Hay-on-Wye you'll find excellent salmon fishing, canoeing on the River Wye, and pony trekking and hiking in the gently rolling hills.

■ **TOURING TIPS** Hay-on-Wye is located about 60 miles north of Cardiff, and about 140 miles northwest of London. Trains leave London's Paddington Station for Hereford (3½ hours), where passengers change to a bus for an hour's ride to Hay-on-Wye. Accommodations in town include the 13th-century Old Black Lion Inn, with a pub and 10 rooms (in one of which Cromwell reportedly slept), several small hotels, and boardinghouses with bed-and-breakfast accommodations.

ROBERT BURNS'S AYRSHIRE

The uncrowded and peaceful countryside of southwest Scotland is Robert Burns country, the gentle land that nurtured and inspired Ayrshire's famed "poet of the common man." Born in Alloway, Burns immortalized many of the region's landmarks in his poems.

You can trace his life and learn more about his work by visiting several towns and villages near Ayr. Begin your quest at Burns's statue, which stands outside the Ayr railway station. Nearby in High Street is the thatched Tam o' Shanter Inn, named in honor of Burns's memorable poem; a brewhouse in the poet's day, it now houses a Burns museum. The 13th-century Auld Brig of Ayr still spans the river.

Alloway. The Burns Heritage Trail begins south of Ayr in the village of Alloway, where the poet was born in a humble gardener's cottage—the "auld clay biggin"—in 1759. Preserved as a Burns museum, the small thatched house and a museum next door contain exhibits reflecting his early life. The Land o' Burns Interpretive Centre is located nearby.

Burns's father is buried in the churchyard in the ruined Auld Kirk of Alloway, where in "Tam o' Shanter" the inebriated Tam watched witches revel. Tam fled on his horse to the Brig o' Doon, a simple arched bridge now flanked by gardens, knowing that the witches chasing him would not dare cross the running stream. A Burns monument overlooks the bridge over the Doon.

Heritage loop. From Alloway, the Burns family moved to Tarbolton, where Burns and his friends formed the Bachelors' Club. More Burns museums are located at Irvine, Kilmarnock, and Lochlea Farm, near Tarbolton.

In 1783 Burns moved to Mauchline, where he met and married Jean Armour in 1788; their Castle Street house is now a museum. You can stop for refreshment at Burns's favorite *howff*, or inn, Poosie Nansie's, which has changed little since his time. A Burns memorial tower stands just outside town.

At Kirkoswald you can visit the cottage of Tam's crony, Souter Johnnie, furnished as it was in Burns's day, with stone figures in the garden depicting characters from the poem.

Dumfries. From 1791 until his death 5 years later, Burns lived in Dumfries. Here he wrote some of his most famous songs, including "Auld Lang Syne" and "Ye Banks and Braes of Bonnie Doon." In Dumfries you can view his statue on High Street outside Greyfriars Church, see manuscripts in his old home on Burns Street (formerly Mill Street), and visit his mausoleum in St. Michael's churchyard. Burns memorabilia are featured in the town museum, at the Globe Inn, and at the Hole in the Wa' Tavern.

■ **TOURING TIPS** Ayr, the most popular holiday resort on Scotland's west coast, is about an hour's train ride southwest of Glasgow or a few minutes' drive south of Prestwick Airport. Information on the Burns Heritage Trail can be obtained at the interpretive center in Alloway or at various Burns museums.

SCOTLAND'S WHISKY TRAIL

One of the most popular of Britain's industrial tours is the Malt Whisky Trail, a signposted 70-mile route through the Spey Valley in the Grampian Mountains of northeast Scotland. To reach most of the distilleries, you'll venture up the tributary glens.

Free guided tours are offered in seven distilleries, representing the most honored names in single-malt whisky. Visitors observe the steps from malting to bottling. Most of the plants are open weekdays from April until October; some are also open Saturday in summer, and two offer tours during the winter.

For more information, write to the British Tourist Authority (address on page 128). Limited accommodations are available in Grantown-on-Spey, Keith, Elgin, and Dufftown.

Sheep claim the right-of-way in rural Scotland. Dogs herd animals along road, responding to shepherd's signals.

HIKING IN THE PENTLAND HILLS

See map page 6

A walk through the moorland pastures of Scotland's Pentland Hills will give you a chance to stretch your legs and to find out just why the Scotsman loves his hills. Robert Louis Stevenson, who wrote nostalgically of the region, lived near Swanston, in the hills southeast of Edinburgh.

The range begins about 3 miles south of Edinburgh and extends some 16 miles to the southwest. Few peaks are over 1,500 feet high. If you use the bus and streetcar services that virtually encircle the hills, you can take walks of 2 to 20 miles.

The charm of Stevenson's treasured "hills of home" lies in their many slopes and glens, in the splatterings of "stone glint" (sunlight on wet rocks), and in the luminous light that seems to radiate from rocks, plants, and streams. Clouds constantly shift and reform with the wind.

You climb the windswept hills, threading your way over rocks and clumps of grass, past sheep and patches of gorse and heather. Daisies, buttercups, bluebells, and yellow coltsfoot brush your ankles. Bracken uncurls its light green fronds in the spring and gleams bright gold in autumn. Only an occasional bird song or the bark of a shepherd's dog breaks the silence.

■ **TOURING TIPS** Tourist offices in Edinburgh can suggest good walking routes in the hills and provide information on bus routes and schedules. Take along a pedestrian's map of the Pentland Hills and Edinburgh District, which you can purchase in Edinburgh bookstores. High-topped, rubber-soled shoes or short boots are preferred footwear for walking in the hills, because the ground is boggy in places. Pack a knapsack with a picnic lunch and beverages.

SCOTLAND'S REMOTE HIGHLANDS

Brightly painted buildings line Tobermory's waterfront on island of Mull. Yachts anchor in harbor here in summer.

Renowned for splendid mountain scenery, the North West Highlands occupy a remote corner of Scotland. From Inverness, capital of the Highlands, roads lead south through the legendary Great Glen toward Fort William, and west into the sparsely populated, rugged countryside.

The Great Glen. The highway through the Great Glen parallels the Caledonian Canal, a 60-mile waterway linking Loch Ness and Loch Lochy, which provides a water route between the North Sea and Irish Sea. Anglers come to this district to fish the lake and river waters, and pony trekkers and hikers head into the spacious hill country.

About 1½ miles southeast of Drumnadrochit, the 16th-century ruins of Urquhart Castle command a promontory overlooking Loch Ness. Like most visitors, you'll probably scan the waters for the legendary Loch Ness monster.

An important touring center for the Western Highlands, the town of Fort William lies at the foot of Ben Nevis, Britain's highest peak at 4,406 feet. To learn more about the Highlands region, its scenic attractions, and its traditions, stop at the West Highland Museum on High Street.

Into the Highlands. From the Great Glen, roads lead west toward the coast, through some of Scotland's wild back country. As you near the shore, the scenery becomes increasingly magnificent.

West of Kinlochewe, Beinn Eighe National Nature Reserve attracts hill-walkers, climbers, and anglers; it preserves a remnant of the once-vast Caledonian Forest.

Two nature tracks start at Loch Maree, a lovely inland lake rimmed by wild mountain scenery. You can picnic or camp here; it's a favorite fishing spot for salmon (April and May) and seagoing trout (July to mid-October). Druids once worshiped on one of the lake's tiny islands.

The road linking Torridon and Kishorn opens up more spectacular mountain views. You veer inland around Loch Carron, then head west to the busy shipping and ferry port of Kyle of Lochalsh. If you follow the coastal route south of Loch Carron, tiny Plockton offers an appealing site at which to pause.

Inland from Kyle of Lochalsh at Dornie, you'll spot the Castle of Eilean Donan on an island connected by causeway to the mainland where three lochs meet. Visitors can tour the interior.

About 2 miles southeast of Glenelg, in Gleann Beag, stand two well-preserved Iron Age *brochs* (stone towers with double walls), probably built by Picts about 2,000 years ago for protection against raiders.

■ TOURING TIPS Tourist offices in Inverness, Fort Augustus, Fort William, and other settlements can help arrange accommodations and provide information on regional attractions and events. In summer, many Highland Gatherings and Games and festive *ceilidhs* (parties with songs) are held at various sites throughout Scotland. You'll find hotels in larger settlements, but this is bed-and-breakfast country; caravans (camper vans) are a popular way to explore without the bother of finding nightly accommodations. Expect sudden shifts in the weather, and be prepared for rain at any time of year. Be sure your car is in good working order before leaving the main routes; repair shops and gas stations are far apart. Hikers should come prepared with Ordnance Survey maps (sold throughout Britain) and insect repellent. If you plan to travel to one or more of the Hebrides Islands, be sure to check in advance for ferry schedules.

THE WINDSWEPT WESTERN ISLES

See map page 18

In the mist-shrouded Inner and Outer Hebrides, romantic legends enhance the islands' awesome beauty and historic ruins dating from the Iron Age. Small fishing villages huddle in sheltered bays along the coast. On remote islands, the old Gaelic way of life survives in language, music, and crafts.

Trains and intercity motorcoaches connect Glasgow, Inverness, and other inland centers with settlements on the west coast. From these coastal ports, interisland car ferries and passenger steamers transport travelers to the main islands offshore. You also can reach the Outer Hebrides by air; scheduled flights from Glasgow land on the islands of Barra, Benbecula, and Lewis, and planes from Inverness also land at Stornoway on Lewis.

Skye. An island rich in myths and legends, Skye is the largest island of the Inner Hebrides, and it contains some of the most glorious scenery in the Highlands. Though it is 50 miles in length, no part of the irregularly shaped island is more than 6 miles from the sea. The stark, steep peaks of the Cuillin Hills dominate its landscape.

Ferries from the mainland port of Kyle of Lochalsh cross a narrow channel to Skye, docking at Kyleakin. Island roads meet at Broadford. To the south lies Isleornsay, a sheltered harbor for yachters, and Armadale, a farm village. At Portree, the island's capital, whitewashed houses are flanked by steep hills above a bay.

North of Kilmuir is the tomb of Flora Macdonald, the Highland heroine who aided Bonnie Prince Charlie's escape from British troops in 1746. Nearby is Isle of Skye Cottage Museum, a renovated, thatched croft house (open April to September).

The village of Uig is the ferry port for the islands of Harris and North Uist in the Outer Hebrides.

Dunvegan village grew up around Dunvegan Castle, a 13th-century fortress and seat of the chiefs of the clan MacLeod. It commands a rock high above the sea inlet. Visitors are welcome from April to mid-October.

Mull & Iona. Mull is a beautiful isle of heather- and bracken-covered moorland, forest, and peaks. Steamers and freighters dock in Craignure's sheltered deep-water bay. Perched on a crag overlooking the water is Duart Castle, ancient home of the chiefs of the Clan Maclean. At the north end of the island is Tobermory, the main town and fishing port. Brightly painted buildings overlook its natural harbor. Thin waterfalls drop down sheer cliffs along Mull's southwest coast.

The small island of Iona lies off Mull's southwest tip. Saint Columba established an abbey here in A.D. 563 and sent out his missionaries to convert Scotland to Christianity. The reconstructed cathedral dates from about 1500. Carved Celtic crosses dot the island. St. Oran's Cemetery was the burial place of 48 Scottish kings.

The Outer Hebrides. Locally called the "Long Island," this wild and rugged group of islands stretches 130 miles from Lewis south to Barra. The islands' western shores absorb the full pounding of the Atlantic. Deep inlets mark the shores, and scattered islets border the coast. Small houses built of stone or peat are topped by thatch roofs held in place by ropes and stones. Most people here make a living by fishing or weaving; the weaving of tweed cloth is still a cottage industry.

Largest of the islands is Lewis, 30 miles long. Simple cottages in scattered coastal villages are often painted in bright colors. At the northern tip, Butt of Lewis Lighthouse stands on rugged cliffs. Inland, small lakes speckle the rolling peat moors. Stornoway, the main settlement, is an important herring port and the center of the Harris tweed industry. In Arnol you can visit the Black House Museum, a traditional island dwelling. Near Carloway is a well-preserved Iron Age *broch*, its double walls of stone standing about 30 feet high on a hilltop. At Callanish you'll see a ring of standing stones dating from about 2000 B.C.

On the island of Harris, the largest village is Tarbert, standing on a narrow isthmus between bays. Stone cairns along the road to Luskentyre mark prehistoric funeral routes. The Toe Head Peninsula, stretching into the Atlantic, is a haven for seabirds. In Rodel village, take a look at the rich carvings in St. Clement's Church.

Wild winds from the sea whip the tiny islands to the south, populated by families of crofters and fishermen. An island road circles North Uist's irregular shore, passing small lakes and standing stones and ruins dating from the Stone Age. Medieval ruins and nature reserves are located on South Uist, celebrated as the birthplace of Flora Macdonald. On Barra, the ancient castle owned by the Clan Macneil faces Castlebay.

■ TOURING TIPS Check ferry schedules in advance, since some vessels offer only seasonal service or do not operate daily. Sundays are strictly observed, both on the mainland and in the islands; most ferries do not operate, fuel is not available, and shops and many restaurants are closed.

In Outer Hebrides, weaver looms handmade fabric in dimly lit workshop at Finsbay, South Harris Island.

Near Clifden, Connemara

Aran Islands farmer

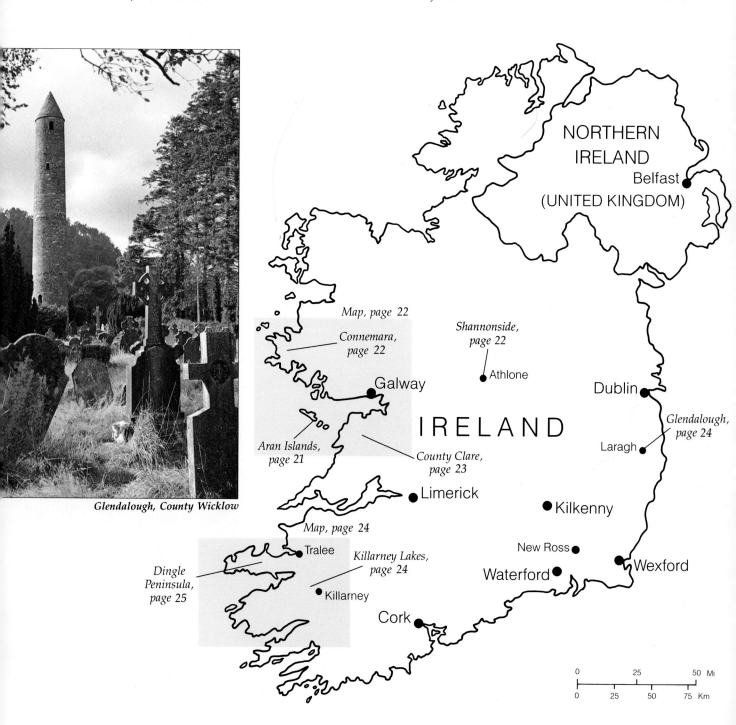

Glendalough, County Wicklow

NORTHERN
IRELAND
Belfast
(UNITED KINGDOM)

Map, page 22

*Connemara,
page 22*

*Shannonside,
page 22*

● Athlone

Dublin ●

Galway ●

IRELAND

*Glendalough,
page 24*

Laragh ●

*Aran Islands,
page 21*

*County Clare,
page 23*

Limerick ●

Map, page 24

*Killarney Lakes,
page 24*

Tralee ●

*Dingle
Peninsula,
page 25*

Killarney ●

Kilkenny ●

New Ross ●

Waterford ●

Wexford ●

Cork ●

0		25		50 Mi
0	25	50	75	Km

IRELAND

The spacious grandeur and haunting beauty of the Irish countryside captivate inhabitants and visitors alike. Generations of writers and painters have tried to capture the appeal of its rugged Atlantic coastline and the changing colors of the Irish hills—shades of brown flecked with the grayish white of granite outcrops, the many greens of forest and field, the subtle hues of purple heather, and the bright accents of golden gorse. Home weavers there thread these subtle hues into their fabrics.

To savor this appealing land for yourself, head for the friendly towns and villages of the West Country. Explore sparsely settled Connemara or the dramatic coastline of Counties Clare or Kerry. Enjoy the Killarney Lakes district on foot or by horse-drawn jaunting car. Settle down in an Irish holiday cottage and become part of the community. Or travel to the windswept Aran Islands west of Galway to experience the traditional ways of island life.

Inland, you'll find destinations to visit on motoring trips, cycling tours, or for a change of pace, cruises on the River Shannon and other waterways. South of Dublin, the wooded glens and dark lakes of County Wicklow offer mystical ruins of a great monastic city.

THE MYSTERIOUS ARAN ISLANDS

See map page 22

The bleak and rugged Aran Islands lie some 30 miles west of Galway near the mouth of Galway Bay. A place of mystery, these windswept isles leave a deep impression on visitors.

The three rocky islands—Inishmore, Inishmaan, and Inisheer—are home to tenacious farmers and hardy fishermen who cling to the Irish language and many ancient customs and superstitions. Island songs and stories are filled with folklore. Some fishermen still sail the chilly Atlantic in the traditional *currach,* a fragile craft of lath and tarred canvas that easily rides the waves. John Millington Synge immortalized these rugged men in his plays *Riders to the Sea* and *The Aran Islands.*

Island dress has changed little in centuries. Almost every man wears a *bainin* (a coat of white homespun) and heavy tweed trousers; some still wear *pampooties* (heelless shoes made of rough hide). Women spin wool and weave their own fabric. Home knitters fashion heavy Aran sweaters and other garments from unbleached wool, knitting decorative motifs and folk symbols into the garments.

The islands have several attractive villages, good sandy beaches, and dramatic scenery. Archeologists are drawn to the stone forts, early Christian churches, and monuments left on the islands by prehistoric inhabitants. Most famous is Dun Aengus on Inishmore, a massive 1st-century fortress clinging to the edge of a 300-foot cliff. Hermit monks came here to meditate in the early centuries of Christianity, and you can explore the remains of several monastic settlements.

■ **TOURING TIPS** Aer Arann planes provide scheduled service from Galway to all three islands. There's also steamer service from Galway to the village of Kilronan on Inishmore, largest of the islands. Most island accommodations are on Inishmore in private homes; some are open year round, but most close from November to March.

IRISH HOLIDAY COTTAGES

If you want to live in the easygoing Irish way, rent a whitewashed cottage built in traditional style and settle down for a week in the scenic West Country or along Ireland's southern coast. It's a perfect choice for a leisurely holiday. Cottage rentals are popular with Irish families and overseas visitors who want to experience life in a small rural community. You stay near the village, shop for food in local stores, have a drink in the village pub, and relax in front of your own open-hearth fireplace in the evening.

Clusters of cottages are located near small communities in counties Clare, Cork, Donegal, Galway, Kerry, Leitrim, Limerick, Mayo, Roscommon, Tipperary, and Waterford. Though traditional in design, they have modern facilities including central heating. Cottages are typically built around a large, modern kitchen with beamed ceiling and open fireplace; they are fully furnished and accommodate up to eight people.

Rates are highest from June through August, least expensive from November through March. For an illustrated directory, write to the Irish Tourist Board (address on page 128).

CYCLING SHANNONSIDE

See map page 20

One of the most pleasant ways to enjoy the attractions of the Shannonside region—counties Clare, Limerick, and north Tipperary—is on a leisurely cycling trip. Using one of the country towns as a base, you can choose from many possible routes, ranging from 10 to 55 miles.

From Limerick you could cycle to Adare, Ireland's most photographed village; along several river and forest routes; and to Bunratty Castle and Folk Park. Departing from Nenagh in north Tipperary, you could visit the wood craft center of Puckaun, tour several abbeys, or cycle through lake and forest scenery.

In County Clare, Ennis is a starting point for trips to several castles and abbeys, to scenic Inchiquin Lake, and to megalithic tombs and stone forts. From Killaloe and Athlone you can cycle beside Lough Derg and to villages along the River Shannon. Routes from Ballyvaughan and Lahinch feature the Burren countryside and coastal attractions.

■ **TOURING TIPS** You can purchase maps and guides to attractions in each county at regional tourist offices; those at Shannon Airport and Limerick are open year round, others are open only from June to September. For information on bicycle rentals and touring suggestions, write to the Irish Tourist Board (address on page 128).

WILD, LONELY CONNEMARA

Wedged between Lough Corrib and the Atlantic Ocean northwest of Galway, this sparsely settled countryside of green hills and rusty bogs has a special appeal. A lonely land of great beauty, Connemara has inspired many artists, writers, and musicians.

Much of Connemara's charm lies in its lack of people. Scattered villages are small, tourist facilities limited, and horses and bicycles are almost as common as automobiles. Often the only person you'll see for miles is a lone turf cutter chopping bricks of dark brown peat and stacking them to dry in the wind and sun. The character-

Pink-cheeked schoolboys pause on their way home. Meeting local people is one of the pleasures of travel in Ireland.

istic blue smoke of peat fires rises from chimneys of low, thatch-roofed cottages.

Your route to Connemara heads west from Galway, through its seaside suburb of Salthill and along the shore of Galway Bay. Small inlets and coves indent the rocky coastline. Barna, center for deep-sea fishing on Galway Bay, also has an excellent beach called the Silver Strand. Spiddal is a delightful little coastal resort with stores selling handknits and tweeds. Largest of the Connemara settlements is at Clifden, site of the annual Connemara pony show in late August.

Inland, you pass through rolling, lake-studded moorland dominated by a range of conical peaks called the Twelve Bens. Heather and broom form patches of purple and gold. Tall fuchsia bushes edge many country lanes; stone-walled fields are bright with seasonal wildflowers.

Nearly 4,000 acres between Clifden and Leenane have been officially designated as Connemara National Park; a visitor center is located at Letterfrack.

■ **TOURING TIPS** Stop at the information office in Galway for suggestions before you depart; from June through August, local offices are also open in Salthill and Clifden. You'll find the largest choice of overnight accommodations in Clifden and other coastal resorts; bed-and-breakfast accommodations are available throughout the region. Irish-style cottages with kitchens may be rented by the week (see page 22).

EXPLORING COUNTY CLARE

See map page 22

Hearty hospitality prevails in Ireland's friendly and informal West Country, where people customarily greet you with a cheery wave and a smile. Stop in a pub, and soon you'll be drawn into the conversation. Ask directions, and you'll get a bit of history or folklore thrown in.

A loop south of Galway offers a look at scenic County Clare, as you follow the scenic coast and return through the bleak region known as the Burren. You can plan an excursion to sample local oysters, banquet in a 15th-century castle, or visit a William Butler Yeats museum.

Along the coast. From Galway, take the route south to Clarinbridge and stop for a platter of Galway Bay oysters (from September through April), traditionally accompanied by wholesome Irish bread and a pint of Guinness stout. In mid-September the Clarinbridge Oyster Festival ushers in the new season.

Overlooking an inlet of Galway Bay is Dunguaire, a beautifully restored 15th-century castle north of Kinvara, built on the site of a 7th-century fortress. Visitors can tour the castle daily from April to September. From mid-May to mid-September, medieval banquets are presented nightly, followed by excerpts from the works by Synge, Yeats, and other Irish dramatists.

The main route follows the coast to the village of Ballyvaughan, then veers southwest over the Corkscrew Road toward Lisdoonvarna, Ireland's favorite spa; an alternative road borders the sea.

Rising up to 668 feet above the sea, Cliffs of Moher stretch for five miles along Ireland's west coast in County Clare.

The famed Cliffs of Moher rise vertically from the Atlantic in a 5-mile wall. Your best viewpoint is from O'Brien's Tower at the northern end, where the cliffs reach their maximum height of 668 feet.

The coast road turns inland along the shore of Liscannor Bay. Golfers head for Lahinch and its championship 18-hole course near the sea.

The Burren. Inland, you enter a strange region of barren limestone hills called the Burren. At Kilfenora you can stop at the interpretive center to learn about the area's unusual rock formations, rare plants, and other features.

Retreating glaciers of the Ice Age left great layers of bare gray rock over a wide area of northern County Clare. Many caves and passageways tunnel beneath the surface, and lakes appear and disappear mysteriously amid the limestone. Delicate wildflowers—normally found only north of the Arctic circle—nestle between rocks. Prehistoric inhabitants left stone forts and a number of dolmens (two or more huge upright stones capped by large horizontal ones); other antiquities date from medieval times.

Thoor Ballylee. One of Ireland's famous writers who loved the West Country was poet and playwright William Butler Yeats, who spent his summers at Ballylee Castle (he called it Thoor Ballylee) in the 1920s. From April to October you can visit this restored tower structure, located 4 miles northeast of Gort.

■ **TOURING TIPS** From mid-March to October, a visitor information center is open at O'Brien's Tower; on a clear day you can see the Aran Islands from the Cliffs of Moher. In Kilfenora, 5 miles southeast of Lisdoonvarna, the Burren Display Centre helps the visitor appreciate the history and environment of the Burren region; it is open daily from mid-March to October.

HISTORIC GLENDALOUGH

See map page 20

The Irish call County Wicklow the Garden of Ireland. Wooded glens and dark lakes lie tucked between its domed granite mountains. Streams tumble down hillsides and cut through its unspoiled valleys.

A region of wild grandeur and haunting beauty, Glendalough (Valley of Two Lakes) stretches west of Laragh deep in County Wicklow. Renowned for both its untamed scenic beauty and its historical and archeological interest, it exerts a mystical appeal on its visitors.

Lying around the lakes' shores are the remains of a great monastic city, once known as one of the important learning centers of Europe. You can trace the glen's history from its ruins—from the monastery founded by Saint Kevin in the 6th century, through the city's golden age of scholarship, to its 9th- and 10th-century plundering by Vikings. In 1398 English troops burned the settlement and left it deserted.

You enter through a gateway that was the original entrance to the monastic city. Though the cathedral is now in ruins, several structures are well preserved. St. Kevin's Church, topped by a steeply pitched stone roof, is typical of early Irish barrel-vaulted oratories. The 110-foot Round Tower is still in almost perfect condition after more than 1,000 years; monks reached the small doorway high above the ground by a ladder, which was drawn up behind them in time of attack.

■ **TOURING TIPS** In summer, sightseeing excursions depart from Dublin for Glendalough and other Wicklow attractions. If you plan to stay overnight in the area, make advance reservations through the Dublin Tourist Office. Good walking trails traverse the valley and its slopes.

CRUISING IRISH WATERWAYS

For a different view of the Irish countryside, do your sightseeing from the water. Nine companies offer cabin cruisers for charter, accommodating two to eight persons. All boats are fitted with refrigerators and gas cooking plates; most have heat, hot water, and showers.

The two main areas for holiday cruising are the River Shannon, navigable for about 140 miles from Lough Key to Killaloe; and the Grand Canal connecting Dublin with the rivers Shannon and Barrow, a distance of about 80 miles.

If you prefer to travel as a passenger, you can take a one- or two-week cruise on the River Shannon aboard the **Shannon Princess,** *which accommodates 12 passengers. In summer, day river trips depart from Athlone and from New Ross (County Wexford). For information, write to the Irish Tourist Board (address on page 128).*

THE KILLARNEY LAKES

Purplish mountains, deep forests for hiking and riding, and historic castles and mansions bless southwestern Ireland's Killarney Lakes district. Killarney, a market town and tourist center, is the starting point for trips along the seacoast and into the lake district, Ireland's first national park.

Ring of Kerry. A famous scenic drive, the Ring of Kerry follows the coastline and features some of Ireland's finest sea and mountain scenery. The 100-mile circuit passes from Killarney through Sneem, Castlecove, Derrynane, Waterville, Cahirciveen, Glenbeigh, and Killorglin. Near Glenbeigh, the beach at Rossbeigh offers a pleasant spot for a stop. Killorglin is the site of the 3-day Puck Fair in mid-August, when a large goat with beribboned horns presides over a livestock fair, dancing, and other festivities.

Killarney National Park. Spread over 25,000 acres with three large lakes, the park has well-defined access areas. Much of the park can be explored on easy day hikes, using Killarney as a base.

Imposing Muckross House, located in the midst of a vast estate about 3½ miles south of Killarney, is a visitor center and a museum of County Kerry history and crafts. Downstairs, weavers, basket makers, potters, and other craftspeople work at their trades. Upstairs, sumptuous rooms reveal how the last wealthy owners lived. From Easter through October, the house is open daily from 10 A.M. to 7 P.M.; in winter, hours are reduced, and it is closed on Monday.

Surrounding the house are handsome gardens, renowned for rhododendrons and azaleas that put on spectacular displays in May and June. Extensive water gardens and a rock garden on the grounds are also worth seeking out.

Visitors traditionally travel around the estate in horse-drawn carts, called jaunting cars, which can be hired in town. Some drivers entertain their passengers with stories during the trip.

Several nature trails offer a closer look at the park. One of the best, an easy 1¼-mile walk, begins near the mansion at the edge of Muckross Lake. The trail is fairly

Oblivious to magnificent coastal scenery, farmer guides horse-drawn hay wagon on slope above Dingle Bay.

level as it meanders under large, sheltering oaks, skirting two bays of the lake, then climbs over limestone cliffs studded with wind-sculpted yew trees. Across the lake you'll see the forbidding, purplish mountains known as Macgillycuddy's Reeks. The trail loops back through an oak wood carpeted with bracken and thick moss.

For a good half-day outing, continue 4 miles south of Muckross House on the Kenmare Road to the turnoff for Torc Waterfall. A short but steep hike leads up to the base of this 60-foot cascade.

Or climb Torc Mountain for another ½ mile or so to a dramatic spot overlooking the main peaks of the park. This is a fair-weather hike: though the trail is sheltered much of the way by dense oaks, it gets slick and muddy after rain.

Just west of the park boundary is the Gap of Dunloe, a wild and rugged gorge between Macgillycuddy's Reeks and the Purple and Tomies mountains. From Killarney, take the Killorglin Road west about 6 miles and follow the signs. You can see part of the gorge in a half-day outing or go deeper on an all-day excursion.

■ **TOURING TIPS** Horse-drawn jaunting cars accommodating four passengers can be hired in Killarney for visits to the park. You can also rent bicycles or hire riding ponies for independent explorations. Weather is changeable; days often start out clear and sunny, with clouds gathering by noon and rain falling in the afternoon. Dress in layers, keep rain gear near at hand, and wear nonskid walking shoes. It's a good idea to rise early and tackle fresh-air outings first; save shopping for later.

DINGLE PENINSULA VILLAGES

See map page 24

If you enjoy the idea of snuggling down for a few days in an Irish village, take a look at the Dingle Peninsula in County Kerry. Jutting into the Atlantic off Ireland's southwestern coast, it is one of several peninsulas offering glorious scenery, homey villages, and interesting ruins. In rural villages, folk customs, craft techniques, and local lore are still passed from generation to generation.

There's an engaging lack of hustle in Irish villages. Mailing a letter in the grocery store or asking directions often takes more time than you expect. Once you settle into village life, you'll have time to relish small pleasures—lingering over a hearty Irish breakfast, watching raincoated women bicycling to market, sharing ideas over a glass of Guinness, joining an evening songfest in a local pub.

The Dingle Peninsula is renowned for the sweeping grandeur of its coast and the archeological remains scattered over its slopes. Mountains of the Slieve Mish range stretch west from Tralee, giving way to the wild, lake-dotted hill country of the central peninsula and a magnificent coastline.

A narrow road leads into the shop- and pub-lined main street of Dingle, the peninsula's chief settlement. Situated on the north side of Dingle Harbour, the town has a quaint Irish charm. Blooming flowers brighten the settlement's plain houses, and tall-masted fishing boats bob in the harbor. You can rent a motorboat or rowboat for a fishing excursion or for coastal exploring. Dingle was the chief Kerry port in the Spanish trading days, and it was a walled town during the reign of Queen Elizabeth I.

Beautiful beaches rim the rocky promontories, though you may have to clamber down a steep footpath to reach the golden sand. Walkers and hikers find no lack of scenic routes.

Studding the green slopes of Dingle Peninsula are archeological ruins—stone- and earthen-ring fortifications, standing and inscribed stones, and other remains. Most unusual are the numerous *clocháns,* unmortared beehive-shaped stone huts reputedly built more than 1,000 years ago. Ancient church buildings are well preserved at Kilmalkedar and 2 miles south at 1,200-year-old Gallarus Oratory.

Magnificent coastal views abound on the road to Slea Head, Ireland's westernmost point; offshore, the Blasket Islands gleam like emeralds in the blue Atlantic. Fishing villages are worth a stop, and you can watch the building of the traditional high-prowed rowboats called *currachs* at Ballydavid.

■ **TOURING TIPS** From Dublin it's a half-day train trip to Killarney and Tralee, where rental cars are available. Government-operated CIE buses depart from these centers for Dingle Peninsula towns. Lodgings range from hotels to family-run guesthouses and bed-and-breakfast accommodations; you can also rent Irish cottages (with kitchens) by the week. Many accommodations close from November to March. Coastal weather is changeable; be prepared for drizzly, foggy Irish "mist" at any time of year.

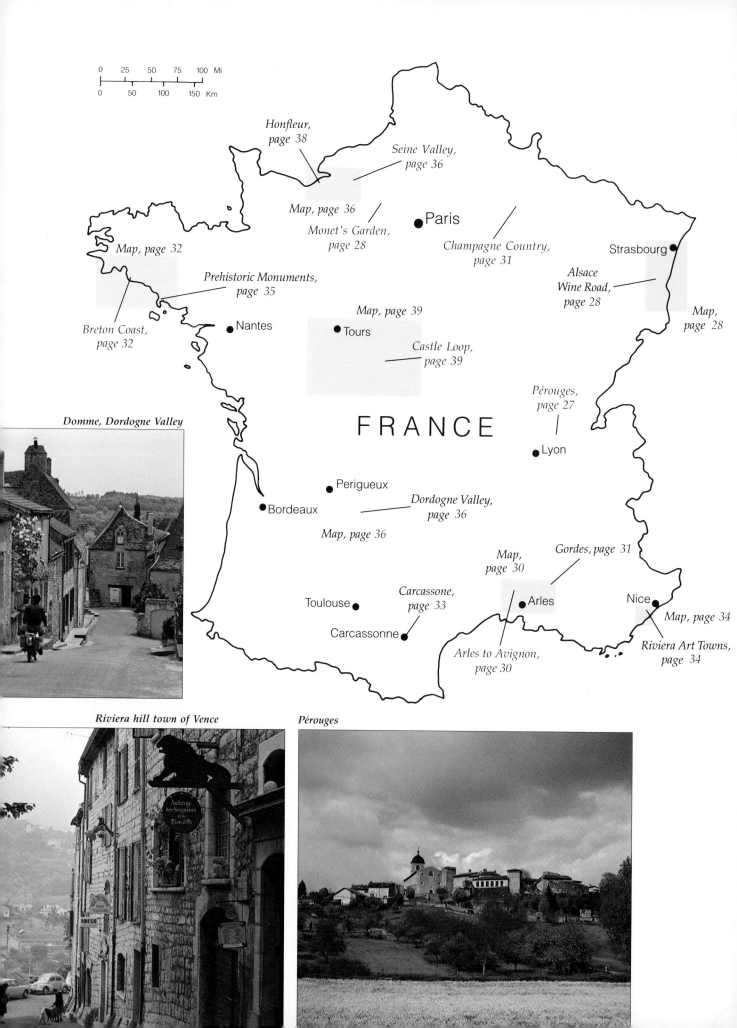

0 25 50 75 100 Mi

0 50 100 150 Km

Honfleur,
page 38

Seine Valley,
page 36

Map, page 36

● **Paris**

Monet's Garden,
page 28

Champagne Country,
page 31

Strasbourg ●

Map, page 32

Prehistoric Monuments,
page 35

Alsace
Wine Road,
page 28

Map,
page 28

Map, page 39

Breton Coast,
page 32

● **Nantes**

● **Tours**

Castle Loop,
page 39

Pérouges,
page 27

Domme, Dordogne Valley

F R A N C E

● **Lyon**

● **Perigueux**

Dordogne Valley,
page 36

● **Bordeaux**

Map, page 36

Map,
page 30

Gordes, page 31

Nice ●

Toulouse ●

Carcassone,
page 33

● **Arles**

Map, page 34

● **Carcassonne**

Arles to Avignon,
page 30

Riviera Art Towns,
page 34

Riviera hill town of Vence

Pérouges

FRANCE

The abundant pleasures of the French countryside offer inspiration, surprise, and delight for every traveler. Our travel suggestions highlight wine country in Alsace and Champagne, prehistoric stone monuments in Brittany, cave art in the Dordogne, castles south of the Loire Valley, Roman artifacts in Provence, and art in the Riviera hill towns and in several other regions.

Intriguing architecture adds interest in all parts of the country—Roman arenas, feudal fortresses, Renaissance châteaux, medieval hilltop villages, half-timbered inns, prehistoric stone bories, towns clinging to vertical cliffs, rich Gothic churches.

PÉROUGES, A HILLTOP FORTRESS

See map page 26

A pocket of tranquillity almost bypassed by the 20th century, the walled village of Pérouges is a French medieval fortress—intact, inhabited, and now restored. It crowns a hilltop some 22 miles/35 km northeast of Lyon.

During the Middle Ages, Pérouges was a settlement of farmers and artisans, primarily linen weavers. A victim of the industrial age, by 1909 Pérouges was virtually dead and scheduled for demolition. To rescue the town, a conservation committee leased the old houses at nominal rent to new owners who agreed to restore them as residences. Exteriors retain 13th- to 15th-century façades, while interiors now have modern conveniences.

You enter Pérouges through the massive Upper Gate, its heavy wooden door now permanently ajar, into a walled village little changed in 500 years. From stone ramparts, you gaze over farmlands toward the Rhône Valley and snowy Alps. Fitted into the perimeter wall are houses and the fortress-church of Ste-Marie-Madeleine; gunports, instead of windows, look out on the valley.

The only way to explore Pérouges is on foot. Curving within the wall is the cobbled Rue des Rondes. Lining the streets are beautiful old houses, some now housing craft workshops. Activity centers around the Place du Tilleul, a pebble-paved square faced with vine-draped stone buildings and dominated by a huge linden tree. One of the 13th-century houses now serves as an inn. Another contains the small but fascinating Museum of Folk Arts and Traditions.

TOURING TIPS To reach Pérouges, drive northeast of Lyon on Route N 84; turn off the highway just west of Meximieux. Avoid visiting on Sunday and, if possible, during the summer peak season; or plan your visit for early morning. Reservations are recommended if you wish to stay overnight in the town's highly regarded inn, Hostellerie du Vieux-Pérouges; other accommodations are located in Meximieux and St-Maurice-de-Gourdans.

MONET'S GARDEN AT GIVERNY

See map page 26

In an era rich in landscape art, Impressionist Claude Monet stood out as a painter of gardens—and as a skilled gardener himself. From 1883 to 1912, he transformed a farmyard at Giverny, on the Seine River about 50 miles/80 km northwest of Paris, with the same zest for color that enlivened his paintings.

The two acres outside his doorstep contain fruit trees, lawns, cut-flower beds, and magnificent flower borders. In 1893, he bought another two acres across the road and enlarged a small pond there to make his Japanese-style water garden. During the 20 years before his death in 1926, Monet painted scores of scenes from the property.

When Monet's son died in 1966, the house and grounds became the property of the Institut de France, and restoration began. They were opened to the public in 1980. From April through October, the garden is open daily except Monday and holidays.

Into the Monet house. Visitors are admitted through the barnlike water-lily studio into the back of the garden. The white simplicity of the studio contrasts with the flood of color outside. As you approach the house, you see rose-covered arches over a nasturtium-lined path, huge sunflowers, and borders exploding with color.

Inside the green-shuttered, brick-pink house, each room has its own monochromatic scheme, from the intensity of the all-yellow dining room to the tranquillity of the ivory bedroom. Doorways were deliberately offset; like Monet, you can watch the effect of changing light and shadow on up to four different rooms at once.

Stroll through the garden. After experiencing Monet's expressiveness with paint indoors, walk through the garden again with sharpened awareness of its unusual juxtapositions of color. Depending on when you visit, you may see rhododendrons the color of blackberry sorbet next to pale peach azaleas; hot orange Oriental poppies against pastel pink roses and yellow iris; red dahlias clustered with pink snapdragons, lavender-pink Michaelmas daisies, and silvery artemesia.

Follow the flower borders from the house to the front avenue and turn right. An underground tunnel takes you beneath the road to the water lily pond, one of the most famous and frequently painted settings of Monet's work. Pause on the wisteria-entwined Japanese bridge, rest at the boat landing, and stroll along rhododendron- and willow-lined paths.

■ **TOURING TIPS** **To drive to the garden from Paris, take the Paris–Normandy Highway through Vernon; cross the Seine River bridge, and head right toward Gasney. Watch for signs and the garden itself. You can also travel to Vernon by train from Gare St-Lazare (the subject of a Monet painting in 1877). The garden is located about 2½ miles/4 km from the train station; you can walk or take a taxi. To prepare for a visit, it's helpful to study an illustrated book on Monet's paintings. In Paris you can see his work at the Orangerie, the Musée Marmottan, and the Musée d'Orsay.**

LOFTY HILLTOP FORTRESS

Castles stand like sentinels on hilltops overlooking the Rhine. One of the most enjoyable to visit is Haut-Koenigsbourg, which crowns a ridge of the Vosges Mountains between Châtenois and Ribeauvillé.

A winding mountain road climbs southwest of Châtenois to the massive 15th-century fortress, which commands the Rhine Valley from its lofty, isolated site. In the early 20th century, Kaiser Wilhelm II restored the feudal stronghold as a summer retreat.

Guides lead you through the castle's magnificent halls and apartments; you can then climb to the castle keep for a memorable view of the Rhine Valley with the Black Forest in the distance.

ALONG THE ALSATIAN WINE ROAD

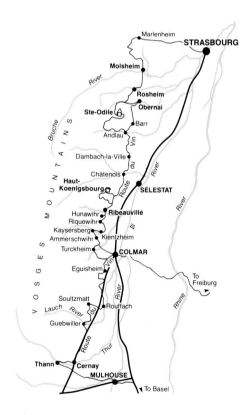

The peaceful vineyards of Alsace cover the eastern flank of the Vosges Mountains, rising above the flat Rhine Plain. Small wine-making towns huddle around steepled churches amid the vine-covered foothills. Lonely ruins of feudal fortresses crown the high rocky outcrops, and trails wind across the wooded slopes.

For centuries Alsace was the buffer between warring powers on opposite banks of the Rhine River. A hybrid civilization grew, combining Gallic culture with Teutonic influences in language, architecture, and cuisine.

Many attractive wine villages are linked by the Route du Vin, which winds for some 75 miles/120 km through the Vosges foothills. A route to be savored leisurely, it begins west of Strasbourg at Marlenheim and meanders south to Thann. Grapes have been cultivated here since Roman times.

Fortifications from the Middle Ages still surround some towns. Medieval and Renaissance churches and timber-framed buildings crowd together on narrow, curving streets. In the mornings, you'll see plump eiderdowns hanging out of gable windows, freshening in the morning air. Ancient gateways, decorated fountains, and charming old inns await discovery.

Northern wine towns. From Marlenheim the road winds south through vineyards on the eastern slopes of the Vosges. Facing Molsheim's central square is the Metzig, a gracious Renaissance building dating from 1525 and decorated in the Alsatian style—multistoried, with steep roof and much ornamentation.

Rosheim contains some of the oldest ruins and ramparts in Alsace. Old houses along the Rue de Général-de-Gaulle date from the 12th century, as does the Church of St-Pierre and St-Paul, built in the characteristically sober and unornamented Rhenish style.

High gabled houses rise along Obernai's small winding streets, and 13th-century ramparts surround the town. On an easy walking tour, look for the attractive market square, belfry, six-bucket well, and 16th-century town hall. Paths wend through the hills.

Roads climb west to Ste-Odile, an ancient pilgrimage town and convent honoring the patron saint of Alsace. From the summit of Mont Ste-Odile, you have a broad view over the plain.

Barr is a wine-producing center below the fortified castles of Landsberg and Andlau. Overlooking vineyards, it boasts handsome old houses and a 17th-century town hall with decorated loggia and sculpted balcony.

Three ancient gateways breach the fortifications of Dambach-la-Ville, a seductive Renaissance town. Dambach's pride is St-Sebastien Chapel, with its ornate 17th-century baroque altar.

Heart of the wine country. Many of Alsace's premier winemakers have settled in towns near Sélestat.

A walk up Ribeauvillé's main street, appropriately called the Grand-Rue, offers enjoyable glimpses into narrow, cobbled side alleys. You'll pass flower-decked fountains and enjoy the well-restored towers and gateways that were part of the town's fortifications during the Middle Ages. Just south of Ribeauvillé is the attractive little village of Hunawihr, where vineyards surround the 15th-century fortified church and cemetery.

In Riquewihr, surprises await you around each curve and corner. Spared by World War II, this charming 16th-century village is a feast of beautiful timbered Alsatian houses, ancient fountains, and curving streets. Flowers spill from window boxes and over balustrades. Vineyards climb the hills behind town. Alsatian folklore

is featured in a small museum in the Dolder, a 13th-century town gate. Another museum features French postal stamps.

The Route du Vin passes through the streets of Mittelwihr, Bennwihr, and Sigolsheim—all rebuilt since World War II. The small fortified town of Kientzheim has typical gabled houses and an Alsatian wine museum.

Albert Schweitzer was born in 1875 in Kaysersberg, a town that, in the Roman era, controlled passage between Gaul and the Rhine valley. The Weiss River flows through town below the fortified castle. Kaysersberg has several handsome churches, a Renaissance town hall, and a 15th-century fortified bridge.

One of the prettiest Alsatian towns, Ammerschwihr was burned by incendiary bombs during the winter of 1944–45 and has been rebuilt in modern Alsatian style. It still has a tall 13th-century gateway and fortifications.

The small village of Turckheim guards its Renaissance character. A wall and three ancient gates enclose its town square, fountain, and old timbered houses.

South of Colmar. Smaller and less crowded than Strasbourg, the old Alsatian town of Colmar is a favorite center for exploring the wine villages. On a walk through its inviting streets, you'll happen upon impressive early buildings such as the old Douane (customs house), and many restored wooden Renaissance houses including the Maison Pfister and the Maison des Têtes. In the quiet district called Little Venice, old houses and overhanging willows border placid canals. The Unterlinden Museum is housed in a former convent.

Back on the Route du Vin, Eguisheim has survived intact since the 16th century. The town is built around an ancient castle and surrounded by vineyards. After you've explored the attractive little village, take a forest drive along the Route of the Five Châteaux to the hilltop ruins of Hohlandsbourg Castle.

Old churches, dating from the 12th century, are highlights in the towns of Rouffach, Soultzmatt, and

(Continued on next page)

Vineyards climb the slopes behind Ribeauvillé, in the heart of the Alsatian wine district.

Guebwiller. Rouffach's Church of Notre Dame is the oldest Gothic building in the Upper Alsace district.

At the south end of the wine road, Cernay has medieval fortifications and a small museum in the Porte de Thann. Towering over Thann are the castle ruins of Engelsbourg. Thann boasts the Collégiale St-Thiébaut, richest in Gothic detail of all Alsatian churches. A regional museum is housed in the town hall.

■ **TOURING TIPS** Express trains south from Strasbourg stop in Sélestat, Colmar, and Mulhouse. Local trains and buses serve some of the smaller towns, but you'll enjoy exploring the region most by car. Some vintners have small tasting rooms where you can sample the light and fruity Alsatian wines and purchase a bottle for a picnic; look for *dégustation libre* (free tasting) signs. Many colorful festivals take place in summer and during the autumn harvest season.

BYWAY FROM ARLES TO AVIGNON

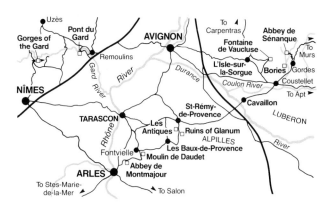

Strolling visitors enjoy timbered buildings and cobbled streets of Riquewihr, a favorite stop on Alsatian wine road.

The sunny valley of the Rhône River is a favored land of mild climate, luminous skies, and balmy days. For centuries the rich delights of this Provençal countryside have been painted by artists and extolled by writers, poets, and troubadours.

This was the "province" of the Romans, who settled in this valley in the 1st century B.C. and for nearly 500 years dominated the region, building great monuments that still endure. In the 14th century, Avignon became the center of the Roman Catholic Church.

Arles. Even before the Romans arrived, Arles was an active port near the mouth of the Rhône River. More than 2000 years later, a strong Roman imprint remains. Centuries of weathering have mellowed stones of the Roman arena, where Provençal-style bullfights are now held. Within walking distance of the arena are the remains of the large Roman theater, the ancient burial ground of Les Alyscamps, other Roman vestiges, and several museums of ancient artifacts.

City activity focuses on the Boulevard des Lices, lined with shops and cafés and shaded by plane trees. On Wednesday and Saturday mornings it becomes a lively open-air marketplace.

The richly-decorated Church of St-Trophime represents the wealth of the medieval era; its richly carved doorway contrasts with a simple interior. You can learn more about Provençal life and folklore at the Arlaten Museum (closed Monday in winter). Near the Rhône, the Réattu Museum features contemporary regional art, including some 60 drawings presented by Pablo Picasso.

Vincent Van Gogh spent his final years in Arles and nearby St-Rémy-de-Provence, turning out numerous paintings of the Provençal countryside.

Avignon. Above the waters of the Rhône at Avignon, the perpendicular lines of the Palace of the Popes stand in severe simplicity, a reminder of the 14th century, when religious power extended around the world from Avignon. Visitors can tour the labyrinth of halls, rooms, and chapels.

See the city's historic quarter on a walking tour; streets are full of handsome old mansions and churches. Along the Rue des Teinturiers (cloth dyers), paralleling a stream, you can still see waterwheels used in the 18th- and 19th-century production of textiles.

Ramparts extend more than 3 miles/5 km around the medieval city. From the viewpoint atop the Rocher of the Doms, you look down on the Rhône River and the Bridge of St-Bénézet.

Highlights of the countryside. North of Arles a splendid route heads northeast past the unfinished Abbey of Montmajour, dating from the 12th century (closed Tuesday). At Fontvielle a side road leads to the windmill of French writer Alphonse Daudet, perched on a hill above a tree-lined road.

Surrounded by desolate landscape, the ghostly stone ruins of Les Baux-de-Provence perch on a hill overlooking an awesome valley that supposedly inspired Dante's *Inferno*. You walk up through the lower town to the site, where jagged foundations recall the ancient town that stood here until 1632, when it was demolished by the troops of Louis XIII.

South of St-Rémy-de-Provence, you'll find the ruins of ancient Glanum. All that remains standing is a pair of magnificent monuments known as Les Antiques—the municipal arch and the mausoleum, one of the most handsome and best preserved in the Roman world.

■ **TOURING TIPS** If you want to seek out sites that Van Gogh painted (many now greatly changed), inquire at the Syndicat d'Initiative (tourist office) in Arles. The best times to visit this region are in spring or early autumn; summer temperatures inland can be miserably hot, and in late autumn and winter the chilling mistral wind sweeps down from the north.

PROVENÇAL SIDE TRIP TO GORDES

See map page 30

Deep in Provence, the attractive village of Gordes perches on an escarpment of the Vaucluse mountains looking toward the Luberon plain. Other villages dot the area, crowning hilltops or hugging slopes.

Near Gordes are three gems: a restored prehistoric stone village, a Renaissance château housing the Vasarély Foundation, and the 12th-century abbey of Sénanque. You can visit them all on a day trip from Avignon.

To get to Gordes, drive east from Avignon on Route N 100 to Coustellet, then go north about 5 miles/ 8 km on routes D 2 and D 15.

Probably built about 4,000 years ago, the restored stone village is located about 2 miles/3 km southwest of Gordes. It has beehive-shaped huts, called *bories,* made with flat stones from the surrounding rough terrain. Such stones are still used as a building material throughout Provence; you'll see many new walls that have been built in the traditional manner.

In the village, high walls protected each hut—lived in by farmers or shepherds and animals—against wolves and brigands. Some bories had second floors for storing hay or provisions, and some included bread ovens and wine presses and vats. You can visit the restored stone village daily.

The charming village of Gordes is dominated by its four-towered, 16th-century château, which incorporates part of a feudal fortress. Displayed inside the château are 1,500 paintings and drawings, representing 40 years' work by the noted Hungarian abstract artist Victor Vasarély. You can visit the castle daily except Tuesday (except in July and August).

On a stroll through town, you'll discover ramparts and vaulted stairways. Modern shops now occupy some of the old buildings along the narrow streets.

Founded in 1148 by the Cistercians, the abbey of Sénanque was used by monks until 1969. Restoration has been going on since that time. In summer, concerts of ancient music are performed. The abbey is open daily to visitors.

■ **TOURING TIPS** A detailed map of the region will help you locate these sites easily. You can pick up supplies for a picnic in the countryside or, if you prefer, enjoy lunch at one of several good restaurants near Gordes.

CHAMPAGNE COUNTRY

See map page 26

The world's most renowned sparkling wine comes from the region of Champagne, centered in the hills between Reims and Épernay, less than a 2-hour drive northeast of Paris. In this district you can explore charming old towns, follow the scenic Route du Champagne through the meandering Marne Valley, and tour some of the caves where the sparkling beverage is produced.

The Route du Champagne begins at La Ferté-sous-Jouarre, on Route N 3 northeast of Paris, and winds along the Marne to Épernay and beyond. Important World War I battles were fought in this area.

Rustic half-timbered houses and sturdy Gothic churches distinguish villages along the way. The hillside corniche road leads to delightful hill towns such as Villers-St-Denis and tiny Châtillon. The birthplace of champagne is a former Benedictine abbey in Hautvillers where, in the 17th century, Dom Pierre Pérignon discovered the principles of making sparkling wine.

Most of the major champagne producers are located near Reims, a city dating back to the era of ancient Gaul. The most interesting cellars are cut into Gallo-Roman chalk pits, called *crayères;* some 2,000 years ago, workmen quarried stone here to build ancient Reims. Most of the major producers have regularly scheduled tours.

After your cellar tour, you can visit the renowned Reims Cathedral; in late afternoon, sun streams through its stained-glass rose window, transforming the interior with magnificent light and color.

■ **TOURING TIPS** On the scenic drive through the Marne Valley, you can alternate between the low-lying valley road and the hillside corniche on the north bank of the river; a detailed road map will help you plan your route. English-language tours are scheduled at many of the cellars; after the tour, you'll visit the tasting room to sample the sparkling wine.

PICNIC AT THE PONT DU GARD

West of Avignon, near the village of Remoulins, the magnificent Pont du Gard aqueduct spans the waters of the Gard River in a superb display of Roman engineering. Built in the 1st century B.C. to carry water to Nîmes—and still in use—the stone bridge is constructed in three arched tiers. It is as beautiful today as when it was first built. Greenery covers the riverbanks, enhancing its setting. You can drive across the bridge or walk on its ancient stones to view construction details close up.

The best views of the bridge are from upriver, on the right bank. If you pick up lunch supplies in Nîmes or Avignon, you can choose a site on the nearby riverbank for a memorable picnic.

ALONG THE BRETON COAST

Beneath an often overcast and always changing sky, life along Brittany's rugged coast is governed in large part by the moods of the sea and the rhythms of the tide. In any port town you'll see tide tables displayed in hotels and on quays. At high tide the coast is beautiful, with waves breaking in foaming spray against the rocky headlands and small boats bobbing cheerily in the harbor. At low tide the same harbor is often a sea of mud.

France's westernmost maritime province shares many ties with Britain's Cornwall across the channel. The Celts, who arrived from Britain in the 5th century, named their new land Little Britain, later shortened to Brittany. Like Cornwall, this is a land where legends thrive and a mystical faith in the supernatural permeates daily life.

Brittany's intense religious fervor is visible not only in the *pardons* (religious festivals) but also in the abundance of churches and church buildings, decorated churchyard calvary monuments, and roadside crosses and shrines. The pardons, most of which occur between late May and mid-September, are popular with visitors. Many Bretons dress for the occasion in their traditional regional costumes. Following the afternoon's procession and ceremonies, the evening is given over to dancing and to wrestling matches.

Quimper and its district. Quimper lies in a valley at the confluence of the Odet and Steir rivers. Since the 17th century, the town's Locmaria quarter has been a center of faïence production; visitors are welcome on weekdays at several of the pottery workshops.

Quimper's historic section is located on streets leading northwest off Place St-Corentin, the cathedral square. The Musée des Beaux Arts in the town hall has a rich art collection. If you're interested in Breton history, folklore, or archeology, visit the Musée Breton, near the cathedral; its collection features costumes from the various towns, samples of Breton furniture, and a display of the distinctive local pottery.

From May to September you can cruise down the Odet River (view it at high tide) to the small seaside resort of Bénodet. The river widens into an attractive estuary lined with numerous mansions and attractive gardens.

To the southwest are Pont-l'Abbé, capital of the Bigouden district, and the Penmarch Peninsula. Because there are no sheltered harbors along this coast, market gardens provide the livelihood. You can see regional costumes in the Bigouden Museum in Pont-l'Abbé (open in summer daily except Sunday and holidays). Near the small resort of St-Guénolé, the Finistère Prehistorical Museum contains antiquities discovered in the district.

Concarneau. If you follow the coastal route southeast, you'll come to colorful Concarneau, one of France's major fishing ports. Sturdy ramparts surround its Ville Close (walled town), an irregularly shaped, fortified island separating the town's inner and outer harbor. Laced with narrow alleys, the island is fun to explore; you can walk along the ramparts, from which you have a view of harbor and fleet, and you can visit a fishing museum.

There's usually some activity along Concarneau's waterfront. Early risers can visit the fish market, which begins each weekday at 7 A.M. along the inner harbor quay. On Monday and Friday morning, women from surrounding villages flock to the town marketplace to buy vegetables, clothing, household utensils, garden plants, and perhaps a baby chick or duck.

Down the coast. A few miles below Concarneau is Pont-Aven, a pleasant little town where Paul Gauguin settled in 1886. He attracted a group of young painters, who became known as the Pont-Aven Group. The Gauguin Museum in the town hall is open in summer only (July to mid-September).

Quimperlé's unusual Church of Ste-Croix is built on the same plan as the Church of the Holy Sepulchre in Jerusalem. Remnants of medieval fortifications may be seen at Hennebont, located upriver from the industrial port and naval base at Lorient.

In 1776 a ship carrying Benjamin Franklin, on his way to negotiate a treaty with France, landed at Auray when it was unable to sail up the Loire River to Nantes. Auray's quay is named for Franklin; a plaque marks the house where he stayed. A wooded hillside overlooks the river, port, and houses of the picturesque old St-Goustan quarter.

From Auray you can branch south to see the prehistoric stone markers around Carnac and Locmariaquer (see page 35). Or you can continue east to Vannes, which has a charming old quarter clustered around the cathedral and partly enclosed by ramparts. The park of the former castle is a city garden and promenade.

South of Vannes, the Gulf of Morbihan cuts deeply into the coast. Many fishing boats and pleasure craft sail among its islands, for the best way to enjoy this small island-studded inland sea is by boat. In summer, excursions depart from Vannes.

■ **TOURING TIPS** Hotel reservations are recommended between June and mid-September, when many French families vacation in Brittany. Off-season visitors find many hotels and attractions closed. Market days are lively in the coastal towns; sometimes you'll see Breton women wearing the white, starched *coiffes* (headdresses) that are part of traditional regional dress. Don't leave Brittany without visiting a *crêperie*; Breton crêpes are large, thin pancakes of wheat or buckwheat, filled with cheese, eggs, ham, or preserves and traditionally enjoyed with cold Breton cider.

Like a setting for a medieval drama, walls and towers of 12th-century fortress of Carcassonne rise along banks of Aude River in southwestern France. City and its fortifications were restored during late 19th century.

THE FORTRESS OF CARCASSONNE

See map page 26

Your first sight of Carcassonne, rising above vineyards with the tips of the distant, snowcapped Pyrénées behind, is a dramatic one. Europe's great medieval fortress, never conquered in battle, commands the plain between the Mediterranean and Toulouse. Its turrets and crenellated battlements tower above the surrounding town like the stage setting for a medieval French play.

Carcassonne's mighty walls, first raised by the Romans, have guarded the route to Spain since the Romans invaded Gaul in the 1st century B.C. The Visigoths built the walls still higher. Time after time, invading armies besieged these ramparts as they reached the Aude River at Carcassonne, but no enemy ever scaled the outer walls. By the Middle Ages, the strong fortress was considered impregnable and nicknamed the Virgin of Languedoc.

Since the town could not be conquered, it was bypassed, then abandoned. Weather and souvenir hunters took their toll. Restoration of the fortifications began in the mid-19th century. Today Carcassonne appears—at least from a distance—just as it did 600 years ago.

Below the fortress is the lower town on the opposite bank of the Aude; it's the commercial center of the region. In the heart of the lower town, plane trees shade the Place Carnot, the market square. Rue Clémenceau, a pedestrian street, runs from one end of town to the other.

You can wander at will, guidebook in hand, exploring the Cité on your own, or you can arrange to take a guided tour of the fortress. The intricate defenses and the quiet little streets provide an awesome glimpse of medieval life.

Dating from various building periods, the fortifications consist of three high walls. The château, which provided living quarters for the nobles of Carcassonne, was the city's defensive stronghold. Winding streets, lined with houses from the Middle Ages and Renaissance, lead up to the Cathedral of St-Nazaire. From the tower behind the church, there's a superb 360° view.

Within the walls lay a self-contained city, able to withstand a long siege. A great storeroom contained hundreds of preserved meat carcasses; a large cistern held a six-month supply of fresh water. There was a mill for grinding wheat, forges that made everything from chain mail to hinges, even a mint for coining money and an open-air theater for entertainments.

In souvenir stalls you may see toy pigs; they commemorate a famous deception that once saved the city. In full view of Charlemagne's besieging army, Dame Carcas herself fed a pig the last of the city's grain. The invaders decided the city must still have an ample food supply and could not be taken by siege, so they withdrew.

The city's most dramatic celebration is the historic *Embrasement* on July 14, when fires are set along ancient city walls. People come from all over the south of France to watch the fiery nighttime spectacle. On July 28, the whole town celebrates Saint Nazaire's Day with a "Donkey Walk"; merrymaking lasts far into the night.

During the off-season it's much quieter. Tourists are scarce, and the Cité seems less like a museum. You pass townspeople going to market for their daily shopping or chatting with friends outside the small shops.

■ **TOURING TIPS** Carcassonne can be reached from Paris by direct trains, some of which provide car-sleeper service. For a guided tour of the walled town, apply at the Château Comtal. Two hotels are located within the city. Guests of these hotels are allowed to bring their automobiles into the narrow streets; all other visitors must park outside the gate and enter on foot.

RIVIERA HILL TOWNS: A TREASURY OF MODERN ART

Behind the narrow coastal strip of the Côte d'Azur rise the undulating hills of the Maritime Alps. Walled towns and villages cling to the slopes and perch on the hilltops, vestiges of the days when Saracen pirates and medieval mercenaries invaded and plundered southern France.

Since the late 19th century, many artists and craftspeople have settled here, bringing creative vitality to the region. Today the hill towns contain a veritable treasury of modern art. Some of the best works remain in the small towns where famous artists lived.

Modern paintings, sculptures, and other works are displayed in indoor-outdoor setting of Maeght Foundation.

Built with stones from the hillsides, the villages blend with the land. Breezes pick up the scent of lavender, wild thyme, and flowers. In the hill towns, tall narrow houses lean protectively against one another, clustering around the central castle or church. Winding lanes and steep alleyways are accessible mainly on foot.

Most of the small towns have a tree-shaded, central square where the local market is held, or where men of the village gather for leisurely games of *pétanque* (outdoor bowling). The region's balmy weather encourages long alfresco lunches and end-of-the-day relaxation at outdoor cafés.

Mougins. An old, fortified market town set atop a hill, Mougins is renowned for its excellent restaurants and its status as the home of Pablo Picasso (1881–1973), who moved to the Riviera after World War II. The town has a 15th-century gateway and traces of the old ramparts.

Vallauris. This town owes its fame to its unique clay deposits, known even before the Roman era, which are used in making cookware and decorative pottery. After settling in the area, Picasso became involved in ceramics and inspired new interest in the local craft during the 1950s. Many potters now work near Vallauris.

Picasso's sculpture *Man with a Sheep* dominates the town's market square; his War and Peace chapel is located nearby in the thick-walled Château de Vallauris.

Biot. This attractive village is known for both its pottery and its interesting glassworks (*verrerie*), where you can watch glassblowers in action.

Bright colors adorn the inside and outside of the Musée Fernand Léger (1881–1955), dedicated to this famous resident of Biot. Paintings, sculptures, ceramics, and collages by the prolific artist illustrate his evolution from Impressionism to a stark and powerful style of Cubism.

Cagnes-sur-Mer. Set in flower-decked countryside, this hilltop town is a favorite haunt of artists. The old town, called Haut-de-Cagnes, is dominated by a fortified castle. The town's business center is below the old town in Cagnes-Ville; nearer the sea is Cros-de-Cagnes, a fishing port and beach resort.

The castle now contains a museum; from the castle tower, there's a splendid panoramic view. Haut-de-Cagnes, the upper town, retains its ramparts, gates, and old streets and houses. Rotating exhibitions of Chagall, Dufy, Vasarély, and others are displayed in the castle's Museum of Modern Mediterranean Art.

Above town you can visit Les Collettes, the house where Auguste Renoir (1841–1919) spent the final years of his life. Preserved as Renoir knew it, the house contains paintings by the artist, and the garden features his sculptures.

St-Paul-de-Vence. One of the region's most charming walled towns, St-Paul has a pleasing medieval atmosphere. An arched gateway frames the worn stone fountain in a tiny plaza. Flowers tumble over iron balconies. Pedestrians take their time strolling along the cobbled lanes and atop the ramparts.

In the early decades of the 20th century, St-Paul's attractions were rediscovered by a number of artists, among them Modigliani, Signac, and Bonnard, and the town continues to attract painters.

Art lovers will want to pause at Auberge de la Colombe d'Or, a luxurious country inn that is a museum in itself. Diners are seated amid a valuable collection of paintings; some were acquired many years ago by an art-conscious proprietor in trade for room and meals from artists who stopped here and later became famous.

The renowned Maeght Foundation occupies a hillside site just northwest of town. Calder mobiles hang in pine trees and Giacometti figures stand amid visitors. The galleries and tiered gardens show off works of art in an indoor-outdoor setting. The superb collection includes paintings, graphics, mosaics, and sculptures by Braque, Léger, Bonnard, Matisse, Tal-Coat, Chagall, Miró, Calder, Giacometti, and other 20th-century artists. Original signed lithographs and limited-edition print reproductions may be purchased in the salesroom.

Vence. Set atop a rocky promontory, Vence is surrounded by cultivated flower fields. You can stroll its old quarter or relax under plane trees in the square.

Henri Matisse (1869–1954) designed and decorated the Chapel of the Rosary in Vence—a simple, dignified place of worship used by Dominican nuns. Visitors are welcome on Tuesday and Thursday. Large black-line murals decorate the chapel's white walls, and light filters in through vivid stained-glass windows. Matisse's original sketches for the chapel are displayed in an adjoining gallery.

Loup River Valley. Northwest of Vence, a scenic loop drive follows the gorgelike valley of the Loup River. Strike out toward the fortified village of Tourrettes-sur-Loup, where outer walls of the houses form the town ramparts.

Paralleling the river gorge, the road heads north from Pont-du-Loup past several waterfalls cascading over the limestone cliffs. When your route intersects road D 3, turn sharply south toward the perched village of Gourdon. You'll have magnificent views over the mountains and the Loup gorge. From atop Gourdon's lofty site, you can see all the way to the Mediterranean.

More art museums. You can also visit other Riviera museums that feature works by a single artist.

Displayed in the Château Grimaldi in Antibes are engravings, ceramics, drawings, and lithographs by Pablo Picasso, inspired during his Riviera period.

Located above Nice in the elegant suburb of Cimiez, the Chagall Museum contains canvases, etchings, gouaches, and ceramics by Marc Chagall—all illustrating scenes from the Bible.

Also located in Cimiez is the Musée Matisse, which contains paintings, drawings, lithographs, sculpture, ceramic panels, and stained-glass work showcasing the varied talents of Henri Matisse.

■ **TOURING TIPS** Planes and fast trains link Paris with the Riviera resort towns, where you can obtain rental cars or connect with buses or tours to the hill towns. Visiting days and hours vary at the art museums; most are closed Tuesday and on national holidays. Accommodations in the villages offer a charming Provençal ambience; some country inns are known for their superior cuisine or garden settings.

BRITTANY'S PREHISTORIC MONUMENTS

See map page 32

Inland from Brittany's rugged coast are great prehistoric monuments, more than 3,000 giant stones placed by a little-known people between 3500 and 1800 B.C. The stones are scattered over the countryside north of Vannes, with the greatest concentration located around Carnac and Locmariaquer.

Single stones called menhirs, often over 20 feet/6 meters high and weighing up to 350 tons/317 tonnes, were set up near ancient tombs and on the slopes of hills. Largest was the Great Menhir, in the village of Locmariaquer. Now broken into several pieces, it was once some 75 feet/23 meters long.

Dolmens—circular or parallel rows of upright stones topped by a flat slab—were probably burial chambers. Originally they were buried under mounds of dry stones or earth, called tumuli. Near the Great Menhir, you'll see the Merchants' Table dolmen, partially covered, with carved designs on the inside walls.

Lines of menhirs are probably the remains of ancient religious monuments. The greatest display, north of Carnac, is called the Alignments of Ménec. Nearly 1,100 upright stones stand in parallel rows, covering a wide area approximately ¾ mile/1,170 meters in length. Running from east to west (apparently to coincide with the lines of sunrise and sunset at the solstices), they end in a semicircle of giant stones.

■ **TOURING TIP** Signs direct visitors to the most important stones, but a detailed regional map will help you locate the lesser monuments. Some are found near roads; others are reached by paths through open fields.

CIRQUE DE GAVARNIE

Long ago, glaciers carved out circular basins high in the Pyrénées Mountains, and waters cut through rocky walls to cascade down from the tributary valleys. One of the most scenic regions is the Cirque de Gavarnie, a glacial amphitheater ringed by high peaks where waterfalls cascade more than 1,000 feet down steep walls.

From the religious center of Lourdes, you drive south to Luz-St-Sauveur along a road that parallels a mountain river, the Gave de Pau. You continue up the wild and beautiful valley to the small mountaineering resort of Gavarnie.

Here you can hire a hiking guide or rent a horse or mule for the trip. From Gavarnie you continue on foot or by animal along a trail to the scenic mountain site. Allow at least a half day for the excursion, and wear sturdy shoes.

ALONG THE WINDING SEINE

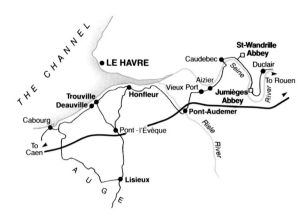

On the final miles of its journey from Burgundy to the sea, the Seine River winds through the rich Normandy countryside. In late April and May, when apple and cherry orchards are in bloom, you'll find this riverside route one of the loveliest in France.

The Seine has always been the vital and historic highway between Paris and the sea. In the days of Gaul, rivers were the main means of travel. Later, occupying Romans built their roads over well-trampled pathways. Monasteries established along the river became the region's religious and intellectual centers. Early in the 9th century, the Vikings sailed up the Seine in their *drakkars* to roam and pillage—and stayed to govern. William the Conqueror, too, knew this land well; it was from Normandy's shores that he sailed for Britain in 1066.

From Normandy's bustling port city of Rouen, take the main highway west to Duclair; then, about a mile beyond, follow the side road (D 65) along the Seine. Fruit orchards, small farms, timbered dwellings, and country homes border this delightful road. Brown-and-white cows graze beneath apple trees.

You can wander at will among the magnificent ruins of Jumièges Abbey. The outlines of the old churches are plainly visible, and arches soar into the trees. Birds trill overhead, and sunlight filters over ancient stone blocks.

Members of the Benedictine order still reside in St-Wandrille Abbey, east of Caudebec-en-Caux.

At Caudebec you and your car are ferried across the widening Seine, then you continue along the southern bank toward Vatteville. A bright green beech forest provides a pleasant change of pace before you are once more among apple trees and thatched, split-timbered Norman cottages.

Many old timbered buildings remain in Pont-Audemer, and several branches of the Risle River flow through town, providing some attractive views. Walkers will find interesting side streets and passageways to explore. From here, you can continue on to Honfleur (see page 38) and other coastal attractions.

■ **TOURING TIPS** **Fast trains from Paris (Gare St-Lazare) take you to Rouen in just over an hour; you can rent a car here for touring Normandy. Guidebooks can direct you to several country inns renowned for their regional food specialties.**

PILGRIMAGE TO ROCAMADOUR

Hanging from the cliffside above the winding Alzou Valley in southwest France, the buildings of Rocamadour appear to defy gravity. Since the Middle Ages, religious pilgrims have traveled here to honor the Black Madonna. From the settlement at the base of the cliff, pilgrims climb the great stairway to the ecclesiastical city; some kneel at every step. If you prefer, you can ascend by elevator. A path marked by stations of the cross leads up to the castle ramparts atop the cliff. The best view of Rocamadour is from the Hospitalet Road.

ALONG THE DORDOGNE

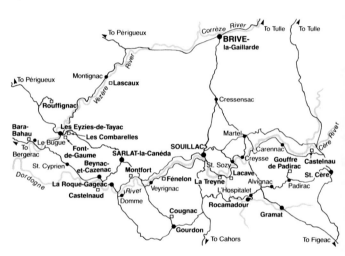

One of the longest rivers in France, the Dordogne is considered by many travelers to be the loveliest as well. From high in the Massif Central, it cuts diagonally southwest through the Périgord, France's unspoiled heartland, past cliffside villages and castle fortresses.

Quiet, flower-filled towns built of yellowish stone dot the Périgord region. Castle-lovers find a rewarding number of châteaux (many of them open to visitors); most of the clifftop castles were built as fortresses to guard the river valleys.

The lovely Dordogne Valley extends from Castelnau west to St-Cyprien. Roads parallel the river, occasionally crossing from one bank to the other.

Follow the river road. The red stone towers and ramparts of Castelnau Castle rise above the trees to command the confluence of the Dordogne and Cère rivers. Built in the 11th century, the large walled fortress is a superb example of medieval military architecture.

Houses roofed in brown tile cluster around Carennac's old priory. At Creysse, you climb flights of steps to

Seeming to defy gravity, Rocamadour's buildings hang from cliffside above the winding Alzou River.

reach vine-covered houses; a steep passageway leads to a church and castle ruins above the town. Reflecting the era of Louis XIV is graceful La Treyne Château, perched on a cliff above the Dordogne.

Market towns. The region's largest towns are Souillac, which grew up around an ancient abbey, and Sarlat, the capital of the district.

Sarlat's fascinating old section is ideal for strolling. Its buildings have been restored but are otherwise little changed since the 17th century. Mellow ocher-colored stone enhances the subtle beauty of the architecture. Some of the handsome gabled houses are ornamented with turrets, carved façades, and mullioned windows. On Saturday mornings, you'll see shoppers heading for the large open-air market.

Castles overlook the river. The Dordogne meanders through hills and woodlands, between cliffs crowned with castles, past lovely cliffside villages at Domme, La Roque-Gageac, Castelnaud, and Beynac-et-Cazenac.

You can visit a pair of castles: Fénelon's 15th-century military fortress, and restored Veyrignac, a 17th-century château. Montfort Castle (not open to the public) clings to a sheer rock above a deep bend in the river.

Attractive Domme crowns a rocky promontory on the river's south bank. Balconies, outside stairways, and climbing vines ornament the ocher stone buildings. Bright flowers bloom everywhere. From a clifftop belvedere, you see the Dordogne valley spread like a green carpet cut by a blue ribbon of river.

Along the north shore, La Roque-Gageac and Beynac-et-Cazenac have awesome perches, clinging to

cliffs that drop vertically to the Dordogne River. The ruins of Castelnaud fortress and several smaller castles rise on the south bank.

Late afternoon sun illuminates La Roque-Gageac's cliff face; its houses are mirrored in the calm waters below. Passageways lined with pretty houses lead to the church on the rock, where you have an excellent view of the meandering river.

Beynac-et-Cazenac's stern 13th-century castle looms atop a sheer cliff overlooking the river and village. You can reach it by climbing the town's narrow streets or by taking the road that begins west of the village.

St-Cyprien's massive church hangs onto the side of a hill near the river.

■ **TOURING TIPS** Fast trains speed south from Paris (Gare d'Austerlitz) to Brive-la-Gaillarde, where you continue on to Souillac. Local trains and buses provide limited service to riverside towns, but driving allows more comprehensive and slower-paced touring. Small country hotels offer Périgord food specialties, frequently flavored with bits of the black truffles for which the region is renowned. Most attractions close between noon and 2 P.M.; many museums also close on Tuesday.

PREHISTORIC CAVE ART

One of the world's richest prehistoric sites is the region around Les Eyzies-de-Tayac, along the Vézère River and its tributary valleys.

Neanderthal tribes roamed these hills and valleys some 150,000 years ago. Much later, Cro-Magnon people, representing a new stage in human evolution, emigrated here. Some 25,000 years ago, these hunting tribes found shelter in caves pitting the cliffs above the river valleys. And in these isolated caves, primitive artists drew pictures of the animals they stalked—horses, deer, bison, mammoths—and left remnants of tools and bones for modern archeologists to discover.

Begin your explorations with a visit to the National Museum of Prehistory in the cliffside castle overlooking Les Eyzies-de-Tayac. Diagrams explain prehistoric chronology, and you'll see objects and works of art discovered locally.

The outstanding Lascaux Cave near Montignac is closed to the public, but an excellent facsimile, Lascaux II, offers a look at replica drawings by artists using Paleolithic methods. Splendid examples of cave art can be seen at Font-de-Gaume and at Les Combarelles. Earliest known drawings are at Bara-Bahau, where animal outlines were carved into cave walls with sharpened flints. You'll explore galleries at Rouffignac by electric railway.

Many of the caves are closed on Tuesday; to preserve the paintings, some also limit the number of daily visitors. Check locally for current information.

MORE GREAT MUSEUMS FOR PARIS

In Paris, a city of great museums, recent additions to the city's arts menu are worth a visit.

A new home for the Impressionist paintings previously housed in the Jeu de Paume is the Musée d'Orsay, a stunning restoration of a turn-of-the-century train station that was spared from the wrecker's ball. It is open daily except Monday at 1 rue de Bellechasse, just across the Seine River from the Jardin des Tuileries. The closest Métro stop is Solférino. A Beaux-Arts entrance invites museumgoers inside, where its collection documents the evolution of French art from 1848 to 1914. The museum bridges the gap between earlier European paintings at the Louvre and modern collections at the Centre Georges-Pompidou.

The Musée Picasso contains only a fraction of the work of the artist. But what an artist! Located in the Hôtel Salé at 5 rue de Thorigny, in the Marais quarter, it offers dramatic testimony to the prolific output of Pablo Picasso. Twenty large rooms are filled with some 200 of his paintings, a group of sculptures, 1,000 prints, and 88 ceramics. Photographs, letters, and memorabilia shed light on his changing relationships with the women portrayed in his art. The Musée Picasso is closed Tuesday. Closest Métro stops are Saint-Paul and Filles-du-Calvaire.

Along Normandy coast, buildings bordering Honfleur's inner harbor are illuminated by late afternoon sun.

CAPTIVATING HONFLEUR

See map page 36

For more than a century, Honfleur has captivated artists. In fact, the Impressionist school of painting was born here on the Normandy coast.

Handsome Norman buildings of wood and slate line the quays rimming the town's enclosed harbor basin, where painters and photographers still come to capture Honfleur's character and charm. Fishing boats and quayside buildings are reflected in the quiet waters.

During the 1860s, Eugène Boudin encouraged his fellow painters—among them Courbet, Monet, Jongkind, and Daubigny—to join him on the Normandy coast, where they recorded their impressions of the region's changing light and mood. They gathered for conversation and fellowship at the St-Siméon inn on the Côte de Grâce.

Spared major war damage, Honfleur has changed little in appearance since the 17th century. Mirrored in the old harbor are colorful boats and tall, slender houses topped by steep slate roofs. Commercial fishermen mend their nets along the river quay, where fishing boats tie up in the tidal estuary.

From Quai St-Étienne you look across to narrow, slate-faced buildings reflected in the water. Fishing boats and pleasure craft rock gently at their moorings. You can learn more about old Honfleur on a visit to the museum now housed in Saint Stephen's church.

At the entrance to the old basin is La Lieutenance, the 16th-century house of the King's Lieutenant, the governor of Honfleur. A nearby plaque commemorates Samuel de Champlain, who sailed from Honfleur early in the 17th century to found Quebec. Narrow cobbled streets lined by typical Norman houses (wood-frame buildings roofed in slate) branch off the harbor quays.

Stroll up the Rue des Logettes to Place Ste-Catherine, which bustles with activity on market days. Facing the marketplace is the unique church of Saint Catherine, constructed by shipwrights entirely of wood (except for its foundations); its interior has twin naves that peak to resemble ships' hulls. Bells ring out from a church bell tower nearby.

You can see some of the luminous seascapes and pictures of Norman peasant life painted by Boudin and his contemporaries in the Eugène Boudin Museum on Rue Albert 1*er* (closed Tuesday and in winter). The museum also displays traditional Norman apparel.

Above town on the quiet Côte de Grâce, you can visit a small, tree-shaded chapel and enjoy the view over the town and Seine estuary.

■ **TOURING TIPS** Frequent trains leave Paris (Gare St-Lazare) for Normandy. In Lisieux, Caen, Deauville, or Le Havre, you can board a bus at the Gare Routière (the bus station) and continue on to Honfleur. If you're driving, you'll enjoy the river route along the Seine (see page 36).

CASTLES IN THE TOURAINE

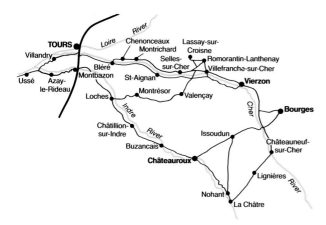

The storybook castles of the French countryside have a magnetic attraction for visitors. Striking in architecture, rich in art treasures and sumptuous furnishings, the châteaux reflect the Renaissance days of dalliance and intrigue, when the court moved from one castle to another at the king's whim. No less delightful is the gentle landscape itself, a pastoral panorama topped by pale blue skies washed by luminous light. Calm waterways mirror castle towers, vineyards line sunny slopes, and blooming flowers add their gracious touches everywhere.

Some of the region's castles flank two main Loire tributaries, the reed-bordered Indre and the meandering Cher, which flow into the Loire River west of Tours.

Castles along the Indre. Near the mouth of the river, the white fortress of Ussé rises above terraced gardens to stand out against a forested cliff. Bristling with turrets and chimneys, it has an intriguing air of mystery. According to legend, Charles Perrault, the French writer of fairy tales, used Ussé as his inspiration for Sleeping Beauty's castle.

Partially built over the Indre River, Azay-le-Rideau benefits from a harmonious setting amid woods and water. Renaissance furnishings decorate its interior.

During the 1830s and '40s, Honoré de Balzac did much of his writing at the castle of Saché; his room has been preserved as a Balzac literary museum. You reach the castle, on the banks of the Indre southeast of Azay-le-Rideau, along scenic route D 17.

At Loches, a notable fortress overlooks the river and medieval town. Many political and religious prisoners were confined in the castle's sinister dungeons.

Between the Indre and the Cher rivers, Valençay château combines Renaissance architecture with touches of classical design. Animals and exotic birds roam freely in its park. An automobile museum on the grounds contains more than 60 vintage models dating from 1898.

Upriver from Châteauroux near Nohant is the 18th-century mansion of French novelist George Sand (born Aurore Dupin). Once a salon for writers, artists, and musicians, it is now a museum. Additional mementoes of this remarkable woman and her friends are displayed in the regional museum in nearby La Châtre.

Cher Valley byways. You'll find more lovely castles along the Cher and its tributaries. North of the river, amid lake-speckled woods near Lassay-sur-Croisne, you'll discover the delightful Château de Moulin, a pink-and-white brick castle surrounded by a moat.

The Cher River mirrors castle towers at Selles-sur-Cher, where a grim medieval fortress contrasts with a gracious Renaissance mansion. Below St-Aignan, take the side road to Monthou, then continue on to charming Gué-Péan castle, an elegant blue-and-white gem set at the end of a peaceful little valley far from any town.

Best known of the Cher castles, Chenonceaux spans the river on a graceful arched bridge. According to legend, Henry II gave Chenonceaux to his mistress, Diane de Poitiers, but on the king's death his widow, Catherine de Medici, claimed Chenonceaux for herself. A splendid avenue of plane trees leads to the château; rich furnishings decorate its interior. You can stroll in the gardens or along the river's wooded banks.

Near the mouth of the Cher, west of Tours, you'll come to Villandry, known for its elegant formal gardens, sculptured hedges, herb-and-vegetable garden, and water displays. From the castle courtyard, you'll have a vista of the Cher and Loire valleys.

■ **TOURING TIPS** Fast trains link Paris with Tours, where rental cars are available. Evening *Son et Lumière* (Sound and Light) performances dramatize history at some of the well-known castles; for information, inquire at the tourist information office in Tours. Smaller castles may be closed to visitors between noon and 2 P.M. and one day a week, usually Tuesday. A detailed map is helpful in locating the smaller castles.

BOURGES, CATHEDRAL CITY

As you approach Bourges from any direction, you see the tall outline of the cathedral soaring above the city. Built between 1192 and 1324, the Bourges cathedral is outstanding, renowned especially for its stained-glass windows and for the carved statues adorning its five doors.

Scattered along the narrow streets of the old town are many medieval buildings constructed with joists and corbels, half-timbered of wide red beams and cream-colored plaster. Most notable of all is the richly decorated Palais Jacques-Cœur, a lavishly furnished 15th-century mansion built by a wealthy merchant who was one of the king's counselors.

The merchant's name has also been given to the Route Jacques-Cœur, a touring circuit through the Bourges countryside that links a number of castle-homes open to the public. You drive along the tree-lined Cher River and through forests and rolling pastureland where white cows graze placidly. For information on the route, inquire at the Syndicat d'Initiative (tourist information office), located across from the cathedral in Bourges.

Giethoorn, Netherlands

Bruges, Belgium

Luxembourg City

Friesland Villages,
page 43

Leeuwarden

Map, page 43

Enkhuizen,
page 42

Zaan District,
page 42

Giethoorn,
page 41

Zwolle

Amsterdam

NETHERLANDS

Bulb Fields,
page 44

The Hague

Utrecht

Utrecht,
page 44

Rotterdam

Arnhem

Antwerp

Bruges

Bruges, page 47

Ghent

Maastricht

Limburg,
page 45

Garden Touring,
page 48

Brussels

BELGIUM

Map, page 45

Hasselt

Namur

Map,
page 46

Meuse Valley,
page 46

Clervaux

Vianden, page 49

Little Switzerland,
page 48

Vianden

Wine Route,
page 49

Mersch

Luxembourg

Map, page 48

LUXEMBOURG

| 0 | | 25 | | 50 Mi |
| 0 | 25 | 50 | 75 | Km |

LOW COUNTRIES

Netherlands ▪ Belgium ▪ Luxembourg

In the heart of Europe, our travels take us to a rich selection of engaging towns, outstanding gardens, unusual museums, and rustic markets.

Holland excursions lead to bulb gardens bordering the North Sea, a town—Giethoorn—where you travel by boat, the pastoral Friesland countryside, and to the castle-studded hills of Limburg. In Belgium you can stroll through historic Bruges, go garden touring near Brussels, or travel leisurely through the scenic Meuse Valley. Luxembourg routes explore its wine country, the wooded ravines known as Little Switzerland, and the Vianden district.

You'll find suggestions for cycling routes, boat trips, hiking excursions, and visits to caves, markets, open-air museums, and World War II battlefield memorials.

BY BOAT THROUGH GIETHOORN

See map page 40

Rustic Giethoorn is unique—a village where nearly all traffic goes by boat. Located northwest of Meppel in West Overijssel, this charming hamlet has no streets, only shallow canals shaped by peat diggers three centuries ago.

Houses topped by thatched roofs sit among trees on individual islands, each reached by boat or a high, narrow, wooden footbridge. Open flat-bottomed boats called punts transport villagers, supplies, and cows through the maze of waterways. The punts are poled along the canals.

If you feel energetic, you can rent your own punt and pole your way through the town's canals, but most visitors join one of the boat trips departing near the parking area.

For a different perspective, take an unhurried stroll along the narrow path beside the main canal. You'll enjoy a more leisurely look at individual cottages and their attractive little gardens.

▪ **TOURING TIPS** If you're traveling by local transport, take the train to Meppel or Zwolle; then board the Noord-Westhoek bus to Giethoorn. Organized boat trips through the village's canals depart near the parking area. You can also rent smaller boats there if you want to explore the canals independently.

ENKHUIZEN'S ZUIDERZEE MUSEUM

See map page 40

The fascinating Zuiderzee Museum in Enkhuizen, northeast of Amsterdam, depicts the everyday life in Dutch fishing villages bordering the Zuyder Zee between 1880 and 1932, before they were cut off from the open sea. In 1932, the completion of the barrier dam, the Afsluitdijk, turned the open Zuyder Zee into an enclosed lake—the IJsselmeer—and transformed the lives of the fisherfolk living along its shores.

In the open-air museum, exhibits in more than 130 houses along streets, canals, and alleys show how families lived and worked—fishing on the open sea, farming on an urban lot, making sails in a sail loft, curing meats in a smokehouse, or running a steam laundry. You also can stroll along Enkhuizen's dike and look out over the IJsselmeer.

Another part of the museum, called the Binnenmuseum, includes a ship hall with 11 old sailing ships and exhibits of traditional village costumes, furnished interiors, model ships, and other displays.

You'll appreciate Enkhuizen's rich past even more on a stroll around the town itself. Landmarks include the Town Hall, the Zuiderkerk (the village church), and the Drommedaris rampart and fortress walls.

Two other West Frisian towns worth a visit are Hoorn and Medemblik; from May through mid-September, you can ride a steam train between the towns. Hoorn's folklore market is held every Wednesday from mid-June to mid-August, and Medemblik has a Saturday morning market.

Visitors can watch craftspeople demonstrate traditional crafts at the Holland Handicraft Centre in De Hout, midway between Hoorn and Enkhuizen; hours are 9 A.M. to 7 P.M. daily from April through October.

■ **TOURING TIPS** Trains depart frequently from Amsterdam's Central Station for Enkhuizen; the trip takes about 1 hour. Visitors arrive at the museum by boat; one departs every 15 minutes from the car park area and from a quay behind the train station. You can return by boat or walk back through the town. The open-air museum is open daily from 10 A.M. to 5 P.M. from mid-April through mid-October. The Binnenmuseum is open from mid-February through December, weekdays and Saturday from 10 A.M. to 5 P.M., and Sunday from noon to 5 P.M.

WINDMILLS ALONG THE ZAAN

See map page 40

During the 1600s, the town of Zaandam was the center of the important Dutch shipbuilding industry. Russia's Peter the Great was one of many who came from other countries to study the Dutch methods.

Hundreds of windmills pumped water from the lowlands. Some industrial mills ground grain and others sawed wood for the shipbuilding industry. Most of the

Distinctive Zaan district houses face canal at De Zaanse Schans. Mail is delivered by young woman on bicycle.

mills are gone now, but you'll still see some along the waterways.

Near Zaandijk, about 10 miles/15 km north of Amsterdam, typical houses and mills of the district have been grouped into a small village called Zaanse Schans, along the east bank of the Zaan River.

Buildings facing the cobbled mall have been converted into small shops, museums, and a restaurant. Near the main entrance, an arched bridge and narrow paths invite you to explore a canal-laced village of compact, green-painted houses, each with its white-painted finial above the front gable. People live in the houses; you may see a home gardener tidying up a neat flower bed or a ruddy-cheeked young woman on a bicycle delivering the day's mail.

Built in 1786, the village's mustard mill still grinds mustard. In summer you can visit the De Kat paint mill, which grinds minerals and wood. Also on the grounds near the river are buildings housing cheese-making equipment, an old-fashioned bakery, and a wooden shoe workshop.

Sightseeing cruises departing from Zaanse Schans offer views of the village's buildings and windmills from the river. There are also pedestrian and cycling paths that lead along the dike to several windmills bordering the Zaan River and then continue on into the countryside.

In nearby Koog aan de Zaan you can visit a merchant's house that has been converted into a windmill museum. Its exhibits focus on mill history and construction.

■ **TOURING TIPS** De Zaanse Schans is open to visitors daily from April through October, on weekends only in winter. It's a 15-minute train ride from Amsterdam's Central Station to the Koog-Zaandijk station; take the "stop train" local heading to Alkmaar. Signs direct visitors to Zaanse Schans. From April through September, cruises on the Zaan River depart hourly between 10 A.M. and 5 P.M.

FRIESLAND VILLAGE LOOP

The province of Friesland lies off the heavily traveled routes, yet this pastoral, lake-studded land has a special appeal. It's an ideal region to explore by boat; canals link the Frisian lakes and lead far inland, offering boaters intriguing perspectives of the countryside.

From Sneek, the yachting center of the Frisian lakes, you venture west to Bolsward, one of Friesland's oldest towns, and on to delightful country villages that proudly preserve the rustic tradition of 19th-century Holland. Your route includes the pottery town of Makkum, the Zuider Zee port of Hindeloopen, and delightful Sloten.

One of Friesland's oldest towns, Bolsward was a member of the Hanseatic League. You can visit the handsome, richly decorated town hall from April through October (closed Sunday); Bolsward is also proud of its famous 15th-century Martini Church with its beautifully carved pulpit and celebrated organ.

Makkum is renowned for its pottery. You can see examples in the Frisian Potterie Museum in the old weighing house from May to mid-September; then visit the pottery at Turfmarkt 61.

Aldfaers Erf Route. In the triangle formed by Bolsward, Makkum, and Workum, you'll discover four tiny villages that preserve the spirit of 19th-century rural life—on the farm and in the family home, village shop, school, bakery, and carpenter's workshop. The route, which means Our Forefathers' Heritage, offers a delightful look at another era. Most attractions are open daily from 9 A.M. to 6 P.M. from April through October.

You follow signposts along narrow roads that twist through the meadows, linking villages and remote homesteads. In Exmorra, you can visit a Frisian agricultural museum and a 19th-century grocer's shop with adjoining village school.

At Allingawier, you can visit an 18th-century farmhouse furnished in period style; inside the barn, you'll see horse-drawn sleighs and carts and restored living quarters. There's also a renovated bakery and a village church nearby.

In Piaam, nestled behind the old dike, the Fûgelhûs (a bird museum) shows the rich variety of bird life that inhabits the polders behind the dike. Meals are available here in a restored 18th-century farmhouse. In Ferwoude, the last of these villages, you can visit a farmhouse used as a carpenter's workshop.

Continue on to the historic town of Workum; among its notable attractions are the handsome town hall, the Weigh House, the medieval church of St. Gertrude, and the Jopie Huisman Museum.

Hindeloopen. Once a Zuider Zee fishing port, this charming canal-laced town has now become a center for wind surfing and other water sports on the IJsselmeer. Crossing the drawbridge near the harbor, you'll probably pass several old sailors discussing their adventures on the "liars' bench" nearby. In summer, the harbor wall provides a good vantage point for enjoying the sun and watching harbor activity.

You'll cross wooden bridges to reach narrow lanes, lined with the brick houses once occupied by sea captains and their families. Examples of old Hindeloopen painted furniture, with its Scandinavian and Oriental influences, are displayed in the Hidde Nijland Museum. In the Frisian Skating Museum, you'll see an unusual collection of ice skates and mementoes of the famous Eleven Towns Race and Tour. Both museums are open daily from May through October.

Sloten. The smallest town in Friesland, Sloten has only 700 inhabitants. It's a charming little fortified town with ramparts, watergates, an old windmill, and a moat.

■ **TOURING TIPS** Information on touring Friesland is available in the VVV tourist office in Leeuwarden, beside the train station; you can get a map brochure showing the Aldfaers Erf Route. Inquire at the VVV office in Hindeloopen for a map showing a suggested walking tour. English translations of both leaflets are available.

MAKKUM POTTERY

For more than 300 years, Holland has been known for its hand-painted earthenware. At one time, more than 70 factories specialized in ceramics.

Pottery has been produced in Makkum since early in the 17th century; today the town is best known for its handmade tiles, which have been produced by a family business—Tichelaar's Royal Pottery and Tile Factory—since 1674.

Visitors are welcome to tour the factory on weekdays from 10 A.M. to 4 P.M. (Friday from 10 to 3); the pottery showroom is open on weekdays until 5:30 and Saturday from 9 to 4.

SAMPLING UTRECHT

See map page 40

Busy Utrecht is Holland's fourth largest city, but its compact center encourages exploration on foot. An encircling canal outlines boundaries of the medieval city. You can explore independently or join a Sunday morning walking tour (see below). For a map, visit one of the city's VVV tourist information offices.

City highlights. If you have only a single day to sample Utrecht's attractions, start with a look at the Dom, its recently restored cathedral. Allow time at the end of your tour to stroll along the quays beside the Oude Gracht, the old canal which cuts through the central city, and to pause in one of the outdoor cafés. Utrecht has many fine museums; here are three superb ones you shouldn't miss:

Museum Het Catharijneconvent, Nieuwegracht 63, contains the largest collection of medieval religious art in the Netherlands and important works by 17th century artists, including Rembrandt and Frans Hals.

The Dutch Railway Museum, currently being renovated, is located in a former train station at Johan van Oldenbarneveltlaan 6. It includes illustrated displays and an amazing collection of Dutch rail cars and trams.

If you've ever enjoyed a Dutch street organ, you'll want to stop at the delightful museum called From Musical Clock to Street Organ, located at Buurkerkhof 10 in a former church. Its automated musical instruments range from clocks and music boxes to elaborate dance hall organs. Guides demonstrate many of the instruments during tours, which begin hourly from 10 to 4.

Utrecht's countryside. If you're driving, you'll enjoy a look at the water-laced landscape of Utrecht province. You can wander at will, discovering delightful small towns, such as Wijk bij Duurstede and Oudewater (southeast and southwest of Utrecht, respectively).

Northwest of Utrecht near Vleuten is De Haar Castle, largest castle in Holland and renowned for its valuable art collection and large wooded park. Visitors are welcome from March 1 to November 15, except from August 15 to October 15, when the owners are in residence. Several smaller castles are also open to visitors.

In summer you can take an all-day boat trip on the River Vecht from Utrecht to Loenen. Near Breukelen, you'll see country mansions built in the late 17th and early 18th centuries by Amsterdam merchants who made their fortunes in the East Indies trade.

The Loosdrecht lakes attract water sports enthusiasts. Sightseeing boats tour the lakes in summer.

■ **TOURING TIPS** City and regional tourist information is available at the main VVV office at Vredenburg 90 or at the VVV booth in Hoog Catharijne shopping center. From mid-May to late September, a guided 1½-hour city walking tour departs each Sunday morning at 10:30 from the main VVV office. All three museums are open Tuesday through Friday from 10 A.M. to 5 P.M.; on weekends, the art museum is open Saturday and Sunday from 11 to 5, while the railway and musical museums are open Saturday from 10 to 5 and Sunday from 1 to 5. On Saturday seven markets dot the city.

Keukenhof Gardens near Lisse is abloom with tulips, hyacinths, and other bulbs from late March to mid-May.

SPRING IN THE BULB FIELDS

See map page 40

The Dutch love flowers, and you'll see blooms everywhere. In the fields, the peak display comes in spring, beginning around the end of March and continuing until mid-May. Along Holland's west coast, inland from the North Sea, millions of blooming bulbs turn the land into one vast garden, a kaleidoscope of color. The largest concentration of flowering bulbs is located between Haarlem and Leiden, but you'll find other bulb areas from Haarlem north to Den Helder and in the countryside near Enkhuizen.

Keukenhof Gardens, near Lisse, is a showplace in spring; its 69 acres/28 hectares are planted with more than 6 million crocus, narcissus, hyacinth, and tulip bulbs each year. Greenhouses contain special displays. From late March through mid-May, the bulb exhibition is open daily from 8 A.M. to 6:30 P.M.

During April and May, bulb grower Frans Roozen welcomes visitors to tour his magnificent display gardens and greenhouses in Vogelenzang daily from 8 A.M. to 6 P.M. Summer bulbs begin to bloom in July.

Blossoming fruit trees add their beauty to the Dutch countryside from mid-April until mid-May. Many orchards are located in the Betuwe region in Gelderland province; in the southern part of Limburg; and in the Zuid-Beveland district in Zeeland. At VVV tourist offices, you can purchase folders that map out the signposted routes and describe nearby attractions.

■ **TOURING TIPS** For information on public gardens and floral events, contact the Netherlands Board of Tourism (address on page 128). Several signposted motoring and cycling routes wind through the bulb country; it's best to do leisurely touring on a weekday during the bulb season. In the spring, Netherlands Railways issues special excursion tickets to Keukenhof that include rail and bus transportation and the admission fee.

HOLLAND BATTLES THE SEA

Over the centuries, the Dutch have labored to reclaim their land from the sea. One of the most ambitious projects ever undertaken has finally been completed in Zeeland, near the delta of the Rhine, Maas (Meuse), and Scheldt rivers.

You can learn more about this massive project —both the background and the work involved—at the Delta Expo exhibit near Westerschouwen. It's located southwest of Rotterdam and west of Zierikzee, at the mouth of the Eastern Scheldt. Video and slide presentations, models, and photographs give a broad picture of the plan's vast scope.

From April through October, Delta Expo is open daily from 10 to 5; in winter it is closed on Monday and Tuesday. Netherlands Railways issues special day excursion tickets; you'll travel by train to Rotterdam, then board the Zuid-West-Nederland bus to reach the exhibit. For more information, contact the Netherlands Board of Tourism (address on page 128).

A LOOK AT LIMBURG

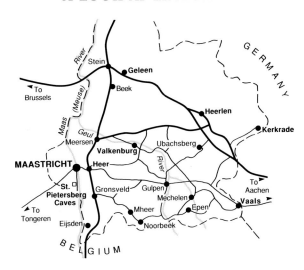

Holland's hilly southern province of Limburg nestles along the Maas (Meuse) River, between the Belgian Ardennes and German Eifel ranges. Near the country's southern tip is the old city of Maastricht, founded by the Romans in 50 B.C. and enriched by later cultures. It's a city with an international flavor, for Germany and Belgium are only a few minutes drive away.

Maastricht is a city to explore on foot. At the VVV Maastricht office at Kleine Staat 1, ask for a brochure that maps a walking tour through the pedestrian streets of the old Stokstraat quarter. Landmarks along the route include several churches, the 13th-century city wall, and Vrijthof square. Outdoor cafés dot the town.

Excavations dating from the Roman era are located in the Derlon Cellar Museum (open Sunday from noon to 4 P.M. or during guided tours) beneath the Hotel Derlon.

In the Bonnefanten Museum at Dominikanerplein 5, above a shopping center, you'll see both archaeological remains and excellent works on religious and secular art.

Boat trips on the Maas River depart from April through September. At the St. Pietersberg Caves, you'll see great underground galleries, carved out of marl limestone, that sheltered people during wartime battles.

Ruins of ancient Valkenburg Castle loom above nearby Valkenburg, a thriving resort in the scenic Geul River valley. Many local buildings are built from blocks of the local yellow marlstone. Valkenburg's casino and excellent restaurants attract many visitors. Soon to be completed on a wooded slope just outside town is Thermae 2000, a hillside spa with extensive facilities.

No visit to south Limburg is complete without a tour through the beautiful Geul Valley. As you drive or cycle along roads near the border, you'll discover delightful villages of white buildings. Several of the region's handsome castles have been converted to comfortable castle hotels or restaurants; others are private homes.

■ **TOURING TIPS** Guided walking tours of Maastricht depart from the VVV office on Saturday at 2 P.M. in spring and fall (daily in July and August and on holiday weekends). For information on castle hotels, contact the Netherlands Board of Tourism (address on page 128). Limburg province not only offers some of Holland's most scenic countryside, but also some of its most highly rated restaurants. Look for regional food specialties on menus; in May and June, locally grown white asparagus is featured at many restaurants. Maastricht is noted for its cozy pub-cafés; for a map and list, inquire at the VVV. Bicycles can be rented locally for day excursions or longer trips.

It's a colorful show: Traditional cheese market draws visitors to Alkmaar each Friday morning in summer.

BELGIUM'S MEUSE VALLEY

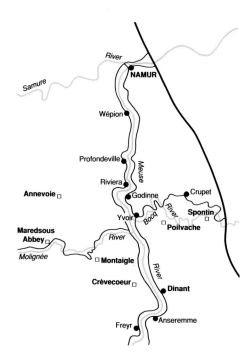

Vacationing Europeans have made southeastern Belgium's Meuse Valley a busy vacation playground. Yet even in summer the tributary valleys are relatively quiet, and everywhere you come upon unexpected villages, castles, and abbeys hidden among abundant flowers and dramatic rock formations.

A leisurely trip from Namur up the Meuse to Dinant, with short detours away from the main valley, offers opportunities to visit several castles and tour a magnificent garden at Annevoie Castle. Massive citadel fortresses in Namur and Dinant offer commanding views of the Meuse Valley; both can be reached by teleferic. In Namur the citadel grounds overlook the meeting of the Sambre and Meuse rivers and offer a scenic panorama south toward Profondeville and Dinant. Visitors can also reach the site by footpath or by car.

From Namur you head south, along the scenic route up the Meuse Valley. Lawns extend to the water's edge, and the river is alive with pleasure craft. In summer, excursion boats cruise between Namur and Dinant, passing through several river locks on a route lined with flowers and fortresses.

Upriver from Namur, the riverbanks gradually grow higher and steeper, becoming crowded with rocks and boulders. Some of these conceal caves. From the scenic road you have good views of riverside villages and romantic ruins perched on hills overlooking the valley.

Attractive Profondeville is the starting point for a number of walks. One favorite path follows the riverbank, where you can enjoy river activity.

Opposite the town of Godinne, at Annevoie Castle, you'll find one of Europe's loveliest gardens. Here seasonal flowers, woodlands, and water displays—fountains, cascades, and pools—transform the landscaped château gardens into a smaller version of Versailles. The gardens are open daily from April through October. Guided visits of the castle last one hour.

Travel east of Yvoir to visit the fortified village of Crupet and the feudal castle of Spontin, the oldest castle in Belgium and still inhabited. Tours of Spontin are available daily (by appointment from November through February).

The Molignée Valley, west of Yvoir, contains one of the prettiest of the Meuse tributaries. You see the ruins of Château de Montaigle on your way to Maredsous Abbey, a Benedictine monastery that dominates the scenic valley.

South of Yvoir you pass the ruins of two more castles. Poilvache was one of the most important Meuse Valley fortresses during the Middle Ages. Across the river on the left bank are the ruins of Crèvecoeur, where legend says three noblewomen leaped from the ramparts to escape invaders.

The town of Dinant clusters below its citadel at the base of rocky cliffs. Boat trips depart on a 3½-hour trip downriver to Namur or head upstream to Anseremme, Freyr, and the French frontier.

■ **TOURING TIPS** **You can tour both the Namur and Dinant citadels. If you wish to enjoy the scenery from the river, you'll find cruises of varying lengths and destinations departing from Namur and Dinant in summer. Guided visits of Annevoie Castle are available daily from Easter through November.**

BATTLEFIELD MEMORIALS

The Low Countries were the site of many famous battles during World War I and II. Several memorials and museums honor those who fought in the conflicts and offer vivid memorabilia of their human and historical aspects.

In central Holland, landmarks and memorials recall the Battle of Arnhem in September 1944. You can visit a museum housed in the former Hotel Hartenstein, Allied headquarters during the battle. A detailed brochure is available from the Netherlands Board of Tourism or at local VVV (tourist information) offices.

During the winter of 1944–45, the Battle of the Bulge was fought in the Ardennes Mountains, which span eastern Belgium and northern Luxembourg. In Belgium, the Bastogne Historical Center and nearby American Memorial mark this bitter battle and honor the American soldiers who lost their lives there. In Bastogne's war museum, dramatic exhibits and a film with commentary in several languages recreate elements of the battle.

Luxembourg museums in Diekirch, Wiltz, Clervaux, and Ettelbruck also have exhibits that commemorate the Battle of the Bulge.

BELGIUM'S BEGUINAGES

*During the Middle Ages, many women entered into a female community known as the **Beguinage** (or begijnhof). Beguines were either women left on their own because of war or the Crusades, or those who wanted a life of religious devotion but were unwilling to take full vows as nuns.*

They lived in small, individual houses protected by an enclosure, which also contained a church, an infirmary, and a weaving center. Consecrated as a parish, the enclosure formed a town within a town, with its own laws and way of life.

Once there were more than 80 beguinages on Belgian territory. Today, about a dozen of these peaceful havens remain. You can visit beguinages in Bruges, Ghent, Kortrijk, Leuven, and in several smaller towns, including Diest, Diksmuide, Lier, and Turnhout.

STROLLING THROUGH BRUGES

See map page 40

A sleepy ambience today pervades Bruges, one of the great trading centers of Europe in the 14th and 15th centuries. Canals meander through the old Flemish town, and narrow cobbled streets lead past façades little changed in hundreds of years. Art museums display paintings from the city's golden age.

In medieval days, merchants traveled to Bruges from all parts of the world, sailing up the Zwin River with rich cargoes—wool from Britain, silks from Asia, and spices from the Middle East. Vast fortunes were made in the sea trade and in the manufacture of woolen cloth. Merchant guilds built impressive meeting halls. Prosperous burghers converted their wealth into handsome houses, monuments, and churches, and they encouraged and supported Flemish artists.

But in the 16th century the Zwin silted up. Merchants and bankers moved on to Antwerp, and Bruges became a neglected backwater.

Heart of the city.   The heart of any Flemish town is its market square. In Bruges, outdoor cafes and ornamented buildings rim the Markt. Here you'll find the city's covered market, and the most famous landmark in Bruges, the belfry. Its 47-bell carillon is one of the most famous in Europe. If you feel energetic, you can climb the 366 steps to the top of the belfry for a spectacular view.

A side street leads from the Markt to the Burg square. The 14th-century Stadhuis (town hall) contains a colorfully decorated Gothic hall used for weddings and important civic events. Other government buildings and the Chapel of the Holy Blood also border the Burg.

Leisurely strolling.   Follow the canal southwest to find the art treasures of Bruges. Among the aristocratic old houses bordering the water is the Groeninge Museum, containing masterpieces by many of the Flemish painters who contributed to the city's renown.

The Gruuthuse Museum, former palace of an aristocratic family, is furnished with decorative and utilitarian objects of the Renaissance. Major works by Hans Memling are housed in the former Hospital of St. John.

Cross the canal bridge leading into the Beguinage, a secluded compound of small whitewashed houses and a chapel bordering a large parklike square. Founded in 1245, it once served as a refuge for devout women whose husbands were away fighting in the Crusades.

Just beyond is the Minnewater, the busy inner port of Bruges during the Middle Ages. A wooded park and massive stone towers of the old city walls frame this peaceful vista.

Another Bruges walk leads northeast from the Markt to the Volkskunde (folklore museum) on Balstraat, where exhibits depict the history and traditions of Bruges and its people. Across the street at Kantcentrum Brugge, the lace center, students learn the fundamentals of bobbin lacemaking, a skill practiced in Bruges for hundreds of years.

On pleasant days, sightseeing boats cruise along the canals; overhanging willows shade the waterways as you glide past ancient buildings and beneath arched bridges. Several houses, once occupied by early merchants, have been converted into small hotels.

■ **TOURING TIPS**   You can reach Bruges by train in less than an hour from Brussels. For a map of the city showing suggested walking routes, stop at the Bruges tourist office, Burg 11. From March to November, sightseeing boats depart for canal tours from docks along the Rozenhoedkaai and Dijver. You can also travel by boat from Bruges to the former outer port at Damme (several round trips daily from April through October).

Golden daffodils dot Beguinage grounds in Bruges each spring. Benedictine nuns occupy perimeter buildings.

GARDEN TOURING IN BELGIUM

See map page 40

Two outstanding gardens outside Brussels offer inspiration for gardeners. Both can be reached easily from the capital.

Tropical and subtropical plants take the spotlight at the National Plant Garden of Belgium, located at Meise, 8 miles/14 km north of Brussels. The plants are displayed in 13 large exhibition greenhouses, laid out according to native geographical areas. A favorite of many visitors is the Victorian glasshouse, where water- and swamp-plants are featured. The garden is open year round Monday through Thursday from 2 to 4 P.M.; from Easter through October, it is also open on Sunday afternoons from 2 to 6.

A delightful rock garden is the main attraction at Huizingen Provincial Domain, located about 7 miles/12 km southwest of Brussels in Huizingen. In this botanical wonderland, more than 1,200 different types of flowers, shrubs, and other plants grow beside brooks and small waterfalls. You'll also discover a garden for the blind containing plants that can be recognized by their scent or shape. The large parkland offers visitors woodland walks, boating on a lake, and other recreational activities. The rock garden and park are open daily from 9 A.M. until sunset.

■ **TOURING TIPS** **Visitors can use public transportation to reach both gardens. To visit the National Plant Garden, take Bus L from Brussels' North Station to Meise. To travel to Huizingen, board Tram 55 (Brouckèreplein-Brussels) and change in Ukkel Calevoet to Bus UB or UH for Huizingen.**

Fortified gateway guards entrance to Mersch. Medieval bastions still command views over many towns and valleys.

OPEN-AIR MUSEUM AT BOKRIJK

Midway between Hasselt and Genk, about 55 miles/88 km northeast of Brussels, the Flemish open-air museum at Bokrijk recreates the Belgium of centuries past. Rural dwellings dating from 1500 to 1920, along with barns, windmills, and even an old Romanesque church, have been assembled and furnished to depict village life. The museum also has an "old town" section.

On the grounds of Bokrijk's large provincial park you'll find wooded areas with footpaths, a rose garden containing about 15,000 shrubs, an arboretum with 3,000 labeled trees and shrubs, sports facilities, a children's playground, and several restaurants.

The open-air museum is open from April through October; the park is open all year.

HIKING IN "LITTLE SWITZERLAND"

Along Luxembourg's northeastern border, the region known as Little Switzerland is a hiker's delight. Bordered by the Sûre River and cut by the Ernz Noire, it is a land of wooded ravines and dramatic rock formations.

Echternach and Berdorf are favorite summer resorts near the entrance to the region. The ancient city of Echternach, founded in the 7th century, boasts architectural ruins dating from the Gallo-Roman period. The medieval buildings, including an elegant town hall built in 1444, form the backdrop for the town's festive Whit Tuesday dancing procession and celebration.

Dozens of well-marked footpaths lead to waterfalls, rocky areas, and scenic viewpoints. A favorite destination is the Gorge du Loup (Wolf's Throat), a fearful-looking rock crevasse. Many visitors come here for fishing and rock climbing. Canoers and kayakers paddle on the Sûre River, and cyclists pedal along bicycle paths through scenic countryside.

Motorists enjoy the scenic forest road that follows the Ernz Noire River from Mullerthal to Grundhof, where it flows into the Sûre. Another pleasant route leads through the woods to Larochette, set in the narrow wooded valley of the Ernz Blanche River. The ruins of two castles overlook the charming old market town.

■ **TOURING TIPS** Accommodations in this popular vacation spot will be found at Echternach and Grundhof in the Sûre Valley and near Berdorf, Mullerthal, and other small towns. Information on hiking trails and other activities is available at the tourist office in Echternach; you can also purchase guides in Luxembourg that offer route suggestions and show how to combine auto or train travel with hiking.

LUXEMBOURG'S WINE ROUTE

See map page 48

Neatly tended vineyards cover the hills bordering the Moselle River along Luxembourg's southeastern border. Beginning in Schengen, at the southern tip, explore the wine district as you travel north through Remich, Grevenmacher, and smaller wine centers like Ehren, Wormeldange, and Wasserbillig.

From spring through autumn you can stop at wine cellars along the route, perhaps buying a bottle of the delicate white wine to go with a picnic lunch of smoked Ardennes ham. Wine tastings, fairs, and festivals enliven many wine district towns from April through September.

This sunny district is popular with European vacationers. You'll see anglers casting from the shore, strollers enjoying tree-shaded walks along the river, and water activities—boating, windsurfing, and waterskiing.

In Bech-Kleinmacher, just south of Remich, a dwelling dating from 1617 has been restored and refurnished as a museum depicting the life of early vintners. You'll see the kitchen with its hooded fireplace, equipment used for buttermaking and spinning, vintner's tools, and a cooper's shop. From Easter through October, the museum is open afternoons daily except Monday.

For a leisurely look at Luxembourg's vineyard district, consider a day excursion aboard the M. S. *Princesse Marie-Astrid,* which cruises the Moselle from mid-April to late September. Schedules vary by day and season; some trips cover only the Luxembourg stretch of the river between Remich or Schengen and Wasserbillig, and others continue down the Moselle to the German towns of Trier or Bernkastel.

■ **TOURING TIPS** Remich and Grevenmacher offer the largest selection of accommodations, but small hotels are located in other towns as well. Bus service links the major towns; trains operate between Luxembourg City and Wasserbillig.

VALLEY OF THE SEVEN CASTLES

One of the most scenic routes in Luxembourg is the valley of the Eisch River, known as the Valley of the Seven Castles.

The route begins at Eischen, northwest of Luxembourg City near the Belgian border. It leads to Hobscheid and on to Septfontaines, starting point for many pleasant walks. This delightful town dates from the 13th century; its trademark is an archaic stone "goat's bridge," arching across the water.

The route continues northeast through Ansembourg and Hollenfels, each with its handsome castle. Northeast of Hollenfels is the Hunnebour (Huns' Spring), a pleasant spot for a picnic. Legend has it that Attila's army camped here.

You can follow the Eisch River northeast to Mersch or, if you prefer, detour east to the Mamer Valley and another castle at Schoenfels.

DELIGHTFUL VIANDEN

See map page 40

The ruins of an immense feudal fortress loom over Vianden, a charming town bordering the Our River near Luxembourg's northeastern border. Recently restored, the castle dates from the 9th to the 15th centuries and is a national monument.

One of the country's beauty spots, Vianden provides a good base for exploring the Ardennes region. The town's narrow main street, called the Grand-Rue, curves invitingly from the hills toward the river.

Luxembourg's only chairlift transports passengers from Vianden high over the river and town to a forest park and restaurant with a panoramic view. After you've gazed over the valley, castle, and town, follow the path through the forest that leads to another viewpoint. The chairlift operates daily from April to late September.

In 1871 Victor Hugo, the French writer, described Vianden as "a jewel set in splendid scenery." During his voluntary exile from France, he lived here in a house near the river bridge; it now contains the Vianden tourist office and a small but interesting Victor Hugo museum.

Vianden's other diversions are quiet ones—exploring the winding streets, strolling beside the river, visiting a small folklore museum, or boating on the Our River. Many paths lead into nearby forest and countryside; one pleasant walk leads upriver to the castle ruins of Stolzembourg and Falkenstein.

■ **TOURING TIPS** Several excellent small hotels make Vianden a pleasant touring center. You can obtain information on activities and destinations in the region at the Syndicat d'Initiative in the Musée Victor Hugo.

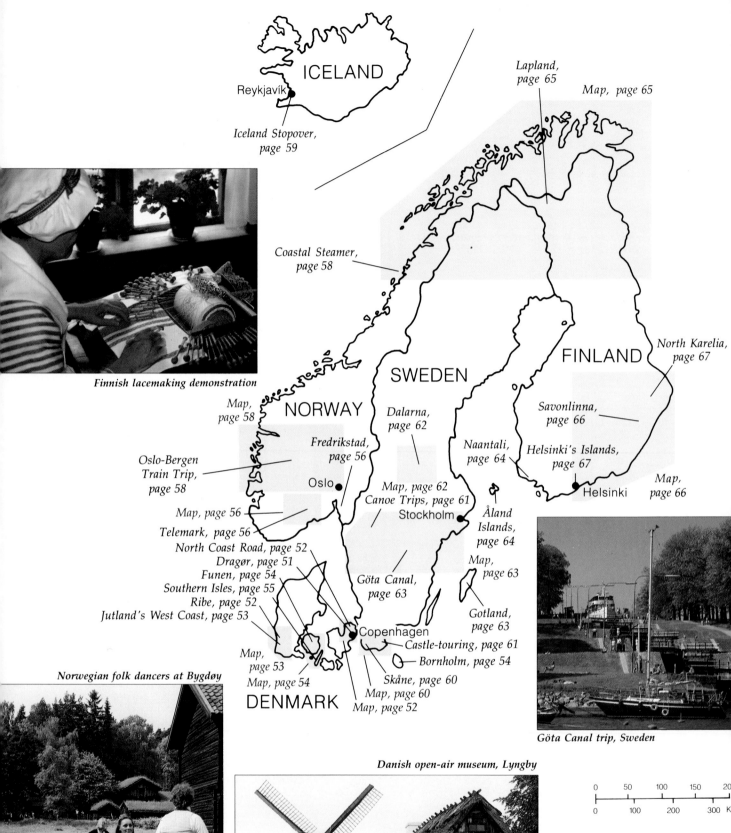

ICELAND

Reykjavík

Iceland Stopover,
page 59

Lapland,
page 65

Map, page 65

Coastal Steamer,
page 58

Finnish lacemaking demonstration

SWEDEN

FINLAND

North Karelia,
page 67

Map,
page 58

NORWAY

Dalarna,
page 62

Savonlinna,
page 66

Fredrikstad,
page 56

Naantali,
page 64

Helsinki's Islands,
page 67

Oslo-Bergen
Train Trip,
page 58

Oslo

Map, page 62
Canoe Trips, page 61

Stockholm

Helsinki

Map,
page 66

Map, page 56

Telemark, page 56

North Coast Road, page 52

Dragør, page 51

Funen, page 54

Southern Isles, page 55

Ribe, page 52

Jutland's West Coast, page 53

Åland
Islands,
page 64

Map,
page 63

Göta Canal,
page 63

Gotland,
page 63

Copenhagen

Castle-touring, page 61

Bornholm, page 54

Map,
page 53

Map, page 54

Skåne, page 60

Map, page 60

DENMARK

Map, page 52

Norwegian folk dancers at Bygdøy

Göta Canal trip, Sweden

Danish open-air museum, Lyngby

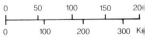

SCANDINAVIA

Denmark ▪ Norway ▪ Iceland ▪ Sweden ▪ Finland

Our Scandinavian travels range from Norway's fjords to Finland's lakes, from Denmark's southern islands to Sweden's highlands and the wilds of Lapland. A visit to Iceland offers an intriguing look at geysers and glaciers.

DELIGHTFUL DRAGØR

See map page 52

For an enjoyable change of pace in a Copenhagen visit, spend a few hours in the tiny port town of Dragør (pronounced Drahwer), on the island of Amager just south of Kastrup Airport. A busy fishing port during the Middle Ages, Dragør became a drowsy waterfront village when the herring fishing declined.

Dragør's old section near the harbor is marked by scattered half-timbered buildings and a charming mix of small cottages, painted in white, ocher, and pastel colors. Many dwellings are topped by thatched roofs. Lanes branch off the shopping street, inviting you to explore. Hollyhocks and other flowers brighten small gardens.

In the 16th century, Dutch farmers settled on Amager, bringing their own customs, language, and love of flowers. To learn about how they lived, visit the Dragør Museum near the harbor. Its exhibits show life on the island from prehistoric times to the 20th century. From May through September, the museum is open afternoons daily except Monday.

Next door you can see pictures and drawings of Dragør in the studio of the late Danish marine artist Christian Molstead (1862–1930).

Furnished room interiors and examples of richly embroidered clothing from the Amager Dutch are located in the Amager Museum a short distance inland in the town of Store Magleby. From mid-May through mid-September, the museum is open daily except Monday; the rest of the year it is open Wednesday to Sunday from 11 A.M. to 3 P.M.

▪ **TOURING TIPS** From Copenhagen's Town Hall Square, take bus no. 30 or 33 to Dragør; the trip takes about a half hour. Hearty meals are available in inns and cafés along Dragør's main street and overlooking the harbor.

Nets of the fishing fleet dry in open air in Gilleleje. Fishermen use time in port to mend nets.

RIBE, DENMARK'S OLDEST CITY

See map page 53

Inland a few miles from Jutland's west coast is Ribe, Denmark's oldest city. Founded in the 9th century, Ribe was one of the main Viking trading centers; it was already an important settlement when its cathedral was built in the 12th century.

In the Middle Ages, Ribe was Denmark's most important western port. Merchants returned here from their long voyages with exotic merchandise. More than 100 medieval buildings have been preserved in the town. You'll find many of them on crooked streets and cobbled lanes off the main thoroughfares.

Hans Tausen's House, a brick-and-timbered building across from the cathedral, contains historical exhibits that depict the history of Ribe from the Stone Age to modern days. To learn about life in Ribe during the medieval and industrial eras, visit the Town Hall Museum in the Town Hall, and the Antiquarian Collection at Quedens Gård, 10 Overdammen.

Works by Danish artists are displayed in the Museum of Art, located on the north bank of the Ribe River. From May to September, boat trips depart from the harbor to tour nearby waterways.

■ **TOURING TIPS** Ribe's cathedral is open from mid-May through September from 10 A.M. to 6 P.M. (noon to 6 on Sunday); the rest of the year, hours are 10 to noon and 2 to 4 P.M. (Sunday from 2 to 4). From the tower, you may be able to spot some of Ribe's nesting storks, which traditionally return each spring. On summer evenings, watch for the night watchman to make his traditional rounds about 10 P.M., chanting songs about attractions along his route.

THE NORTH COAST ROAD

One of Denmark's classic excursions is the drive along the coast road north of Copenhagen to Helsingør, and on to the summer resorts at Hornbæk, Gilleleje, and Tisvilde. If you explore in leisurely fashion, you'll discover a museum of modern art, craft workshops, delightful country inns, and busy fishing ports.

At Humlebæk, art lovers stop at Louisiana, a museum of modern art that occupies a wooded site above the Øresund. Sculpture is featured in an outdoor park. Works by renowned 20th-century artists dominate the art collection. Special events are also held here.

Helsingør's main attraction is magnificent Kronborg Castle, a great fortress commanding the waterway between Denmark and Sweden. Legends link the castle with Holger the Dane, the national hero, and with Shakespeare's Hamlet. Take time to explore Helsingør's delightful old quarter near the waterfront, where many buildings have been restored. For a local map, stop at the Helsingør tourist office at 93 Strandgade.

Continue along the coast road west of Helsingør to Hornbæk, site of the region's most popular beach. In the fishing ports of Gilleleje and Hundested, early risers can watch the fish auctions when the boats come back from the Kattegat fishing grounds. Tisvilde's beach also is popular with vacationing families in summer.

On a loop trip from Copenhagen, you can also visit inland attractions. Don't miss the royal palaces of Frederiksborg Castle at Hillerød and Fredensborg Palace, the summer residence of the royal family; and the old country town of Lyngby with its lakes and museums.

■ **TOURING TIPS** For information on North Sealand, stop at the Copenhagen tourist information office at 22 H.C. Andersens Boulevard, or at local tourist offices in larger towns. The Copenhagen Card is valid for travel on all trains within the metropolitan region, which extends north to Helsingør; it also covers admission to many attractions in the area.

ALONG JUTLAND'S WEST COAST

Travelers who love the wide open spaces find Jutland's west coast a perfect side trip. Long sandy beaches backed by high grassy dunes edge the North Sea, where centuries ago Viking ships sailed forth on distant raiding and trading expeditions. Side trips lead to two offshore islands and to a group of delightful villages.

The windswept coast.   Jutland's long, clean, west coast beaches are Denmark's vacationland. As soon as the cold weather is over, Danes get the seasonal urge to jump into the water for a swim. In summer, everyone, regardless of age or shape, plunges in. Bathing is the country's national sport, and the Danes and their guests make maximum use of the beaches and the sea.

In May and September you may well have this spectacular coast almost to yourself. You can stride over the smooth white sands in the invigorating air or soak up the warm sun from a sheltered hollow in the dunes.

Esbjerg is West Jutland's largest town, with one of Denmark's longest pedestrian streets. On weekday mornings at 7 you can watch the lively selling activity in the fish auction hall at the harbor.

Island side trips.   The two offshore islands along this southwestern coast are favorite resorts.

Fanø, southwest of Esbjerg, is accessible by a 20-minute ferry ride from Esbjerg. The island has two towns, Nordby, where the ferry docks, and the fishing village of Sønderho, near the island's southern tip.

Handsome cottages line Nordby's narrow streets. In summer the town bustles with activity as Danish families enjoy the splendid 10-mile-/17-km-long beach. The tourist office here can suggest island excursions. Buses run to all parts of Fanø.

In Sønderho, on Fanø's southern end, you recall Fanø's seafaring past as you visit the small church hung with model ships and walk along narrow streets past old skippers' cottages. You can also visit an old mill.

West of Skærbæk is the island of Rømø, connected to the mainland by a 6-mile/10-km causeway. Denmark's widest beach is located along its western shore. The island also includes areas of marshland, heathland, and forests; the tidewater areas are rich in animal life. An 18th-century farm has been restored as a museum, the Kommandørgården, which recalls some of the island's whaling traditions. You can also visit the fishing harbor in Havneby.

Border villages.   Several enticing villages cluster in Denmark's southwestern corner, in fertile marshlands only a few feet above sea level. Once periodic floods caused tremendous damage and loss of life here, but now the region is protected from the sea by great embankments.

Largest of the marshland towns is Tønder, renowned for both its lacemaking industry and its attractive houses. If you stroll down Uldgate, Østergade, or Vestergade, you can see small mansions and town houses with the characteristic gabled roofs, projecting bay windows, and artful doorways. Tønder's fine laces once brought great wealth to the town.

Three miles to the west you'll find the drowsy village of Møgeltønder. Thatched, bay-windowed houses and sweet-smelling lime trees line its attractive main street. You'll find the village church and an 18th-century baroque manor house nearby in a large park.

In Højer you can see splendid West Scheswig houses; the town's windmill is now a museum.

The center of Rudbøl's main street marks the Danish-German border.

■ **TOURING TIPS**   To avoid the summer crowds, time your beach visit for May or September, before or after the school holidays. Many Danes consider June to be the best beach month; summer days are delightfully long and sunny. On the third weekend in July, the Fanø towns of Nordby and Sønderho celebrate with festive outdoor fairs. Bus and ferry timetables are available from local tourist offices.

FOURTH OF JULY AT REBILD

For more than 75 years, Danes have celebrated the Fourth of July in the heather-covered hills of Rebild National Park, near Ålborg in northern Jutland. Some 40,000 Danes and their Danish-American guests gather annually for a great party with plenty of food and drink, music, speeches, dancing, and general merriment.

The festival began in 1912, after a group of Danish-Americans purchased land at Rebild and presented the deed to Denmark's King Christian X. Their only condition was that a Danish-American festival be held every year on July 4. The festival pays tribute to the Danes who emigrated to the United States and strengthens ties between the two countries.

BORNHOLM, A VIKING STRONGHOLD

See map page 50

A favorite of Scandinavian vacationers, the Danish island of Bornholm lies in the Baltic about 105 miles/ 170 km southeast of Copenhagen off Sweden's south coast. Runic stones, fortified round churches, and castle ruins are reminders of less idyllic times. Bornholm was controlled by Sweden and later by the Hanseatic city of Lübeck before passing to the Danes about 1660.

Most towns border the coast, so you can combine island attractions into a circular loop. Bornholm has some of the most attractive bicycle routes in Denmark. When you've had ample sightseeing, you can go for walks, sail or fish off the coast, or relax on sandy beaches.

Black-shingled, conical roofs top Bornholm's famous round white churches, fortified hundreds of years ago against pirates who plundered the coast. In times of trouble the people took refuge in the fortified upper chambers. Handsome 14th-century Biblical frescoes often decorate the beams. Largest of the churches is at Østerlars, south of Gudhjem. Others are located at Nyker and Nylars, both near Rønne; and at Olsker, south of Allinge.

Displays in Rønne's museum feature island history, shipping, and bird life. You can follow the coast road north to Hasle, past eroded cliffs, to mysterious Hammershus, where you can walk amid the ruins of a large medieval castle. Near the island's northern tip are Sandvig and the fishing village of Allinge. Paths traverse pine-covered hills, and you can see old rock engravings.

In quiet Gudhjem, colorful cottages—many of them half-timbered or thatch-roofed—nestle against the hillside, each with its small garden. Good beaches edge the nearby coast, and pleasant walks follow the wooded cliffs.

Continue to Svaneke and Neksø, two attractive port towns on the east coast. Turn inland to explore the wooded Paradise Hills and, north of Åkirkeby, the forest of Almindingen, with its many delightful paths. On the south coast, beaches and sand dunes rim the sea near Dueodde, and megalith tombs can be seen at Arnager.

■ **TOURING TIPS** Rønne, the island's thriving capital, is 30 minutes by air from Copenhagen. You can also reach Bornholm by car ferry from Copenhagen or from Ystad, Sweden. Accommodations range from comfortable hotels in the larger towns to inexpensive pensions and seaside guest houses. In late July and early August, Bornholm hosts a summer music festival.

FUNEN, DENMARK'S GARDEN ISLAND

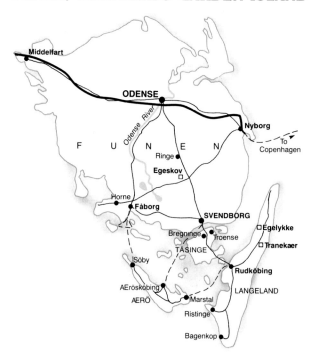

Uncrowded Funen is Denmark's garden island, a tranquil land brightened by hollyhock-splashed cottage gardens, half-timbered farmhouses, square-towered country churches, and elegant old manor houses. The countryside is at its prettiest in summer, when the wheat stands golden, the oats green, and mounds of drying hay mark the meadows.

Funen's largest town, Odense is best known as the birthplace of Hans Christian Andersen, Denmark's great writer of fairy tales. According to tradition, he was born

Black conical roof tops Østerlars Church south of Gudhjem, largest of Bornholm's handsome fortified churches.

Hollyhocks along Ærøskøbing street tower over passing children. Pastel colors brighten many island houses.

in 1805 in the house at Hans Jensensstræde 39, the son of a cobbler and a washerwoman. Here you'll see mementoes of his life and writings, including his writing desk, top hat, and famous umbrella. He spent his childhood in the humble house at Munkemøllestræde 3.

Rail buffs will enjoy a visit to the Danish Railway Museum at Dannebrogsgade 24. One of Europe's largest railway museums, it includes rolling stock, a museum square, films, models, and other exhibits.

In summer you can take a boat ride on the tree-lined Odense River; a footpath borders the river.

Funen Village (Den Fynske Landsby) is located in a wooded riverside site south of Odense. This delightful collection of about 20 rural buildings has been reconstructed as a typical Funen settlement of the 18th and 19th centuries. Open daily from April through October (Sunday and holidays only in winter), the village can be reached by bus from Odense.

Towered and turreted Egeskov Castle, near Ringe, resembles a proper fairy-tale palace. Mirrored in its encircling moat and reached by drawbridge, the rosy brick castle was built about 1554 as a private fortress during a period of civil war. The parklike gardens include a fuchsia garden, herb gardens, and a maze; there's also a museum that features antique cars and aircraft.

On Funen's south coast, the old sailing town of Svendborg is still devoted to commerce and the sea. You can visit a regional museum, Anne Hvide's Gård at Fruestræde 3; the old Church of Saint Nicolas dedicated to the patron saint of sailors; and a zoological museum.

Surrounded by wooded rolling hills, Fåborg overlooks its own fjord. At Horne is an unusual round fortress-church, the only one of its type on the island. North of Horne, a 500-year-old water mill has been turned into a museum.

■ **TOURING TIPS** Express trains link Copenhagen and Odense, Funen's largest town; a spur line extends south from Odense to Svendborg. Buses serve the main towns. You also can rent bicycles for independent exploring; tourist offices in larger towns can suggest routes.

ISLAND-HOPPING IN THE SOUTHERN ISLES

See map page 54

On Funen's southern coast, Svendborg and Fåborg are jumping-off towns for the southern islands. From Svendborg you can reach Tåsinge and Langeland by bridge, but you'll need to take a ferry to Ærø and the smaller islands in the archipelago. Cycling is a great way to see the islands.

Tåsinge, an idyllic island of billowing grain fields and thick beech groves, has few villages breaking its flat horizon. In Troense, the main town, thatched roofs add a cozy touch to many whitewashed and half-timbered houses. Denmark's days of naval glory are recalled in maritime museums here. You can visit the privately owned 17th-century Valdemar Castle, which contains furnishings and art collected through many generations.

Largest of the archipelago islands, Langeland is linked by bridge to Tåsinge. Attractive beaches draw swimmers and sunbathers. In Rudkøbing, the main town, you'll find charming old houses lining Brogade and Østergade. The road north passes Tranekær Castle, built as a royal fortress about 1200, and Egelykke Manor.

Ærø's old seafaring town of Marstal, home port of many of Denmark's ships, has the tang of tar and saltwater. Displays in its museum recall the era when some 400 ships used to sail from here. In delightful Ærøskøbing, time stands still. Crooked old houses line cobbled streets lighted by gas lamps. You can mail postcards in a 1749 post office.

■ **TOURING TIPS** Main ferry routes link Svendborg and Ærøskøbing; Fåborg and Søby; Marstal and Rudkøbing. Motorists traveling on weekends and during vacation periods should reserve ferry space to avoid delays. Bicycles can be rented in many Danish towns; cycling tours offer the opportunity to pedal at your own pace, with arrangements for equipment rental, lodging, meals, and ferry passage handled for you. For cycling information, contact the Danish Tourist Board or local tourist information offices.

STAYING IN A KRO

One of the delights of the Danish countryside is the opportunity to spend the night in a kro, one of the numerous charming country inns that dot the rolling green countryside. Accommodations range from rustic-but-comfortable to luxurious. In the inns' cozy pubs and restaurants, travelers can obtain well-prepared food, including local specialties.

Many of these cheery roadside guesthouses are several hundred years old; some have been operated by the same hospitable family for generations. For information on country inns, contact the Danish Tourist Board (address on page 128).

OPEN-AIR FOLK MUSEUMS

In the Scandinavian countries, museum towns are a special pleasure. Open-air folk villages preserve the architecture and life of an earlier time. Most of the museum towns assemble rural buildings from throughout the region or country, but some re-create 18th- or 19th-century town life.

Depending on the country and museum, you may see thatched cottages or sod-roofed log cabins, timbered brick houses or plank-sided dwellings. Many of the buildings have been furnished in period style, including utensils and tools. Shops sometimes announce their business with interesting wooden or wrought-iron signs: candles, a boot, a wooden cask, or a baker's pretzel.

On arrival at the museum, check the day's events. Sometimes you can get an overview with a guided tour or a ride around the grounds in a horse-drawn cart.

Some museums offer demonstrations of old-time crafts, such as spinning, weaving, lacemaking, pottery making, glass blowing, printing, or bookbinding. A fiddler's tunes may draw you to a program of folk dancing and music, particularly on weekends and during the peak tourist season (mid-June through mid-August).

Most of the folk museums are open only in summer, usually from May to September. Local tourist offices can provide information on the attractions and how to reach them.

FREDRIKSTAD'S FORTRESS TOWN

See map page 50

The first Norsemen settled about 10,000 years ago in the district now known as Østfold, south of present-day Oslo, where Oslofjord opens to the sea. Located near the Swedish border, the district was often a battleground. Among its many historical attractions is Fredrikstad, Scandinavia's only preserved fortress town, built to guard the mouth of the Glomma River.

Fredrikstad was built on the Glomma estuary in 1567, after the nearby town of Sarpsborg had been burned to the ground by Swedish troops. In the 1660s, permanent fortifications were constructed; at the peak of Fredrikstad's glory, some 200 cannons guarded the site. However, by 1814 its troop strength had been considerably reduced; when Swedish forces attacked Fredrikstad, the garrison was forced to surrender, and the town was handed over to the Swedes. The fortress was decommissioned in 1903.

The old 17th-century fortified town is encircled by ramparts and a moat with a drawbridge. Gateways guard the town on all sides, and bastions overlook its borders.

Begin your walking tour in the cobbled King's Square near the center of the old town, where a statue honors the town's founder, King Frederik II. You can visit the church, which dates from 1779, and the main guardroom and old convict prison; built in 1731, the prison is now the municipal museum. Norway's military forces occupy some of the buildings. You'll see a few cannons mounted overlooking the water.

Artists and artisans of PLUS, an arts and crafts organization, have workshops in some of the buildings. You'll see their work in shops as you stroll through the walled town. Inquire at the information center to learn which ones welcome visitors to their workshops. You can also visit a glass-blowing workshop outside the walls, near the drawbridge.

Kongsten Fort occupies a lonely bluff east of the walled town. Guides take groups into the fort's underground chambers.

■ **TOURING TIPS** Located about 60 miles/100 km south of Oslo, Fredrikstad can be reached in 1½ hours by express train from Oslo's Central Station. The fortress is on the opposite bank of the river from the modern town. At the Fredrikstad Tourist Office, ask for a descriptive map brochure showing the layout of the fortress town and describing its many well-preserved buildings. You can also inquire about guided tours of the Old Town and workshop visits; to see artisans at work, it's best to visit Fredrikstad on a weekday.

TOURING IN TELEMARK

Some of Norway's most spectacular scenery is found in the Telemark district. You can enjoy its dense forests and pastoral farmlands from May through September, but if you plan to venture into the higher elevations, wait until June. Tradition remains strong in the inland valleys, but you'll also find tourist hotels and giant power stations that harness the nation's abundant water energy.

In Skien, on Norway's south coast, the Telemark Museum in Brekke Park offers visitors a broad cultural introduction to the region. Open from mid-May to mid-September, its collections show traditional Telemark architecture and Norwegian arts and crafts, such as wood carving, weaving, and silverwork. Born in Skien in 1828, dramatist Henrik Ibsen was a native son; you can visit Venstøp Farm, his childhood home just north of town.

Telemark Canal. One of the most enjoyable ways to approach the heart of Telemark is by boat. In summer, the *Victoria* and *Vildanden* make all-day trips from Skien inland to Dalen, in the heart of Telemark.

The longest waterway still used in southern Norway, this 65-mile/105-km route links several long finger lakes. On the memorable all-day trip, your boat passes through 18 manually operated locks, climbing from sea level to about 235 feet/72 meters into thick forests and a mountainous wonderland.

You'll pass through the Norsjø-Skien Canal, originally opened in 1861. Farther inland, your boat enters the Bandak-Norsjø Canal, which looks almost as it did when it was opened in 1892. You'll glide along rivers and broad woodland lakes, past a riverside sawmill and scattered farmsteads, and into the mountains where waterfalls cascade.

Other highlights. If you're traveling by car, detour north of Lake Norsjø to the Heddal stave church just west of Notodden; dating from about 1147, it is one of Norway's largest and most beautiful stave churches (open daily in summer). The Heddal District Museum is nearby.

Near Rauland you can see old villages and farmsteads preserved in natural surroundings. Artisans and craftsmen here produce ceramics, silver, and pewter objects. Scenery is spectacular in this corner of Telemark. Hiking and fishing can provide a pleasant change of pace.

From Rauland you follow the edge of Lake Møsvatn down to Rjukan, at the foot of Mount Gausta, where a cable railway transports visitors up the mountain. During World War II, the Nazis produced ''heavy water'' here for use in atomic bomb experiments. In a daring raid, Norwegian commandos sabotaged the plant.

From Rjukan you can return via Notodden to Oslo by train, or travel by bus around the lake and across the mountains to Kongsberg, where you continue to Oslo by rail.

By train and bus through Telemark. You can drive through Telemark on surfaced roads, but you may prefer to travel by rail, boat, and bus, sitting back and enjoying the view. Pay close attention not only to the scenery, but also to the timetables.

Trains departing from Oslo's Central Station (Oslo S) and Western Station (Oslo V) run across the southern part of Telemark. The Sørland Line stops in Nordagutu, Bø, and Lunde; at Nordagutu station, other rail lines branch north to Notodden and south to Skien and other coastal towns. Rail service at Lunde coordinates with boat service on the canal.

Well-preserved stave church in village of Borgund, east of Sognefjord near Laerdal, dates from about 1150.

Bus lines and rail services meet at Bø, the transportation hub of central Telemark. Local bus routes link the main valleys and villages. You can travel through the Morgedal district—where modern skiing originated—on to Vrådal, a quiet lake resort, or Dalen, center of the giant Tokke hydroelectric project (guided tours June to August daily except Sunday). Buses will take you deeper into Telemark and all the way to Bergen.

■ **TOURING TIPS** If you're traveling by train and bus, get detailed schedules in Oslo or Bergen before you begin your Telemark adventures. Keep a few snack items in your bag to stave off hunger pangs if you're traveling in sparsely settled country. Trips on the Telemark Canal operate several times weekly (daily in peak season) from early June through mid-August. It's possible to take part of the Telemark Canal trip on a long day excursion from Oslo: You take the early morning train to Lunde, taxi or walk down to the canal lock, and board the downstream boat in early afternoon; in Skien, take a taxi to the rail station and board the evening train back to Oslo.

NORWAY'S STAVE CHURCHES

Ranking among Norway's most unusual attractions are the richly carved wooden stave churches, with their dragons' heads and serpent ornaments, scattered over the countryside. Of the original 750 churches built during the Middle Ages, only a few remain. Information on the stave churches and a suggested tour can be obtained from the Norwegian Tourist Board (address on page 128).

BY COASTAL STEAMER TO NORTH CAPE

See map page 65

The majestic scenery of Norway's fjord coast has lured generations of travelers. Vast forests, deep fjords, shimmering lakes, plunging waterfalls, and snow-capped mountains provide awesome panoramas. Most travelers, sailing along the coast, delight in the bustle of waterfront activity as the ship pulls into small ports. For others, the primary destination is North Cape, Europe's northernmost outpost. The lonely cliff rises nearly 1,000 feet/about 300 meters above the Arctic Ocean, at 71° North latitude.

Travelers who enjoy sightseeing without fuss or formality enjoy exploring this shore by coastal steamer. Throughout the year, a ship sails north daily from Bergen on an 11-day trip along Norway's spectacular fjord coast. It stops briefly at more than 30 coastal towns to deliver passengers, mail, and freight, then sails past North Cape to Kirkenes. In summer, many cruise ships also sail along Norway's coast.

On the coastal steamer you'll stop at larger towns, including Trondheim, Bodø, Narvik, and Hammerfest, but most of the ports are small ones. Ferries and fishing boats enliven port activity, and often people will wave as your ship passes. Modern buildings mark the small northern towns, many of which were bombed or burned during World War II. In the small fishing villages, you'll see tidy wooden houses painted in bright blue, orange, and yellow, with lace curtains at the windows.

There's a relaxed informality to life aboard one of the coastal steamers, as you sail in and out of small ports, delivering the mail and cargo. Shore excursions are available in several towns and from Honnigsvåg to North Cape. Travelers preferring a shorter trip can disembark or board at Trondheim.

■ **TOURING TIPS** A warming Gulf Stream moderates Norway's coastal climate. If you're traveling between June and early August, you'll have daylight nearly 24 hours a day. Travelers can also explore Norway's northern coast by land, traveling by bus or car on the Arctic Highway. From early June to mid-September, the Nord-Norge-Bussen (sometimes called the Polar Express) makes a 3-day run from Fauske, east of Bodø, to Kirkenes; overnight stops are made at Narvik and Alta. (The rest of the year, the bus operates between Fauske and Hammerfest.) If you plan to drive, allow 3 travel days between Trondheim and North Cape.

OVER THE TOP OF NORWAY

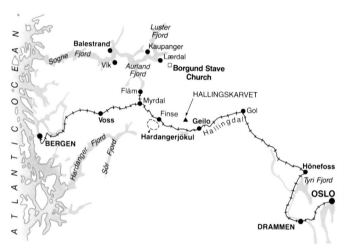

One of Europe's most scenic rail routes climbs across Norway's mountainous spine, which links Oslo and Bergen, the country's largest cities. During the fascinating 6½-hour trip, the train wends from agricultural valleys through pine forests, up into the bleak tundra and icy mountains, and dips into western Norway's beautiful fjord country.

Completed in 1909 and totally electrified, the railroad is an engineering feat. More than 60 miles/100 km of track lie above timberline, in country covered by snow most of the year. Passing waterfalls and glaciers, trains go through about 200 tunnels and 18 miles/29 km of snowsheds. Several of Norway's best-known ski resorts are located along the rail line.

The Bergen Line. Leaving Oslo, the train heads for the lakes, woods, and hills of Nordmarka, where Oslo families go on country outings. Later you pass through the Hallingdal district, a region where Norwegian peasant culture still survives.

West of Geilo, one of Norway's major ski resorts, the railway enters the high mountain zone, crossing near the base of Hallingskarvet, an impressive mountain wall about 21 miles/34 km long. The Hardangerjökul glacier

In the Sognefjord country in western Norway, farmer cuts high grass by hand with a scythe.

comes into view near Finse. High snow fences and covered snowsheds shield the tracks, a necessity at this elevation (about 4,300 feet/1,300 meters). Sod-roofed farm buildings and storehouses dot the tundra.

Just before Myrdal, look for one of the trip's best sights: a view down more than 1,000 feet/300 meters to the Flåmsdal, a huge ravine yawning at the foot of towering mountains. The Flåm Line departs from Myrdal to descend to the Sognefjord.

The Bergen Line continues to Voss, where the railway enters fjord country; between the many railway tunnels, you'll get brief glimpses of some of Europe's most spectacular scenery.

The Flåm Line. For an exciting variation, get off the train in Myrdal, take the short but spectacular ride on the Flåm rail line, and continue to Bergen by fjord steamer.

The steep (to 55°) Flåm Line is the shortest and most scenic of Norway's mountain rail routes. In about 12 miles/20 km, the railway descends to the town of Flåm on Aurlandfjord. It drops 2,800 feet/850 meters, passes through 21 tunnels, and completes a circle inside a mountain tunnel to reach the valley. Emerging from the tunnel, the train crosses the thundering Kjosfoss Falls, stops for passengers to take photographs, and continues down to the village at the edge of the fjord.

From June through August, travelers can board an express ferry that connects with the train and cruises along the Sognefjord to Bergen, arriving about 6½ hours later. The rest of the year, travelers stay overnight in Flåm and continue next day by ferry to Bergen.

■ **TOURING TIPS** Obtain seat reservations for the rail trip in advance, particularly if you're traveling Friday through Sunday. Travelers departing from Bergen from June through August can also make the same one-day trip in reverse; you'll take the early morning ferry from Bergen to Flåm, climb the Flåmdal by train, and catch the late-afternoon train from Myrdal to Oslo. If you wish to see more of this country, you'll find hotels in resorts along the rail line and in Flåm. Skiing lasts from Christmas through April at most resorts.

LOFOTEN ISLANDS HOLIDAY

If you're looking for an unusual destination, consider a visit to the Lofoten Islands, where life focuses on the sea. Tourist anglers can fish from a small boat, join a fishing excursion, or cast from shore. Other visitors—bird-watchers, artists, and mountaineers—come to enjoy the islands' abundant bird life and rugged topography.

Some visitors stay in the typical red-painted fishermen's cabins that ring the harbors of most Lofoten fishing villages. Once housing fishermen who arrived to work during the annual spring fishing period, they now provide simple and reasonably priced tourist accommodations. The old cabins were primitive, but those rented today have modern conveniences.

AN ICELAND STOPOVER

See map page 50

See map page 50

In Iceland, travelers find a land of amazing geographical variety, one where nature's primeval forces are close at hand, shaping the land and being utilized by its people. Icy glaciers carve high mountain valleys, and geysers, hot springs, and volcanic activity hint at the restless geothermal energy beneath the surface. Along Iceland's rugged coast, dramatic fjords and stark cliffs are further evidence of powerful forces at work. Geothermal energy heats the towns, and glacial rivers power giant turbines.

Visitors land at Keflavík Airport, located on a volcanic peninsula on the island's southwestern coast. You'll drive into the capital city of Reykjavík through a moonlike volcanic landscape devoid of vegetation. At Krísuvík, a hot springs area shows geothermal activity in its bubbling mud pools, steam blowholes, and colorful sulphur-encrusted deposits.

Reykjavík surprises many visitors. Though it dates from the 9th century and is rooted in fishing and agricultural traditions, Reykjavík is a modern, technological city. The clean lines and bright colors of its buildings testify to a thriving economy; all its buildings are heated by geothermal energy, in the form of hot water piped directly from the city's drill holes.

Most of the traditional buildings are located near the town's center. Here, too, are the town's lakes, where you can usually see arctic terns and other wildfowl.

Urban activity is centered in Reykjavík, where you can dine on Icelandic mountain lamb and freshly caught fish, enjoy nightlife in publike bars and discotheques, and swim in thermally heated outdoor pools at any time of year. There's good salmon fishing within city boundaries.

The tranquillity and grandeur of Iceland's magnificent unspoiled countryside draw those who love the outdoors. Near the city you'll find good skiing facilities, trails for hiking across the countryside, and trout fishing in many lakes and rivers. You can go pony-trekking, see awesome displays of bird life, and explore lava fields and glaciers. Along the coast, you can visit busy fishing ports and watch trawlers and smaller craft unload their catch.

From Reykjavík, you'll set out on day trips or longer excursions to see this varied land. On day trips you can follow a circle route that includes the scenic highlights of Gullfoss (Golden Falls) and Geysir's erupting hot springs; take a highland road between the glaciers; fly north to Isafjordur and the western fjords; or explore the glaciers and bird rookeries along the south coast. Other day trips offer pony-trekking excursions on Icelandic ponies, trout fishing trips, flight-seeing trips over the volcanic and glacial countryside, and flights to nearby islands. Many 2- to 6-day excursions also tour the rugged countryside.

■ **TOURING TIPS** Icelandic Air offers a number of inclusive stopover plans for visitors with only a few days to see the country; for information, contact the Iceland Tourist Board (address on page 128). Other itineraries focus on Icelandic life and culture, bird-watching, farmhouse holidays, fishing trips, pony-trekking tours, walking trips, and camping tours.

SWEDEN'S SUNNY SOUTHERN COAST

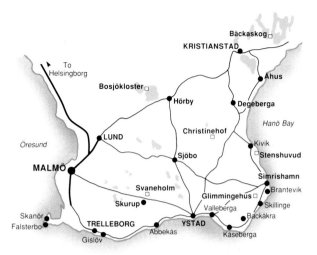

What the Riviera is to France, Skåne is to Sweden. From June to September, this province of fertile farmland edged with sandy beaches becomes Sweden's vacationland. Relics of Viking days are scattered along its shore.

Sweden's southern provinces belonged to Denmark for centuries, joining the Swedish kingdom only in 1658. Many Danish influences remain, particularly in the style of architecture, language, and way of life.

Malmö, the province's commercial center, is the starting point for a loop along Skåne's coast.

Coastal towns. In July and August coastal resorts teem with visitors in search of sun, sea, and sights, but in June and September you'll be able to enjoy the towns in more leisurely fashion. Several—Ystad, Simrishamn, Kristianstad—have preserved numerous medieval half-timbered buildings. Relics of Viking days include rune stones, ancient stone monuments, and grave fields.

South of Malmö on a small peninsula are the charming twin villages of Falsterbo and Skanör. Between Trelleborg and Ystad, the coast road passes several attractive fishing villages, such as Gislöv and Abbekås. Ystad is another popular resort, with a fine curving stretch of wide sandy beach. More than 400 half-timbered buildings line the town's winding streets.

Take the coastal road between Ystad and Simrishamn to reach Valleberga, site of Skåne's only remaining round church, and Ales Stenar (Ale's Stones), most impressive of the ancient stone monuments on the southeastern coast. Located near Kåseberga, Sweden's largest grave field dates from the early Viking Age. Its vertical stones form the outline of a ship, more than 70 yards long, pointing out to sea.

Farther east is the old farmstead of Backåkra, purchased by Dag Hammarskjold as a home for his retirement years. The late U.N. secretary-general died in a plane crash in 1961; the residence was restored and furnished after his death. The property on the Kåseberga ridge overlooking the Baltic Sea is now a Hammarskjold memorial and nature reserve (open to visitors mid-May through August).

The east coast. Along the eastern shore you can visit fishing villages like Skillinge and Brantevik, and Glimmingehus, a medieval stronghold built about 1500.

One of the most pleasant towns along the Skåne coast is Simrishamn, a seaport that is popular with artists. A town of small, well-preserved houses, it is also a busy port. Visit the 12th century, step-gabled Saint Nikolaus Church, where ship models are suspended from the ceiling, and Bergengrenska Trädgården, a charming park located off Stortorget.

One of the landmarks along Hanö Bay is Stenshuvud, a high granite peak that offers superb views and the remains of a castle. Kivik, in the center of orchards, has an ancient royal grave dating from 1400 B.C. This Bronze Age monument, a huge mound of boulders and stones, was excavated in the 1930s and yielded tomb furniture, grave carvings, and fragments of bronze. Another attraction is Kivik's great market fair each July.

Inland at Degeberga, you can see the Forsakar Waterfall in a thick beech forest near the main highway.

Although its population multiplies during the summer tourist invasion, Åhus has retained a charming small-town character.

Kristianstad was founded in 1614 as a fortified Danish merchant town; only the moat and outer walls of the fortress remain. The city's most striking sight is the impressive Trefaldighets Church, which dates from the 17th century. Beyond the town, bird life flourishes in the reeds, bog-meadows, and shallow lakes formed by the Helgeån River.

■ **TOURING TIPS** Country inns offer a chance to order Swedish food specialties, including pickled herring and various eel dishes. Boats depart from Ystad and Simrishamn for the Danish island of Bornholm. Tourist offices are located in larger towns along the coast.

WHERE CRYSTAL IS KING

Swedish glassworks, whose names are known around the world, are concentrated in Småland province between Växjö and Kalmar. You can visit the factories of Orrefors, Boda, Kosta, and others—17 glassworks produce some of the world's most beautiful glassware within this small district.

Begin your tour with a visit to the Glass Museum in Växjö. Tourist offices in Kalmar or Växjö can provide maps and touring information. Several of the towns can be reached by train.

During guided tours, you watch glassblowers at work, visit a glassware museum to see exceptional pieces, then finish your visit in the shop, where you can select first-quality pieces or seconds with minute flaws. Tax-free shopping and gift shipments can be arranged in the shop.

Glassblowers usually work weekdays between 8 and 3. Some factories close during July, but the shops and exhibition rooms remain open.

Sign of golden bun over entrance identifies bakery in Skansen's open-air museum in Stockholm.

CASTLE-TOURING IN SKÅNE

See map page 60

One of Skåne's greatest attractions is the large number of castles and manor houses scattered over the province. More than 150 dot the gentle, rolling countryside. Most are inhabited and can be visited only by special arrangement. These four are open to the public in summer.

Bäckaskog Castle, six miles east of Kristianstad just off Route 15, is a 700-year-old castle with hotel and restaurant facilities, centered around a medieval cloister. Located between two lakes, the château is surrounded by a large park with gardens and woodland. A biblical garden features plants mentioned in the Bible.

Bosjökloster Castle, northwest of Hörby, is a former Benedictine convent. Surrounded by green parklands, the white, step-gabled castle occupies a thin strip of land separating the Ringsjön lakes. Exhibits of handicrafts and contemporary art are featured in the Stone Hall. The castle is especially noted for its handsome gardens.

Christinehof Castle lies a few miles northwest of Eljaröd near the Ystad-Kristianstad road. Built in the 1730s, the castle is fully furnished and has never been altered or modernized.

Svaneholm Castle, north of Skurup, was built as a 16th-century fortress around a central courtyard; later it was partially remodeled to resemble an Italian palazzo. Set in a rural lake district, it now displays 18th- and 19th-century furnishings, paintings, and tools.

■ **TOURING TIP** In summer, these castles are usually open daily, though some close on Monday; for information on hours, check locally.

CANOEING ON SWEDISH WATERWAYS

See map page 63

Canoeing through southwestern Sweden's lake region is one of the best ways to sample the stunning beauty of the Scandinavian countryside. A favorite of many paddlers is the century-old Dalsland Canal, a 170-mile-/270-km-long waterway linking lakes, rivers, and canals. It is now used solely by recreational boaters.

Canal locks operate from June through August; paddlers pay a small fee at each station (the 29 locks are scattered on short stretches of canal between the lakes).

Whether you plan to paddle on your own or with a group, you'll enjoy the long days of the northern summer while gliding past farms, lumber mills, idyllic small villages, wooded islands, and lake shores dotted with brightly painted summer homes. Along the way, you may meet Swedes hunting for edible berries and mushrooms—a favorite summer pastime.

If you plan to travel on the Dalsland Canal, you'll travel by train to Åmål, the lake region's main rail connection. You can arrange at the local tourist office for accommodations in towns along the lakes and canal. If you plan to camp, you can pitch a tent either in designated campsites along the canoe routes or, with certain restrictions, just about anywhere. Camping equipment (except for sleeping bags) can be rented at several lakeside locations in the region.

Rental firms also offer guided family camping tours and adults-only trips, all suitable for beginners. Prices include canoes, guides, lock station fees, food, tents, stoves, and maps. Group size is usually 15 to 20 people.

■ **TOURING TIPS** For information on canoe trips in north Dalsland and southwest Värmland provinces, contact the Swedish Tourist Board (address on page 128). You can reach Åmål in about 7 hours by train from Stockholm, 2 hours from Göteborg or Oslo. Peak season rental rates for equipment apply from mid-June through early August. Usually the warmest and fairest weather occurs in July and August, but be prepared for rain at any time.

HIKING IN THE HIGHLANDS

Northern Sweden is part of Europe's only remaining wilderness. Hikers head for the highlands, where the Swedish Touring Club has marked hiking routes, built bridges, and provided simple accommodation facilities in Lapp-type huts; it also arranges group hiking tours. Many areas of the highlands are virtually uninhabited, so good physical condition and good equipment are essential for hikers. The Swedish Tourist Board (address on page 128) can provide information on routes, national parks, suggested equipment, and transportation in the northern provinces.

THE HEART OF SWEDEN

Midsummer mist fails to dampen spirits of Dalarna nuptial party. Bridal pair wears traditional wedding costumes.

Swedes call Dalarna the heart of Sweden. In summer and winter, they come here on holiday, drawn by the province's scenery, outdoor sports, and rural folk culture. Most of the principal resorts—Leksand, Tällberg, Rättvik, and Mora—rim Lake Siljan.

This is a land of lakes and fir forests, separated by narrow cultivated valleys speckled with bright red farm buildings. It is also the nation's oldest industrial center— Dalarna's mineral wealth financed Sweden's imperialistic adventures several hundred years ago.

Tradition still remains strong in Dalarna. On festive occasions, Swedish women often wear traditional local dress. Rural fiddlers play for local dances, and crafts such as weaving and wood carving remain popular. You'll see the brightly painted Dala horse displayed frequently.

You can learn more about Dalarna farm life at several open-air museums near Lake Siljan. Groups of wooden farm buildings typical of an earlier era show handcrafted details like carved gables and decorative folk paintings.

Falun district. In summer you can visit Falun's open-pit copper mine, which has yielded minerals since Viking days. It supplied Europe with copper before the Swedish kingdom was established. To visit the mine, you descend by elevator and follow a guide through underground chambers and passages that have been in use since medieval days. The mine is open daily from May through August.

In nearby Sundborn, visitors can tour the home of Swedish watercolor artist Carl Larsson, who died in 1919. His home is open daily from May through September.

Leksand. Attractive resort towns border Lake Siljan's shore. One of the oldest settlements is Leksand, where the lakeside church is built on the site of a pagan temple.

In early days, parishioners traveled to church in long, oar-powered "churchboats." This tradition is celebrated on the first Sunday in July, when crews from various lakeside parishes compete in churchboat races, followed by folk dancing to a fiddler's tunes. Another July event is the 10-day run of *The Road to Heaven*, an open-air miracle play, based on Dalarna folk traditions.

Tällberg. A favorite vacation village, Tällberg occupies a magnificent site on the lake's southeast shore. Water sports lure summer visitors; in winter you can ski, ice skate, practice your curling, or take a sleigh ride. Among the creative people who settled here was the late Swedish artist Gustaf Ankarcrona; his farmhouse is now a museum where you can see works by folk artists.

Rättvik. Another popular lakeside resort is Rättvik, which has a good selection of hotels. At its Gammelgård open-air museum on the outskirts of town, you can tour an old Dalecarlian farmstead with buildings decorated in rural folk art. The museum is open from mid-June to mid-August; folk dancers and musicians entertain twice weekly in July and early August. An artists' village has been established at Rättviks Hantverksby.

Mora. This Dalarna town is closely associated with Sweden's most famous painter, Anders Zorn (1860–1920). The Zorn Museum contains many of his best paintings, as well as works by other Swedish and international artists from his private collection, and exhibits of Dalarna handicrafts and rural art. The home of this impressionist painter is also a museum. Near the museum, about 40 timber buildings, typical of Swedish rural architecture, house art and craft studios and boutiques. You can watch craftspeople at work at Balder-Lisselby, a craft center. A Santa complex in Mora is a family favorite where visitors meet "Santa" and tour his house and busy workshop.

■ **TOURING TIPS** Trains travel from Stockholm to Falun in 3 hours and to Mora in 4½ to 5 hours, with stops at Borlänge, Leksand, and Rättvik. Local buses also connect Dalarna's larger towns. In summer, tours of the Lake Siljan district depart from Leksand, Rättvik and Mora; for information, inquire at the local tourist bureau. On the weekend nearest June 23, visitors can join in Midsummer Eve celebrations in lakeside towns.

CRUISING ACROSS SWEDEN

Summer visitors to Sweden can enjoy a unique excursion: a scenic cruise through the Swedish countryside on the Göta Canal. From late May to mid-September, three vintage boats make the 4- or 5-day trip along the historic route linking Göteborg, Sweden's main North Sea port, with Stockholm, on the Baltic Sea.

Built between 1810 and 1832, the Göta Canal links several rivers and large freshwater lakes as it cuts through scenic, ever-changing countryside. Stately old trees along the canal embankment cast their shade across the open decks of the slow-moving ships, and there's plenty of opportunity to relax in a deck chair and enjoy the passing scenery.

Your boat cuts through green meadows, crosses the glistening waters of sunlit lakes, passes beneath overhanging trees, and cruises along the coast through an island-studded sea. Along the route you'll see many small waterside communities, where the passing of the excursion boats is an important event, and people wave and smile as you pass. You'll maneuver through 58 locks, which lift your boat from sea level to an elevation of nearly 300 feet/92 meters and lower it back to sea level.

Passengers boarding in Göteborg will stop at Trollhättan to see the waterfalls, at the medieval town of Vadstena on the shore of Lake Vättern, and at Motala to visit the Museum of Canal and Navigation History. At Berg, you can watch as your boat descends through a series of locks leading into Lake Roxen. Your final stop is at the medieval town of Söderköping.

If you depart from Stockholm, your boat will stop for sightseeing in Nyköping, at the Berg Locks, and at Motala. On the western section of the canal, you'll stop at Lyrestad to see a restored harbor warehouse, now a regional museum. At Trollhättan, early risers can see cargo boats passing through the canal locks.

■ **Touring Tips** The Göta Canal is open only in summer. See your travel agent or contact the Swedish Tourist Board (address on page 128) for information on Göta Canal excursion schedules and fares. Day excursions on the Göta Canal depart from many towns from mid-May until early September. Private canal boats can be rented by the week at Sjötorp and Söderköping. In Sweden you can purchase a canal guidebook with detailed information on attractions along the route.

SUNNY GOTLAND

See map page 50

Sunny Gotland lies about 60 miles/100 km off Sweden's east coast, about a half-hour by air and 700 years in time from Stockholm. Largest of the Baltic islands, Gotland is lushly green in the interior with rugged cliffs edging the west coast. Woolly sheep graze everywhere. The island's swimming beaches are among the best in Scandinavia.

Visby, the island capital, rose to glory in the Middle Ages as the cultural crossroads of Scandinavia and a key trading center of the Hanseatic League. Its magnificent city wall, built in the 12th and 13th centuries, is largely intact and surrounds the town on all but the sea side.

Inside the wall, narrow half-timbered houses roofed in red tile line cobbled streets. Sudden glimpses of flowers, fountains, and tumbled cathedrals delight the eye. Impressive buildings reflect Visby's medieval wealth: merchants' stepped-gable houses along Strandgatan, the main street during Hanseatic days; the old Apothecary; and Saint Mary's Cathedral, the only one of the town's 17 medieval churches still in use.

Gotland's Fornsal is one of Europe's best provincial museums, devoted to the island's rich cultural history and medieval religious art.

In the countryside you'll see many ancient churches built during the great medieval commercial era; many are still in use. Most are covered with unusual ornamentation, and the interiors often contain some artistic or architectural treasure—paintings, crucifixes carved of wood, stained-glass windows, or stone sculptures.

Gotland also has prehistoric and Viking remains—tumuli, fortresses, and burial grounds. The island's natural features include unusual limestone sculptures called *raukar*, shaped by the Baltic's waves and winds, and the stalactite caves of Lummelunda.

■ **Touring Tips** Daily flights from Stockholm's Bromma Airport reach Visby in about 35 minutes. Car ferries leave the mainland from Nynäshamn and Oskarshamn, and from additional ports in summer. Gotland is the warmest of Sweden's provinces; its Mediterranean climate lasts into October, and roses bloom until Christmas.

SWEDISH EMIGRATION MUSEUM

If your ancestors migrated from Sweden, you might like to visit the Swedish Emigration Museum in Växjö. Its research staff has compiled an impressive record on the emigration of Swedes to America, beginning about 1850. The museum has a wealth of information about Swedish genealogy and artifacts concerning the migration. It is open weekdays from 9 A.M. to 4 P.M., Saturday from 11 to 3, and Sunday from 1 to 5. Sweden-America Day is celebrated annually on the second Sunday in August.

AN ÅLAND ISLANDS STOPOVER

See map page 50

If you've always wanted to snuggle down in a small cottage on a wooded island, spending your days fishing, boating, or just relaxing by the sea, consider a holiday in the Åland Islands, an archipelago of 6,429 islands and islets in the strait separating Sweden and Finland. Swedish is the official language of the Åland people, but the islands are an autonomous province of Finland.

The most natural way to reach Åland is by sea, as immigrants have for many centuries. The islands were densely populated during part of the Bronze Age, and again during the Viking era. Their strategic location made them a stop on early trading routes.

Situated on a small isthmus between two harbors, Mariehamn bustles with activity in summer. An outdoor market is held on the Torget square, and you might hear an outdoor concert in town. Mariehamn has several museums to visit; the major ones are the Maritime Museum and the new Åland Museum and Art Gallery.

In summer you can rent boats of various sizes, from yachts to motorboats to canoes; rental cars, motor scooters, and bicycles are also available. Cycling is a great way to see the islands; roads have little traffic, and several bicycle ferries transport cyclists between islands. You can also rent fishing and windsurfing equipment, plan a picnic, arrange a guided fishing excursion, board a sightseeing cruise, or visit craftspeople in their island workshops. Day sightseeing trips by bus and ferry depart from Mariehamn.

■ **TOURING TIPS** Daily ferry service links the main town of Mariehamn with Stockholm and Kapellskär in Sweden, and Turku and Naantali in Finland; in summer, there's also service from Grisslehamn, Sweden. In the archipelago, northern and southern ferry routes link the islands. Hotels, guest houses, and bed-and-breakfast accommodations are available, but many families rent small holiday cottages by the week. Summer reservations should be made at least 6 months in advance. Early-season weather is cooler, but wildflowers bloom in the meadows and woods and along the roads. Autumn weather is mild but rather windy; deciduous trees and shrubs turn to flaming hues of red, orange, and golden yellow.

RELAXING AT NAANTALI

See map page 50

One of Finland's oldest towns, the resort of Naantali is a favorite destination along the country's south coast. In summer, windsurfers flock to this port, and the boat harbor is lively with water sports. The president of Finland has a summer residence on a nearby island.

Beginning in the mid-15th century, Naantali grew up around Saint Birgitta's Convent and flourished as many wealthy pilgrims made the trip to this shrine. After the convent was closed in 1527, the town fell upon hard times, but it didn't die. In 1863 a spa opened, and once again the town thrived.

Naantali today. Curving through the historic town are narrow lanes. Many of Naantali's old wooden buildings, which date mainly from the late 18th and early 19th centuries, now house workshops and small boutiques.

Near the harbor you'll see the Church of Saint Birgitta's Convent, the only remaining building from the 15th-century convent, and the Merisali and Kaivohuone restaurants, part of the old spa. In summer, visitors can tour the convent church daily from noon to 6 P.M. (noon to 4 P.M. in September); the rest of the year, the church is open only on Sunday from noon to 4 P.M.

To learn more about Naantali's history, visit the Naantali Museum at Katinhäntä 1 (open every afternoon from mid-May through August). It is housed in three wooden dwellings with outbuildings, all dating from the 18th and 19th centuries.

Luonnonmaa Island. Across the bay from the convent church on Luonnonmaa Island is Kultaranta, summer residence of the president of Finland. Visitors are welcome to visit the surrounding park on Fridays from 6 to 8 P.M. Its splendid rose garden contains more than 3,500 bushes.

Also on the island is the Käkölä Farm Museum, which is open to visitors on Sunday from noon to 6 P.M. A bridge links the island with the mainland.

■ **TOURING TIPS** If you want to swim in Naantali, there's a sandy beach behind the church. Band concerts occur on summer weekends in Kaivopuisto Park. You can also rent bicycles during the summer season. Naantali is located about 10 miles/15 km west of Turku. Direct trains and buses link the resort with Turku and Helsinki; in summer there is also steamboat service between Turku and Naantali. Ferries travel daily between Naantali and Sweden via the Åland Islands.

LAPLAND'S NATURE RESERVES

Because the wildlife and landscape of Lapland are particularly vulnerable, large areas of Finland's north country have been preserved as national parks and nature reserves.

Five parks have been set aside in Finnish Lapland: Pallas-Ounas in Western Lapland and Lemmenjoki, Pyhätunturi, Riisitunturi, UKK-park, and Oulanka in Eastern Lapland. In Pallas National Park, between Muonio and Enontekiö near the Swedish border, there's a new guide center, with a geological and zoological collection.

Seven nature reserves have also been reserved for serious scientific research. Specially marked trails cross three of the reserves: Malla in Western Lapland, and Kevo and Sompio in Eastern Lapland. With special permission, backpackers can follow these marked routes to observe the protected wildlife, flowers, and plants. Nights can be spent in Lapp-style log huts, which have been built along wilderness hiking and skiing routes.

NORTH TO LAPLAND

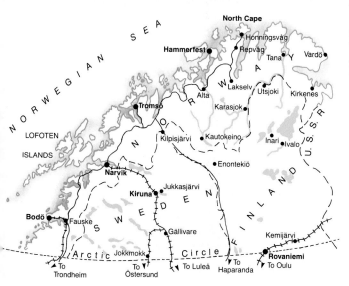

Europe's last wilderness lies north of the Arctic Circle—the vast land of the midnight sun. Spectacular vistas of snow-capped mountains and the fjord-indented coast are punctuated by sparkling lakes, tumbling rivers, pine and birch forests, and wild tundra.

Stretching across the northernmost regions of Scandinavia, the wild tundra of Lapland is inhabited mainly by Lapps (who prefer to call themselves Sami), a self-sufficient people with their own language, cultural traditions, colorful red and blue apparel, and handicrafts. Most families have given up the traditional nomadic life, but some still follow the reindeer herds.

Among the more accessible settlements are Karasjok and Kautokeino in Norway; Jokkmokk, Gällivare, and Jukkasjärvi in Sweden; and Rovaniemi, Enontekiö, Kilpisjärvi, Inari, and Utsjoki in Finland. In cultural museums you can learn about the Lapps' history, way of life, and handicrafts.

Summer in Lapland. Spring appears suddenly in Lapland. In May the first flowers peek through melting snows, and rivers thunder with ice floes. From first thaw to first snowfall, Scandinavians devote nearly every spare waking hour to outdoor activities.

Hikers enjoy a network of trails in the highlands and across the fells and tundra. The season begins after Midsummer Day and lasts into September. Insects appear in hordes as the snow recedes, so bring repellent.

Fishing is excellent in Lapland's lakes and rivers and in the Swedish highlands. Guided fishing and hunting trips are available, with air taxi service to remote areas. You can fish for salmon in several rivers or go deep-sea fishing from Hammerfest.

You can also run the rapids on Norway's Alta River and in Finland's Kuusamo district (east of Rovaniemi), and take boat trips on some of the larger lakes. Canoe trips on northern rivers begin in Ivalo and Inari.

A minor gold rush began here nearly 100 years ago. If you like, you can pan for gold in the Karasjokka River,

upriver from Karasjok on Norway's Finnmark plateau; or in remote tributaries of Finland's Lemmenjoki and Ivalojoki rivers west of Ivalo, and at Tankavaara south of Ivalo. There's a gold museum at Tankavaara.

The train ride between Kiruna and Narvik on the scenic "iron-ore route" makes an interesting day trip. Ore is mined in Kiruna (visitors are welcome June to August) and shipped by rail to the Norwegian port of Narvik. The railway provides the only access to some scenic areas of the Swedish highlands.

Winter above the Arctic Circle. Early in September, the first autumn frosts usher in the brief *ruska* period. Deciduous trees, plants, and heather explode almost overnight into tumultuous color, which vanishes a few days later.

Snow starts falling in October and soon covers the whole landscape, transforming Lapland's hills, lakes, and birch-studded tundra. Temperatures drop far below freezing, but no one goes into hibernation.

Cross-country skiing draws an increasing number of visitors; the best skiing comes between March and May—what the locals call "spring winter," and spring skiers enjoy long days beneath the midnight sun.

Winter visitors can join a guided "reindeer safari," exploring the Lapp wilderness by reindeer-drawn sleigh. If you prefer, you can do your wilderness sightseeing by snowmobile or join a cross-country ski trek.

■ **TOURING TIPS** Scandinavian Airlines and Finnair have scheduled flights to larger cities north of the Arctic Circle; train lines also head north from Oslo, Stockholm, and Helsinki. In the far north local buses fan out from the main bus and rail routes to remote areas. Best months for driving are from late June through September (spring thaw makes some roads impassable until mid-June). Hikers and other visitors find regular summer boat service on some Lapland lakes.

Inquisitive reindeer in Lapland, near Rovaniemi, nuzzles visitor's hand in search of a snack.

SAVONLINNA EXCURSIONS

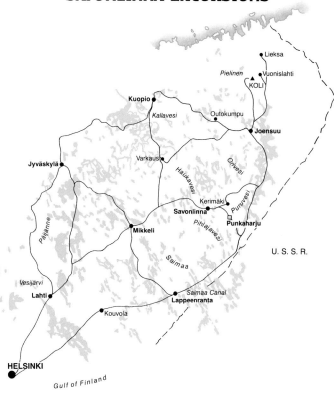

In southeast Finland, boating on a tree-rimmed lake is a relaxing way to spend a sunny day.

Founded in 1639, the attractive lake resort of Savonlinna is the oldest city in eastern Finland and the commercial and cultural center of the eastern Savo region. The town's superb natural setting and central location make it a fine headquarters for exploring the lake district. Savonlinna is built on several islands and a cape jutting into the water, and it has a quiet natural park in the heart of town.

Savonlinna attractions. Olavinlinna Castle, Savonlinna's best-known landmark, is a well-preserved medieval fortress built on a small island guarding the Kyrönsalmi Straits. The town grew up on islands surrounding the castle.

Built about 1475, Olavinlinna was a bastion that protected the eastern frontier of the Swedish kingdom (which ruled Finland until the early 1800s) and supported colonists who moved here to develop the land. Visitors can tour the castle daily; guided tours in English are available. In July, the courtyard of the 500-year-old castle serves as a stage for the Savonlinna Opera Festival, which has been performed here since 1912. Other musical and dramatic events are also presented at the castle.

When Finland was ruled by Russia (between the Napoleonic Wars and 1917), wealthy families from St. Petersburg (now Leningrad) traveled to the holiday and health resort of Savonlinna. On Kasinonsarri Island you'll find Casino Park, with its baths, saunas, and other modern spa facilities.

Your Savonlinna visit should also include a look at the cathedral, built in 1879, and the lively open-air Savo

Market, centrally located near the harbor. In the Savonlinna Museum you'll see museum ships like the restored 19th-century steam schooner *Salama*, which once sailed on Lake Saimaa.

Excursions from Savonlinna. In summer, many regular sightseeing cruises depart from Savonlinna to destinations in the island-studded lake district. The following are among the most popular trips.

Punkaharju, about 25 miles/40 km southeast of Savonlinna, is a famous Ice Age ridge that forms a narrow causeway between lakes Puruvesi and Pihlajavesi. Now a scenic reserve, Punkaharju is accessible from Savonlinna by boat (summers only), bus, or train. Also in Punkaharju is the Retretti Art Centre, a large concert and conference hall and exhibition center constructed in underground caves.

Kerimäki, about 16 miles/25 km northeast of Savonlinna, is the site of Finland's largest wooden church (open June to mid-August). Built in 1847, it can hold 3,300 people. From Kerimäki, boats transport visitors to the Hytermä nature reserve and museum islands, where a large folklore collection is on display.

Rauhalinna, a Byzantine-style private villa built by the Russians about 1900, overlooks the lake from a wooded site near Lehtiniemi, about 11 miles/18 km east of Savonlinna. The intricately decorated, 20-room wooden manor house is now used as a summer hotel and restaurant (open June through mid-August).

■ **TOURING TIPS** Two Valtionhotelli hotels near the Russian border recall the era when Finland was a Grand Duchy, and this region was a popular travel destination. One is a romantic, castlelike hotel by the falls at Imatra. The other, located at Punkaharju, is Finland's oldest hotel; recently restored, it was the holiday home of the Czar and his family. From Savonlinna, steamers cruise south through Saimaa waterways to Mikkeli and Lappeenranta, and north to Kuopio.

HELSINKI'S ISLANDS

See map page 50

Helsinki is a peninsula city, shielded by an archipelago. On its nearby islands, you'll find a national park and open-air museum, swimming beaches, an island fortress, and Helsinki's zoo. All are easily accessible by bus or boat from Helsinki in summer.

Seurasaari.　Just west of central Helsinki, this island is a national park. Its open-air museum offers a look at the Finland of yesteryear, with nearly 100 furnished farmhouses and other buildings from various parts of the country. The museum is open daily from May to September. On many summer evenings, a fiddler plays for folk dancing.

Pihlajasaari.　South of the city, two small wooded islands form a popular summer retreat, with sandy beaches, clear waters for swimming, and smooth rocks for sunbathing. The islands are linked by a footbridge.

Suomenlinna.　Located southeast of Helsinki, this 18th-century fortress covers a cluster of five rocky islands. Now a national monument, it served as part of the nation's defenses until 1973. Visitors see the main fortifications on the islands of Susisaari and Kustaanmiekka; in summer you can take guided tours of the fortress and visit several museums and the Nordic Arts Centre on Susisaari.

Korkeasaari.　Helsinki's zoo is located on this island east of the city. Its collection includes a number of northern European animals, including reindeer, Siberian tigers, northern owls and many other mammals and birds from Europe and Asia.

■ **TOURING TIPS**　In summer, restaurants and other tourist facilities are open on all four islands. Outdoor performances of folk dancing, folk concerts, and a traditional Midsummer Festival are held at Seurasaari.

SCANDINAVIAN DESIGN

Beginning in the 1930s, Scandinavian designers have created an outstanding array of well-designed articles for the home, renowned for their innovative design, flair, and superior craftsmanship. Many have become design classics. No visit to Scandinavia would be complete without a look at the newest creations in glassware, ceramics, textiles, jewelry, furniture, and articles crafted in metal and wood.

In the capital cities, design centers display the newest creations by renowned and upcoming designers. Local tourist offices can direct you to craft centers and other displays of regional work.

A LOOK AT NORTH KARELIA

See map page 66

The Karelia region, with Joensuu as its center, maintains a strong traditional culture. Following a brief war in 1939–40, part of eastern Finland was ceded to the U.S.S.R. Some of Karelia's historic buildings and other cultural treasures were relocated from the Lake Ladoga district. North of Joensuu, Lake Pielinen and the Koli Hills offer opportunities for hiking, fishing, and skiing. Several regional museums contain Karelian collections.

Joensuu.　The only sizable town in North Karelia, Joensuu was founded in 1848, at the mouth of the Pielisjoki River. It is a flourishing university town and the center of its district. The renowned Finnish architect Eliel Saarinen designed Joensuu's Town Hall in 1914. The Joensuu Art Museum includes works by Finnish and international artists and a collection of Chinese art.

You'll see examples of Karelian clothing and textiles, folk art, and crafts in the Northern Karelia Museum at Siltakatu 1, which includes the collection of the Lake Ladoga district museum. East of Joensuu at Ilomantsi village is another center of Karelian culture.

Koli Hills.　About 43 miles/70 km north of Joensuu, the Koli Hills rise along the western shore of Lake Pielinen. The Koli region is gaining popularity as a holiday center. Well-marked hiking paths cross the forested fell. Visitors enjoy good fishing in the lake and excellent canoeing on the Pielisjoki River. In winter, the Koli district draws both downhill and cross-country skiers.

Many summer travelers take the train north from Joensuu along the lake's eastern shore to Vuonislahti or Lieska and travel by boat across the lake to Koli. You also can reach Koli by local bus.

Lake Pielinen district.　Lieska, on the eastern shore of Lake Pielinen, is the most populous town along its shore. In the Pielinen Open-Air Museum at Lieska are about 60 traditional buildings from rural Karelia; the museum is open daily from mid-May to mid-September. Northeast of Lieska, wilderness boat trips run the Ruunaa rapids.

Nurmes is situated on a ridge at the north end of the lake. In the old district, north of the business center, you'll find attractive old wooden houses and birch-lined streets. Just outside town at Ritoniemi is the Bomba Karelian Village. A traditional log-built Karelian house, handsomely decorated in the regional style, forms its centerpiece. Accommodations are available here in cottages, and Karelian foods are served in the village's restaurant.

■ **TOURING TIPS**　The summer tourist season is concentrated between mid-June and mid-August. In Joensuu and Lieska, regional tourist offices are open daily (except Sunday) in summer to help visitors arrange sightseeing tours, accommodations, and guided trips. Boat trips on the lakes operate from the first half of June to mid-August. Summer visitors can arrange to rent bicycles, fishing equipment, canoes, motorboats, rowboats, sailboats, and windsurfing equipment. Guided fishing and canoeing trips are available.

Zell, Mosel Valley

Street sign, Enkirch

GERMANY

Lübeck

Hamburg

Bremen

Hannover

Map, page 76

Goslar

Einbeck — Harz Mountains, page 75

Einbeck, page 74

Essen

Kassel — Fairy-tale route, page 76

Cologne

Lauterbach/Hesse

Mosel Valley,
page 72

Koblenz

Frankfurt's Sachsenhausen,
page 73

Map,
page 72

Frankfurt am Main

Trier

Würzburg

Trier, page 73

Heidelberg

Rothenburg
o. d. Tauber

Nuremberg

Rothenburg ob der Tauber

Romantic Road, page 77

Map, page 74

Map, page 77

Stuttgart

Rottweil

Augsburg

Freiburg

Munich

Map, page 70

Königsee, page 69

Black Forest,
page 74

Füssen

Berchtesgaden

Ludwig's Castles,
page 70

Garmisch-
Partenkirchen

Bavarian Alps, page 71

0	25	50	75	100 Mi
0	50	100	150 Km	

GERMANY

Stretching from the North Sea to the Bavarian Alps, Germany offers a range of intriguing destinations.

Sturdy medieval towns and vineyard villages offer delightful glimpses of country life. Or you can venture into the uplands, where forest roads and footpaths await you in the Black Forest or the Harz Mountains.

You can board a sightseeing boat and glide across the placid lakes tucked amid the foothills of the Bavarian Alps, or you can relax as you cruise on river highways through the vineyard districts.

In Bavaria you can tour magnificent castles built by a mad king. You can even stay in a castle yourself; many now house travelers.

A CRUISE ON THE KÖNIGSSEE

See map page 68

Tucked in the easternmost corner of the Bavarian Alps is the old market town of Berchtesgaden, a popular center for enjoying the rocky, forested slopes along the Austrian border. Old buildings facing the town's triangular central Schlossplatz retain the appeal of earlier eras. Berchtesgaden developed around an Augustinian priory, and later it became the summer residence of the Bavarian ruling family. The Obersalzberg region east of Berchtesgaden gained notoriety as the domain of Adolf Hitler during his rise to power in Germany.

Berchtesgaden offers numerous excursion opportunities, but none is more enjoyable than the boat trip on the Königssee, a long, narrow lake hemmed in by steep escarpments. Lake cruises depart from the village of Königssee, about 3 miles/5 km south of Berchtesgaden.

Rounding a deep curve, you suddenly see the entire lake hemmed in by its mountain backdrop. Snow dapples the sheer cliffs. Waterfalls plunge from great heights into the lake's deep, emerald waters. The area surrounding the Königssee is a wildlife preserve, so few buildings disturb the pristine shore. Only rowboats and electrically-powered boats are allowed on the lake, to maintain the quiet and sense of solitude.

The highlight of the boat ride is a stop at the gleaming white Chapel of St. Bartholomä, topped by several bulbous red domes and surrounded by thick maple trees. Now maintained by caretakers, the distinctive church at different times has been a chapel, a royal Bavarian hunting lodge, and a mountain inn. From the church, you can continue on to the head of the placid lake or return directly to the village of Königssee.

■ **TOURING TIPS** Excursion boats depart frequently during daylight hours year round, except when the lake is frozen. If you'd enjoy a leisurely picnic along the lake shore, pick up lunch supplies before departure.

LUDWIG'S MAGNIFICENT CASTLES

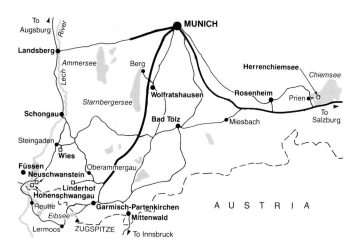

Wooded mountains rise dramatically behind Linderhof Castle, a palatial villa built by Ludwig II as a hunting lodge.

Eccentric European monarchs have added a colorful touch to the history and landscape of the Continent. Among the strangest was King Ludwig II of Bavaria, who had two great passions: the building of extravagant castles and a lifelong infatuation with composer Richard Wagner and his music.

On a loop south of Munich, you can visit four royal castles: Hohenschwangau (the country palace of the Bavarian royal family) and Ludwig's three exuberant structures (Neuschwanstein, built atop a mountain; Linderhof, nestled deep in the forest; and Herrenchiemsee, rising on an island in the middle of an Alpine lake). Begin your journey at Hohenschwangau, once the rural retreat of the Bavarian royal family. The castle rises on a wooded spur overlooking a small lake rimmed by mountains.

Hohenschwangau. Built in the 1830s by Maximilian II of Bavaria, Hohenschwangau has the warmth of a lived-in castle. Young Ludwig spent his summers here, dreaming of Teutonic legends. The walls and ceilings are elaborately decorated; many murals portray medieval heroes. The family's swan motif appears frequently.

Wagner visited Hohenschwangau many times. Mementos of the long association are displayed in the music room on the second floor.

From his bedroom window at Hohenschwangau, Ludwig could watch through a telescope the building progress at Neuschwanstein.

Neuschwanstein. Perched on a craggy rock above dark green pines, Neuschwanstein exemplifies a child's fantasy of a fairy-tale castle. Grayish white towers and turrets give the feudal-style keep a dreamlike appearance.

As you walk up the long approach road, you begin to appreciate the difficulty of constructing such a massive project on this isolated site. (Tired sightseers can arrange to ride up the hill in a horse-drawn cart.)

Neuschwanstein's interior is equally remarkable: rooms decorated with marble, gilded paneling, heavy tapestries, magnificent chandeliers and candelabras.

You'll see Ludwig's artificial grotto and the great Singer's Hall (a pair of triumphant shrines to Wagnerian heroes), the unfinished throne room, and the castle kitchens.

Linderhof. Built in the 1870s, this small, creamy white villa nestles in a wooded valley west of Oberammergau. Although it was used primarily as a royal hunting lodge, Linderhof is a palatial gem combining Italian Renaissance and baroque styles. Opulent decorations adorn the interior.

Surrounding the castle is a magnificent park containing formal gardens, fountains, and pools. Don't miss the Moorish pavilion and artificial grotto that Ludwig used whenever he decided to play Oriental potentate.

Herrenchiemsee. Ludwig's last palatial indulgence was Herrenchiemsee, built on a wooded island in the Chiemsee, largest of the Bavarian lakes. Visitors reach the island by boat from the Prien-Stock dock.

Inspired by a visit to the palace of Versailles, Ludwig began construction on this castle in 1878. In the next seven years he spent 20 million marks, virtually exhausting the royal treasury.

Herrenchiemsee's royal apartments are lavishly decorated. On Saturday evenings in summer, chamber music concerts are presented by candlelight in the magnificent Hall of Mirrors as giant fountains play on the terrace.

■ TOURING TIPS Most travelers visit the castles on excursions from Munich. If you wish to stay in the area, you'll find the widest range of accommodations in Garmisch-Partenkirchen and Füssen; a more limited selection is available in Oberammergau and Mittenwald near Linderhof, and in Rosenheim and Prien near Herrenchiemsee.

CASTLES & HISTORIC HOTELS

If you like to seek out castle hotels and other historic inns with special charm, you'll find rich opportunities in Germany. A number of castles and fortresses have been converted into comfortable hotels. Many belong to the Gast im Schloss (Guest in a Castle) Association; other historic hotels are members of the Romantik Hotels & Restaurants organization.

Guides to these historic hotels are available from the German National Tourist Office (address on page 128). Travelers can stay in individual hotels or plan a personalized tour. The Gast im Schloss Association offers a special program for hikers, who walk unencumbered while their luggage is transported by vehicle.

GERMANY'S MOUNTAIN PLAYGROUND

See map page 70

The snowy peaks of the Bavarian Alps form an awesome backdrop to mountain lakes and chalet villages along Germany's southeastern border. Bavarian resort towns are at their busiest in winter, when crowds flock to Garmisch-Partenkirchen and smaller towns for skiing, skating, and other winter sports. Summer visitors find many choices: charming villages to explore, Alpine trails to hike, and snowy peaks to climb. Chair lifts and aerial tramways provide access to the heights.

Bavarian towns have a special appeal. Houses with wide eaves and flower-filled balconies line the streets; paintings depicting religious or folk scenes adorn many façades. Slim belfries rise above stately churches.

Garmisch-Partenkirchen. Germany's leading winter sports center, this resort was the setting of the 1936 Winter Olympics. Its excellent skiing and skating facilities attract an international crowd. In summer, life is quieter; days are usually spent outdoors—in the mountains, by the lakes, or strolling around the twin towns.

If you want to do some hiking, take the cable car from the village of Partenkirchen up the Wank, a low peak (5,840 feet/1,780 meters) traversed by paths. You look down on towns snugly encircled by great peaks.

Another excursion leads up the Partnach Gorge south of Partenkirchen. Be sure to take along a raincoat. The rocky path crosses the gorge in two narrow places where spray from the waterfalls mists hikers.

If time limits you to a single mountain goal, it might as well be the highest one around—the 9,731-foot/2,966-meter Zugspitze. Its spectacular panorama has been called the finest in Europe. A large deck offers you a quick tan in the clear, thin air and a view of the skiers on the slopes below. If the weather turns cold or windy, you can retreat to the glass-enclosed restaurant. You can make the ascent in two ways: by narrow-gauge cog railway from Garmisch or by aerial tram from the Eibsee.

Mittenwald. Nestled in a valley near the Austrian border, Mittenwald is protected by the rocky wall of the Karwendel. Many of the town's houses are painted with historical or Biblical scenes.

Skilled craftsmen have made stringed instruments in Mittenwald for more than 300 years, and a museum shows the evolution of the craft.

Oberammergau. This attractive town is renowned for both its fine woodcarving and its Passion Play, presented every 10 years (next in 1990). A Biblical atmosphere pervades the town; many façades display murals with Biblical scenes, and streets bear names from the Bible. Originating in 1634, the Passion Play fulfills a vow by the people of the village to present a play depicting the Passion of Christ once each decade if the ravages of a widespread plague were ended. All of the participants come from the town, and more than a half-million spectators witness the all-day performances each decade.

Wies church. Northwest of Oberammergau, off the main roads, you'll find the exuberantly adorned church of Wies, considered by connoisseurs to be the most beautiful rococo church in Germany. Set amidst meadows, the church is backed by thickly forested slopes. Its simple exterior contrasts with the rich but harmonious decorations found inside. Light streams through the windows, highlighting frescoes painted by Dominikus Zimmermann in the mid-18th century; wood carvings and gilded ornamentation enhance the beauty.

■ **TOURING TIPS** Trains link Munich and other German cities with Garmisch-Partenkirchen and Mittenwald; buses serve smaller resorts. From April until late October, bicycles can be rented from many railway stations.

Window boxes burgeoning with colorful blooms add a festive Bavarian touch to this Oberammergau hotel.

Navigable for nearly 170 miles/270 km, the Mosel is a watery highway busy with barges transporting freight. From May to early October, excursion boats cruise along the Mosel, offering day trips between Koblenz and Cochem and longer cabin cruises between Koblenz and Trier.

Vineyards and castle ruins. The most scenic stretch extends from Bernkastel-Kues to Cochem. Here the valley walls become steeper, the foliage more abundant, the river more twisting in exaggerated bends. Often you'll see anglers and picnickers along the river. Roads and trails lead up to castle ruins and into the hills.

Below the 11th-century ruins of Burg Landshut, Bernkastel faces its twin town of Kues across the river. Narrow cobbled lanes wind between timber-and-stone buildings to Bernkastel's delightful little market square, where an angel tops the 17th-century fountain.

Downstream, on the west bank, Ürzig's timbered houses are topped by tall gables. Handsome 17th- and 18th-century houses face the Mosel at Kröv.

The figure of a maiden carrying grapes stands atop Traben's fountain. Across the river, the ruins of Grevenburg Castle tower above Trarbach, the wine capital of the central Mosel. North of Trarbach, detour into quiet Enkirch, where whimsical carved and painted signs identify streets near the Marktplatz.

Guarded by old fortifications, Zell stretches out along the east bank of the Mosel; on the opposite bank, Alf lies below the Marienburg and Arras castles. If you're weary of vineyards, seek out the small spa of Bad Bertrich west of Alf. At Beilstein, a tiny market town tucked below the ruins of Burg Metternich, you'll see one of the small ferries that operate on the lower Mosel.

Cochem to Koblenz. A popular stopping point on the Mosel's west bank, Cochem has a pleasant riverside promenade. A path leads up to the ruins of Burg Cochem.

It takes extra effort to reach Burg Eltz, in the hills above Moselkern at the end of the wild Eltz Valley. It's a 45-minute walk through woods to the castle, one of the finest in Germany. Bristling with towers, the fortress looms through the trees. (Before the castle tour begins, ask for an English translation of the guide's comments.)

East of Brodenbach, you'll see the ruins of once-powerful Ehrenburg, built on the remains of a Roman fortress. The ruins of two castles overlook Kobern, and vast vineyards surround Winningen.

The Mosel flows into the Rhine at Koblenz, a busy tourist center. Cruises on both the Mosel and Rhine depart from Koblenz, and railways branch in all directions. If you stop here overnight, you might visit the Weindorf, along the Rhine just upriver from the main bridge, to enjoy local wines and music in an open-air garden.

■ **TOURING TIPS** Trains zip through the valley, stopping at Bullay and Cochem; local buses serve other river towns. Cochem, Bernkastel-Kues, and Traben-Trarbach offer the widest choice in accommodations; you'll also find excellent hotels in the Eifel and Hunsrück mountains. Reservations are usually necessary in summer and fall, especially on weekends. Many wine festivals take place in the district; the German National Tourist Office (address on page 128) can provide a listing.

Burg Cochem offers lofty viewpoint over Mosel Valley. From Cochem, footpath leads through vineyards to castle.

MOSEL VALLEY WINE TOURING

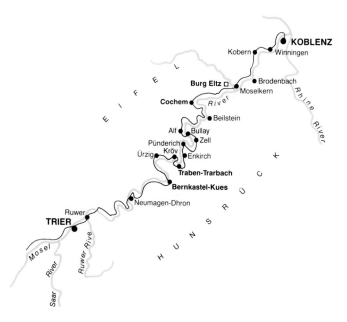

Wine fanciers savor Germany's lovely Mosel Valley, where the river cuts a twisting course between steep slopes planted with terraced vineyards. Life along the Mosel moves at a leisurely pace. Diversions are simple— river towns to explore, footpaths through vineyards and woods to castles and ruined fortresses, marvelous delicate wines.

A STROLL AROUND OLD TRIER

See map page 72

Trier is one of Germany's oldest cities. Though it was officially founded by the Romans in 16 B.C., legends claim the town originated before 2000 B.C. as an Assyrian settlement. Trier's heyday extended from the 3rd to the 5th century, when the city was the capital of Gaul, northern gateway to the Roman Empire, and one of the imperial residences. Ramparts were built, as were impressive civic and religious structures.

Today Trier is a busy commercial center for wine made from grapes of the Mosel-Saar-Ruwer region. You'll enjoy exploring the town's historic district on foot, and you can also take a self-guided tour to learn more about its vineyard district.

Historic Trier. The city's landmark is the magnificent Porta Nigra, a splendid fortified gate built in the 2nd century. It was assembled from large mortarless limestone blocks held together only by a few iron fasteners. Over the centuries, a dark patina formed on the limestone, giving the monument its name. Arcades, guarded by outside towers, lead to an exposed inner court where hostile intruders could be attacked on all sides. You can climb to the upper floors, where you'll have good views of the town.

After a stop at the tourist information office, walk up the Simeonstrasse to the Hauptmarkt, where open-air markets have been held for more than 1,000 years. On all sides, buildings reflect Trier's history—the Porta Nigra and other remnants of the Roman era, churches dating from the Middle Ages, baroque and half-timbered burghers' houses echoing more recent prosperity.

From the Hauptmarkt, your route leads past the Renaissance-style Electoral Palace to the palace gardens. The Landesmuseum, known as one of Germany's leading archeological museums, contains artifacts from the prehistoric, Roman, and early Christian periods. Nearby you can see remnants of the medieval city wall and ruins of the imperial baths. On slopes farther east are the remains of the Roman amphitheater, which could seat more than 20,000 spectators for gladiator competitions.

Along the Mosel River, near the Kaiser Wilhelm Bridge, take a look at the Mariensäule column and Zurlauben, a lane of 18th-century houses. In summer, cruises on the Mosel depart near the bridge. A cable car ascends from Zurlauben to the Weisshaus terrace for a view of the valley.

Wine district. To learn more about Mosel vineyards and wine making, visit the suburb of Olewig, just east of the Roman amphitheater ruins. A brochure outlines a self-guided 2-mile/3-km wine trail through the nearby vineyards and lists local vintners who welcome visitors for wine tasting.

■ **TOURING TIPS** To obtain map brochures of central Trier and the "Trier Wine Teaching Path," stop at the city's tourist information office near the Porta Nigra. Bus routes 6 and 16 link the central district with the wine-making suburb of Olewig.

FRIENDLY SACHSENHAUSEN

See map page 68

Frankfurt's most charming quarter is Sachsenhausen, a center of culture and conviviality south of the Main River. Best known for its apple-wine taverns, the old district also contains the city's main museums, interesting shopping, and the only remaining tower of the city's original fortifications.

Centered around the Affentorplatz, Sachsenhausen has a captivating atmosphere drawn in part from its medieval buildings, narrow pedestrian streets, and the cozy taverns that dispense freshly barreled cider. All of the inns press and age their own apple juice or obtain it from farms near Frankfurt. A pine wreath hanging outside is your signal of hospitality within.

You'll join residents and other visitors at long tables to enjoy the tart *Ebbelwei*; in good weather you can sit in the courtyard under shade trees. With the tangy drink you'll nibble crisp pretzels or order hearty specialties.

Seven riverside museums—called the *Museumsufer*—line the Sachsenhausen side of the Main River in parklike surroundings. Each focuses on a single specialty: art, sculpture, applied arts, architecture, film, ethnology, and post office paraphernalia.

Shoppers come to browse in Sachsenhausen's specialty stores, antique shops, and used bookstores. Along the Schweizer Strasse, many buildings have facades dating from the 1870s. Frankfurt's flea market takes place Saturday morning in the former Schlachthof, south of the Flösserbrücke.

■ **TOURING TIPS** From central Frankfurt you can travel to Sachsenhausen by bus or streetcar; you can also take the *U-bahn* (subway) to the museum district and the Schweizer Strasse shopping area. Passengers purchase tickets from blue ticket-vending machines before boarding; you can also purchase a day ticket (*Tageskarte*) good for 24 hours of travel within the metropolitan Frankfurt area.

MUSEUMS FOR EVERY INTEREST

Travelers often find that unplanned experiences bring unexpected pleasure. In that spirit we suggest you seek out some of Germany's delightful small museums, most devoted to a single topic.

The German National Tourist Office (address on page 128) offers a brochure, "Technical Museums in Germany," listing more than 125, ranging from the commonplace to the arcane. Here's a sampling: medieval criminology, brewing, violin-making, historical toys, model ships in bottles, tobacco and cigars, Gutenburg's printing, X-ray technology, birdcages, caves, windmills and water mills, mining, book design, clocks, bells, dolls, and mechanical musical instruments.

BLACK FOREST BYWAYS

Though its name may sound foreboding, Germany's Black Forest is no more sinister than the cuckoo clocks it produces. Nestled in an elbow of the Rhine River, it stretches for more than 100 miles/160 km north to Karlsruhe. Dark evergreens cover the slopes of the smoothly rounded mountains, giving the region its name, but the valleys are lighter green with open fields.

Generations of European families have come to this year-round holiday area to enjoy bracing air, mountain scenery, and rustic charm. Hiking, water sports, and appealing towns make this region a delightful spot to pause for a few days. Blossoming trees and wildflowers brighten the green slopes in late spring, and colorful foliage enhances autumn scenery.

Hikers work off hearty meals roaming countless miles of well-maintained footpaths—through woodlands, across lush meadows, up winding ridges, and down wild gorges. Marked trails lead into the woods from villages and forest parking areas. Families head for the southern mountain lakes—especially Titisee and Schluchsee—where sailors and swimmers enjoy water sports activities. When snow falls, ski touring and sleigh riding dominate outdoor activities.

Dotting the countryside are large wooden farmhouses, each sheltering people and animals under a single roof. In some districts, such as the Gutach and Kinzig valleys and several Hoch Schwarzwald (Upper Black Forest) villages, residents still don traditional dress for festive occasions.

In Triberg's Heimatmuseum you can learn about Black Forest history, customs, folk dress, and crafts. Or you can follow the path from the Gutach bridge up the shaded ravine to beautiful Gutach Falls. Old Black Forest

farm buildings have been assembled in the Gutach open-air museum north of Hornberg.

Furtwangen's clock museum displays cuckoo clocks and other historic timepieces. Farther south, the Titisee is a jewellike lake set in thick forest; more than 60 miles/100 km of posted hiking trails branch out from this lake village. From Titisee or Freiburg you can explore the wild and rocky Höllental (Hell Valley), the bucolic Glottertal, or the Feldberg, the highest mountain in the Black Forest.

■ **TOURING TIPS** No single route dominates the region; instead, main roads follow several river valleys. Allow ample driving time—at least half a day between Freudenstadt and Freiburg. Many forest roads are narrow and winding, and main routes are often crowded. Marked trails lead into the woods from villages and forest parking areas.

EINBECK, AN OLD BREWERY TOWN

See map page 76

In the Middle Ages, Einbeck earned fame as the home of 600 breweries, which provided all of Germany with Einpöckisches Bier (from which the variety known as Bocksbier derives its name). Today this town east of the Weser

Carved and painted ornamentation enhances façades of many wooden buildings in old brewery town of Einbeck.

Valley is better known for its handsome 16th-century wooden houses.

Einbeck's most distinctive buildings are grouped around the Marktplatz. Well maintained, they lend an elegant and traditional aspect to the heart of the town. Carvings touched with color brighten the wooden façades. Many have large attic vents, indicating that hops and barley were probably once stored there.

Stroll along the Marktplatz, now a pedestrian plaza, to see the *Brodhaus*, the *Rats-apotheke,* and the *Ratswaage* (weighing house) festooned with carved ornamentation. The *Rathaus* (town hall) has a distinctive silhouette: two buildings topped with conical projections.

More of the fine old buildings can be seen along the Tidexerstrasse, beyond the Marktkirche tower, and bordering the Marktstrasse, near the church.

■ **TOURING TIPS** Einbeck's Marktplatz has been converted to a pedestrian plaza, so visitors can admire the old buildings without worrying about traffic; parking areas are located several blocks away. If you want to extend your explorations, you can see part of the town's old perimeter walls.

HOLIDAY IN THE HARZ MOUNTAINS

See map page 76

If you enjoy the outdoors, you may wish to join others who have made the Harz Mountains a popular holiday area. Visitors flock to its resorts and spas and hike through its pine forests. Biking and hiking paths link the towns and villages, and many mountain trails take off from roadside parking areas. Miniature cottages in wooded glens remind you of Hansel and Gretel. In winter, snow blankets the wooded hills.

Of the many towns at the foot of the mountains, the most important is the imperial city of Goslar, more than 1,000 years old and one of Germany's classic medieval cities. You can easily spend a full day exploring.

Goslar. Once a favorite residence of the emperors of the Holy Roman Empire, Goslar began to boom when rich ore deposits were discovered in the Harz Mountains. In the early 16th century, prospering merchants and skilled craftsmen built an impressive town hall, mighty churches, richly decorated guildhalls, and timber-fronted houses with elaborate oriel windows. Moats and high walls, with sturdy towers and gates, encircled the town. The area began to decline about 1550, and it remained substantially undisturbed for several hundred years.

Goslar is a city for strolling—through street after street of handsome old buildings, along the Gose Stream that flows through town, and past remaining sections of the medieval town walls. You'll enjoy lingering amid the lively market stalls and perhaps even climbing the tower of the *Marktkirche* (Market Church).

Begin your explorations in the dignified Marktplatz, the town's central gathering place. Here you'll find the arcaded *Rathaus*, the church, and the traditional old (1494) Hotel Kaiserworth, one of several historic struc-

framed in timber and roofed in slate, face the square and line narrow side streets. Models of medieval Goslar are displayed in the Goslarer Museum; paintings and imperial mementos can be seen in the Imperial Palace.

Harz Mountains loop. Rising suddenly out of the north German plain, the rugged, wooded hills of the Harz region top all the surrounding foothills and straddle the border between West and East Germany. The highest point is Mount Brocken in East Germany; according to legend, witches ride broomsticks to Brocken's summit on Walpurgis Night (April 30) for revelry until dawn.

A half-day trip south from Goslar provides a sampling of the Harz region; on a full-day trip you can add a picnic and a hike along one of the forest trails.

Clausthal-Zellerfeld was once the mining capital of the upper Harz. Exhibits in the museum in Zellerfeld depict some of the local mining methods. The church in Clausthal, built entirely of wood, is also worth a visit. In Osterode, take a look at the Kornmarkt square, framed by half-timbered houses; sculptor Tilman Riemenschneider was born in this town.

St. Andreasberg was a silver-mining center; the mine has been reopened for tourists. The resort of Braunlage offers access to nearby parks and a cableway up the Wurmberg south of Mount Brocken. The road climbs through woods to Torfhaus, where you detour west on the Altenau road.

North of Altenau you follow the Oker Valley downstream, passing a large reservoir and dam. Below the dam, the valley narrows sharply and the torrential outflow tumbles down its rocky valley.

■ **TOURING TIPS** In Goslar, stop at the tourist office facing the Marktplatz for a map and sightseeing information. In the mountains, you'll find the best selection of accommodations in Braunlage; however, most towns have a few small family-run hotels and pensions.

VISITING BERLIN

You can reach West Berlin by plane, train, bus, or car from major cities in West Germany. Visitors traveling by surface transport need a valid passport to enter the German Democratic Republic (East Germany). Transit visas are issued at border checkpoints and on all trains into Berlin. Foreign motorists in East Germany need liability insurance, which can be purchased at border-crossing points. For more information, contact the German National Tourist Office (address on page 128).

Travelers wishing to enter East Berlin can obtain information at the Berlin Tourist Office at Tegel Airport or near the Zoo Railroad Station. Half-day bus excursions with an English-speaking guide are available from West Berlin; tour price includes the visa fee.

CHRISTMAS MARKETS

The Christmas season is a particularly joyous time in Germany. In a number of German towns, the opening of the Christkindlmarkt *signals the start of the holidays.*

Families come to see trees decorated with twinkling lights and to buy Christmas ornaments and other decorations, toys, gingerbread men and Christmas confections, Advent calendars, and other surprises. Stalls open in late November or early December and remain open until a few days before Christmas.

Largest of the German Christmas markets is in Nuremburg; others are held in Frankfurt, Munich, Hamburg, Heidelberg, Stuttgart, Trier, Lübeck, Essen, Freiburg, Augsburg, Rottweil, Lauterbach/Hesse, West Berlin, and other cities.

GERMANY'S "FAIRY-TALE ROUTE"

Brave princes and captivating golden-haired princesses, mean stepmothers and wicked witches, industrious dwarfs and bewitched animals—these characters popularized by the Brothers Grimm originated in the folktales of central Germany.

In the early 19th century, Jacob and Wilhelm Grimm lived in Kassel, working as court librarians while gathering legends and traditional stories in the surrounding villages. They collected some 200 tales featuring such classic characters as Hansel and Gretel, Snow White, Rumpelstiltskin, and Little Red Riding Hood.

To sample this land of once-upon-a-time, explore the rolling hills and unspoiled villages of the Weser Valley. A meandering route called *Die Deutsche Märchenstrasse* (The German Fairy-Tale Road) extends from the brothers' birthplace in Hanau, east of Frankfurt, about 350 miles/600 km north to Bremen. Signs picturing a smiling princess mark the route.

Start your tour in Kassel with a visit to its museum dedicated to the lives and works of the Brothers Grimm. It contains manuscripts, original illustrations, letters, and mementos to rekindle your childhood memories.

The river route. In its upper reaches, the Weser River is a scenic stream, bordered by a number of delightful small towns and villages that resemble illustrations in a children's storybook.

Towns large and small abound with lovely old houses—elegant timber-framed buildings (*Fachwerkhäuser*) as well as sandstone ones built in the local architectural style, known as Weser Renaissance, with characteristic scrollwork and pinnacles on the gables. Gray slate or weathered pink limestone tiles cover the roofs. Frescoes or folk sayings occasionally ornament the façades.

Hannoversch-Münden lies at the confluence of the Fulda and Werra rivers, which join to form the Weser. A park and commemorative stone, the Weserstein, mark the point. After a look at the gabled *Rathaus* (town hall), stroll the nearby streets to admire some of the town's 450 half-timbered houses. You can stroll across the old Werra Bridge, built in 1327, and up to the Weserliedanlage monument overlooking the confluence of the rivers and the wooded hills. In summer, passenger boats cruise the Weser River between Hann.-Münden and Hameln.

Overnight in a castle. The route follows the river north toward Karlshafen. If you like, veer northwest from Veckerhagen into the wooded Reinhardswald toward a pair of medieval castles, both now hotels.

Twin black-domed towers rise above romantic 14th-century Sababurg (locally called "Sleeping Beauty's Castle"), deep in the forest northeast of Hofgeismar, off the main road. Even older is Trendelburg, a 12th-century castle perched on a wooded hilltop above its village and the Diemel Valley. The ruins of Krukenburg overlook the town of Helmarshausen.

Riverside towns. You rejoin the Weser at the thermal springs resort of Karlshafen, a town that has preserved its Huguenot heritage. Identified by pictorial signs, the fairy-tale road winds leisurely north through the tree-covered hills of the Weserbergland. At several points between the larger towns, small ferries transport cars across the Weser.

The pleasant riverside town of Höxter is a stroller's delight. It's filled with colorful houses ornamented with decorative woodwork; many have folk sayings or proverbs inscribed on their façades.

In Bodenwerder, a museum displays mementos of the town's best-known resident, the legendary Baron

Hieronymus von Münchhausen, renowned for his tall tales of adventure.

A special place in German folklore belongs to Hameln and its famed rat catcher, the Pied Piper. In summer, townspeople dramatize the legend each Sunday at noon in the old town. (Rat-shaped souvenirs are a local specialty.) Many handsome old houses cluster around the medieval town center.

■ **TOURING TIPS**   Obtain a copy of the "German Fairy-Tale Road" map brochure from the German National Tourist Office (address on page 128) for additional touring ideas. Trains and buses serve the larger cities and towns, but you'll find driving the best way to enjoy the region. Passenger boats cruise the Weser between Hann.-Münden and Hameln from mid-April to early October.

ALONG THE ROMANTIC ROAD

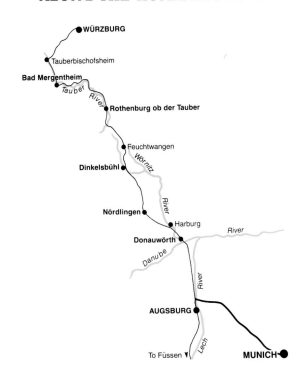

Germany's delightful *Romantische Strasse* wends south from Würzburg through flat valley farmland toward the Austrian border. Highlights along this ancient route are a trio of medieval gems—Rothenburg ob der Tauber, Dinkelsbühl, and Nördlingen. These venerable walled towns thrived in the 13th and 14th centuries as free imperial cities; they escaped destruction during the devastating Thirty Years' War (1618–1648) and survived World War II bombing raids nearby.

High ramparts studded with gates and watchtowers surround the towns. You pass through thick gates into a medieval world of gabled buildings and cobblestone streets. Wrought-iron signs announce the shops. Each town is a large, open-air medieval museum. Obtain a town map at the local tourist office, then let your whims guide your explorations.

Crowd in Rothenburg's Marktplatz awaits the hour; when clock strikes, mechanized wooden characters depict town's legend.

Rothenburg ob der Tauber.   Captivating Rothenburg has been called Germany's best-preserved medieval town. (It's a popular stopping place, however, so traffic and crowds can be a nuisance in summer and on weekends.) Facing the Marktplatz is the imposing town hall and the Ratstrinkstube tavern. Hourly between 11 A.M. and 3 P.M., wooden characters in a gable clock enact a local legend—how a drinking feat by the mayor saved the town from destruction. Gabled mansions built by prosperous burghers line the Herrngasse, which leads to a garden overlooking the valley. Allow time for a leisurely walk along the ramparts surrounding the town. The St. Jakob-Kirche contains a magnificent carved altarpiece by Tilman Riemenschneider.

Dinkelsbühl.   Quiet waters of a reed-bordered moat reflect Dinkelsbühl's walls and watchtowers. Inside the ramparts, tall gabled buildings brightened by blooming flowers face the main square. You can climb to the top of the church bell tower for a view over the town.

Nördlingen.   A remarkable perimeter wall completely encircles Nördlingen. Many of its fortified gateways and towers are topped by helmet-shaped roofs. Another striking asset is the baroque 15th-century church, whose majestic tower rises nearly 300 feet/100 meters above the red roofs. Narrow cobbled streets stretch like spokes from the Marktplatz to various old market districts and craftsmen's quarters, buildings reflecting Nördlingen's medieval wealth and local pride.

■ **TOURING TIPS**   You'll enjoy the route most if you travel by car, stopping where and when you like. No trains reach these towns, but Europabus operates daily service from mid-March to early November. Express buses travel from Wiesbaden and Frankfurt to Munich, stopping at main towns along the route. Local service follows the Romantic Road from Würzburg south to Füssen, with Munich-bound travelers changing buses at Augsburg. Stops are brief, so you may wish to plan at least one overnight stay.

Appenzell pastures

Valle Maggia near Locarno

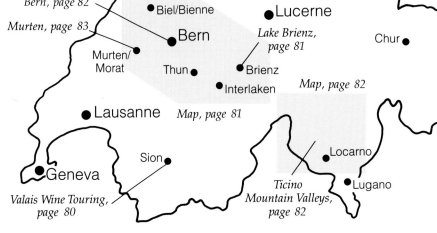

Rhine River Boat Trip, page 79

Zürich Countryside, page 80

Schaffhausen

Kreuzlingen

Basel

Zürich

St. Gallen

Appenzell District, page 83

Appenzell

SWITZERLAND

Day Hiking near Bern, page 82

Biel/Bienne

Lucerne

Map, page 80

Murten, page 83

Bern

Lake Brienz, page 81

Chur

Murten/Morat

Thun

Brienz

Interlaken

Map, page 82

Lausanne

Map, page 81

Locarno

Sion

Ticino Mountain Valleys, page 82

Lugano

Geneva

Valais Wine Touring, page 80

| 0 | | 25 | | 50 Mi |
| 0 | 25 | | 50 | 75 Km |

Murten

SWITZERLAND

Nestled in the heart of Europe between the Rhine River and the Alps, Switzerland offers many destinations that showcase its magnificent scenery.

In the following pages you'll find routes that take you into pastoral countryside, through the Rhône Valley wine country, by boat along rivers and lakes, and to interesting country towns.

Among other excursions are day hikes in the Bernese countryside, a look at a fine open-air museum, a cogwheel train ride with a panoramic view, trips by postal bus up Alpine valleys, and visits to traffic-free towns.

RIVER ROUTE ALONG THE RHINE

See map page 80

Steamers ply the Rhine from Schaffhausen upriver to Kreuzlingen on the Bodensee (Lake Constance), a splendidly scenic half-day cruise through unspoiled countryside.

Your boat departs from the Schifflände in Schaffhausen, on the Rhine River below Munot Castle. You'll cruise upstream between greenery-lined banks, past Diessenhofen with its covered bridge.

You may decide to disembark in Stein am Rhein, one of Switzerland's prettiest medieval towns. It is renowned for its array of colorfully painted buildings, many of them decorated with oriel windows. The heart of the old town is the Rathausplatz, where the town hall presides over some of Stein am Rhein's loveliest buildings. An ornamented fountain and window boxes teeming with red geraniums add to the town's charm. The ancient cathedral stands east of the town hall.

After you've strolled down the main street, enjoying the painted houses and wrought-iron signs, you can wander along the Rhine promenade or stop at a riverside cafe. Roads and trails lead into the countryside and up to the old Hohenkingen Castle, perched behind town with a commanding view of the Rhine.

Upstream from Stein am Rhein, the scenery changes constantly, as you pass wooded hills and vineyards, tidy villages, and ancient hilltop castles.

Above Steckborn, the Rhine widens into the Untersee. More castles crown the hills above attractive villages as you cruise on to Kreuzlingen.

■ **TOURING TIPS** Local tourist offices can provide departure times for the boat trip and for train travel. Roads and a rail line closely parallel the river's southern bank; auto bridges cross the Rhine River at Diessenhofen, Stein am Rhein, and Konstanz.

Colorful paintings, oriel windows, and scarlet geraniums adorn the façades along main street in Stein am Rhein.

ZURICH TO THE RHEINFALL

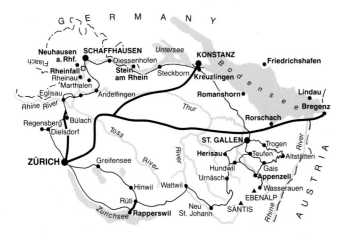

The pastoral countryside north of Zurich invites leisurely exploring. Farmhouses dot the gentle green hills on which dairy cows placidly graze. Country roads lead to tiny villages (each grouped around its small church). On this rural route, you'll visit Regensberg, a medieval gem, then wend your way to the Rhine River and Europe's most powerful waterfall.

North to the Rhine.   From Zurich, take the road north to Dielsdorf, about 10 miles/16 km northwest of the city. A side road leads to captivating Regensberg, which rises above vineyards and farmlands along the crest of a hill.

Follow its one long street through an archway into the tree-shaded main square, where small gardens front many of the steeply roofed houses. The 16th-century castle was once the home of the barons of Regensberg, who ruled the town and environs. You can climb the round watchtower for a view over the town.

Return to Dielsdorf and take country roads northeast through Bülach to Eglisau. Upriver, trees and shrubs grow in lush profusion along this little-known stretch of the Rhine.

Continue on through Flaach, a May destination for asparagus lovers, to see Andelfingen's half-timbered houses and wooden bridge. In these rural villages, barns adjoin the houses with the barnyard facing the road.

Rheinfall.   Since the Middle Ages, the Rhine has been an important river highway. Steamers and barges ferry passengers and freight more than 250 miles/400 km inland from the North Sea, passing through Holland and Germany and along Switzerland's northern border. In medieval days, Schaffhausen grew as a depot for river cargoes, which had to be unloaded and portaged around river rapids and the powerful waterfall.

Above the Rheinfall, the river is nearly 500 feet/175 meters wide. Rounding a deep curve, it suddenly narrows, surging in thundering, foamy cascades around three shrubbery-covered rocks to plunge some 70 feet/22 meters into a wide river basin.

You can view the river from either bank, but you get the closest look directly below Schloss Laufen on the left bank. Stairs lead from the castle courtyard down to a viewing platform suspended over the water. Spray from the waterfall is heavy in spring and early summer, so bring along a raincoat. Adventurous visitors can take a wet boat ride to the main rock in midriver.

Schaffhausen.   North of the Rhine you'll find the old city of Schaffhausen, which received its city charter in 1045, and its industrial suburb, Neuhausen. You can easily spend several hours touring Schaffhausen's medieval quarter. Along its old streets you'll see many fine houses with characteristic oriel windows and frescoes; best known is the Haus zum Ritter on Vordergasse.

Also distinctive are its churches, guildhalls, medieval watchtowers, and ornamented fountains. Dominating the town and river from atop a hill is the massive 16th-century Munot Castle, linked with the old quarter by a stairway and covered passageway.

■ **TOURING TIPS**   If you're traveling by train, you can reach the Rheinfall by trolley bus from the Schaffhausen train station in about 15 minutes. Maps for a walking tour of Schaffhausen are available at the tourist office (*Verkehrsbüro*) at Vorstadt 12 on weekdays and Saturday mornings.

WINE TOURING IN THE VALAIS

See map page 78 ·

Many travelers to Switzerland enjoy the local wines, typically the white Fendant and red Dôle vintages—but Swiss winemakers offer a broader variety. If you'd like to learn more about Swiss wines, consider a visit to the Valais district, which contains almost 40 percent of the country's vineyards. Most are on the sunny, south-facing slopes of the Rhône Valley between Lake Geneva and Sierre.

The Valais Wine Route follows the right bank of the Rhône River for about 30 miles/50 km between Loèche and Martigny; it is clearly marked in both directions.

If you'd like to visit some of the Valais *caves* to meet the vintners and sample the local product, contact the OPAV (Office de Propagande pour les Produits de l'Agriculture Valaisanne) at avenue de la Gare 5, 1950 Sion, a day or two in advance of your proposed visit.

■ **TOURING TIP** For information about Swiss wine touring, write to the Swiss National Tourist Office (address on page 128) or inquire at the OPAV office in Sion.

RELAX ALONG LAKE BRIENZ

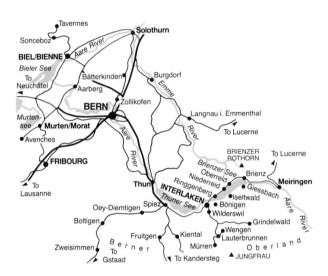

Centrally located in Switzerland, the Brienzersee stretches east from Interlaken to the town of Brienz and beyond. Lakeside resorts dot its shore. Many Bernese Oberland destinations lie within easy distance, or you can plan more wide-ranging excursions using a Swiss Holiday Card (see page 130).

Bönigen, just 5 minutes by bus from Interlaken Ost, is a lakeside resort with many old timbered houses, some dating from the 16th century. Brienz, on the north shore, is a wood-carving center also worth leisurely exploration.

Brienzer Rothorn. From Brienz you can board a cogwheel railway for the climb to the summit of Brienzer Rothorn. The hour-long trip is a delight as the train ascends through woods and alpine meadows. From the summit, your view spans the snow-crested Bernese Alps and Lake Brienz below. With a stopover—or perhaps a picnic—on the summit, the round trip takes about 3 hours. Trips depart approximately hourly during daylight hours from early June to late October.

Open-air museum. Typical rural buildings from various regions of Switzerland have been assembled at the Schweizerisches Freilichtmuseum at Ballenberg, near Brienz. Footpaths through the woods and fields link more than 50 dwellings and farm buildings, arranged in regional groupings that represent the Jura, Central Switzerland, the Ticino, the Grisons, Eastern Switzerland, and the Alpine cantons. Buildings are added each year.

Exhibits include lowland and mountain farmsteads, a vintner's house, an alpine cheese dairy, and a grain mill. Furniture and utensils are displayed inside the houses; gardens and cultivated fields reinforce the rural atmosphere. Often you'll see demonstrations of rural crafts—breadmaking, weaving, spinning, carving, and basket weaving.

The museum is open from mid-April to late October; hours are 10 A.M. to 5 P.M. daily (9:30 to 5:30 from June through September). Buses depart hourly from the Brienz railway station for the short trip to the museum's west entrance; some afternoon buses return to Brienz from both the east and west entrances. A forest path links the east gate with the Brienzwiler rail station.

Giessbach. On the south shore you can visit Giessbach, whose thundering waterfall tumbles into Lake Brienz. Perched above on the wooded hillside is the Grandhotel Giessbach, a castlelike retreat to stir the heart of any romantic.

Visitors arriving by lake steamer board a funicular railway for a brief ascent to the hotel. You can also reach Giessbach by road from Brienz.

Open from May to October, the hotel is more than a century old and has sheltered emperors and kings. Today it's a favorite site for weddings.

■ **TOURING TIPS** Lake steamers stop at Ringgenberg and Brienz on the north shore, and at Bönigen, Iseltwald, and Giessbach along the south shore. Trains stopping at north shore settlements depart from the Interlaken Ost station. Most of the lakeside accommodations are in Bönigen and Iseltwald on the south shore, both accessible by lake steamer or bus from Interlaken Ost, and from Brienz on the north shore.

SWISS HANDICRAFTS

Skilled craftspeople in various regions of Switzerland maintain many of the traditional Alpine crafts. Shoppers can find their output at Schweizer Heimatwerk *shops in major Swiss cities. In Zurich, you can look over a variety of handcrafted items at three Heimatwerk shops downtown (and another at the airport). Regional Heimatwerk shops in Basel, Bern, Luzern, and St. Gallen also offer an extensive selection of handmade goods. You'll find Swiss handicrafts in many other shops as well.*

Look for woven textiles, lace, painted pottery, and toys from the Bernese Oberland; wood carvings and Christmas ornaments from Brienz; and folk art and embroidery from the Appenzell district.

TRAFFIC-FREE TOWNS

If you're seeking a peaceful rural retreat, consider a holiday in one or more of Switzerland's traffic-free towns, where all or most automobile traffic is barred. Some of these towns are accessible by road to the village entrance; others can be reached only by mountain railroad, aerial cable car, or chair lift. Towns range from well-known resorts to hamlets. For more information and for directions to specific towns, write the Swiss National Tourist Office (address on page 128).

TICINO'S MOUNTAIN VALLEYS

Drivers in Switzerland must keep their eyes on the road—a pity in a country with such spectacular scenery. One alternative is the comfortable Swiss postal bus, which goes many places even trains don't go.

In the sunny southern canton of Ticino, the bright yellow coaches take mail and passengers between rail terminals and remote hamlets in the mountain valleys. The vehicles stand out against the mountainsides as they twist their way from village to village, sounding a motif from the Overture to *William Tell* as they confidently round the blind curves.

Little frequented by tourists, Ticino's scenic mountain valleys are flanked by steep rock outcrops where tiny, centuries-old villages hang precariously from mountainsides. Houses are built of native stone in an architectural style unique to the region: their stark rock façades are often softened by hand-carved wooden balconies. Stone churches with square campaniles add an Italian touch—appropriate, since the language here is Italian and the food is similar to that of northern Italy.

From Locarno, postal buses depart several times daily on various routes. Distances are relatively short; you can usually catch a bus in the early morning, tour the town or go for a hike, and take the coach back at the end of the day. You can buy freshly baked bread and local cheese in small village shops; sometimes there's a cafe or simple restaurant. Well-marked trails lead off through forests or to sun-splashed mountain meadows.

A favorite trip leads up the Val Verzasca to the medieval "donkey's back" arched stone bridge at Lavertezzo. It continues to Brione, with its 14th-century frescoed church and four-towered castle, and to the hamlet of Sonogno at the end of the road.

Northwest of Locarno, you can venture up the Valle Maggia, changing to another bus in Cevio or Bignasco to explore the more remote Campo, Bavona, or Lavizzara valleys. Postal buses also travel to the Valle Onsernone and the nearby Val di Vergeletto. Or you can travel by train northeast to Biasca, then by coach up the Val Blenio to Acquarossa or Olivone.

■ **TOURING TIPS** Local tourist offices in Locarno, Tenero, Maggia, Biasca, and Acquarossa can offer suggestions on attractions and hiking trails. You'll want transportation schedules, available at any Swiss train station, and a good local map. You don't need to buy tickets for postal buses in advance.

DAY HIKING NEAR BERN

See map page 81

You don't need to be a mountain climber to enjoy hiking in Switzerland. Marked trails suitable for casual hikers meander across the countryside—through woodlands and vineyards, along lakes and rivers, and into the hills and mountains. You usually reach the trailhead by train, postal bus, lake steamer, or mountain chairlift. At the end of the hike, you return by public transportation.

Several easy day hikes begin near Biel (Bienne). One traverses woodland and vineyard country above the lake (Bielersee), along a ridge of the Jura between Biel and La Neuveville. Another begins northwest of Biel at Sonceboz and follows an old Roman route to Tavannes.

From Bern you can hike to the Fraubrunnen area, between Zollikofen and Bätterkinden, or through forest and meadows to the Frienisberg Plateau and Aarberg. Numerous trails link the hills and valleys cut by the Emme and Aare rivers and their tributaries.

In the Bernese Oberland you can also find hikes without significant changes in elevation. One lakeside route begins at the castle in Spiez and traces the south shore of the Thunersee to Interlaken. Another begins near the Interlaken West train station and follows the Aare River and the north shore of the Brienzersee.

Relatively level mountain routes include a hike through shady woods from Kiental to Frutigen, a trail in the Lower Simmental from Diemtigen to Boltigen, and a walk along the Lütschine River from Wilderswil to Lauterbrunnen.

Contact the Swiss National Tourist Office (address on page 128) to learn more about hiking routes and guided walking and hiking tours. Some groups shelter in mountain huts and tent camps; others stay at first-class or tourist-class hotels or country inns.

■ **TOURING TIPS** In Switzerland, check with local tourist offices for maps and guides to regional walks and hikes. Trail signs indicate hiking times based on an average speed of 2.6 miles/4.2 km per hour, excluding rest breaks. Yellow signs mark the easy routes, suitable for all hikers. On difficult routes, marked with red-and-white signs, hikers should wear solid, nonslip footwear and carry waterproof clothing. Hikers are expected to keep to marked paths and to carry out their own litter.

PASTORAL APPENZELL

See map page 80

Pastoral traditions still thrive in the rolling green hills of the Appenzell country. Dairy cows graze placidly on the rich grass. Cause for local celebration is the annual spring trek of cows to the Alpine pastures and their triumphal return in the autumn, cowbells clanging and horns entwined with flowers and ribbons. Traditional dress of the region is often worn on holidays and other ceremonial occasions.

Some visitors tour at a leisurely pace by car, stopping at charming country hotels and cozy inns that offer good value in meals and accommodations. Others prefer to use the efficient Swiss transportation system. From St. Gallen, narrow-gauge trains—sometimes only two or three cars long—climb into the heartland to link the few settlements. Overlooking the valleys you'll see farmhouses built in traditional style: barn and gabled house combined in a single building.

Hikers descend footpath from Wildkirchli rest stop on Ebenalp, near Wasserauen in the Appenzell district.

Worth a stop is the market town of Gais, whose main square is faced by ranks of gabled houses adorned with carved woodwork. Trogen has many frescoed 18th-century houses. Pedestrian arcades give Altstätten's main street a medieval air; above, its steeply gabled houses present a jagged skyline. Rustic Urnäsch is one of the canton's oldest communities.

Tucked in a valley below the Alpstein Massif, the town of Appenzell is relatively busy and just the right size to explore on foot. Shops along the Hauptgasse display embroidery and cowbells along with cheesemaking implements and the traditional Appenzell honey cakes (*Biber*). Whimsical painted or carved designs decorate many buildings. There's a folklore museum in the old town hall.

Above the town, craggy mountains jut skyward. You can ascend both the Ebenalp and the towering, 8,209-foot/2,502-meter Säntis, renowned for its panoramic views over eastern Switzerland. Marked footpaths traverse the slopes of the lower Alps, opening the woods and sunny, flower-strewn hills to walkers and hikers.

■ **TOURING TIPS** The Appenzell district is known for its chocolates, baked goods, and folk paintings. Neighboring St. Gallen is a textile and embroidery center. In the town of Appenzell, you'll find regional specialties in shops along the main street, the Hauptgasse, and in other towns. Try to pick a clear day for your trip up the Säntis; it offers wide vistas of eastern Switzerland, from the Bernese Alps and the Grisons north to the Bodensee and Germany.

MEDIEVAL MURTEN

See map page 78

Encircled by ramparts and towers and guarded by its castle, medieval Murten (also called Morat in this bilingual region) overlooks a lake that bears its name. One of the most handsomely preserved of Switzerland's old towns, it's a delightful destination for a day trip from Bern or for an overnight visit. Founded some 800 years ago by the dukes of Zähringen, Murten successfully blends its historical appeal with the attraction of a busy modern town.

In the Middle Ages, defensive walls and fortified gates protected Murten. Today you can stroll atop the city ramparts, enjoying views over the roofs and down into the streets and gardens of the old town. Many of the buildings date from the 15th to 18th centuries.

Shopping arcades line the handsome main street, the Hauptgasse, that runs through the center of the old quarter. You can visit the 13th-century castle; from its inner courtyard, there's a fine view of the lake and Jura foothills. The Historical Museum is housed in an old mill adjacent to the castle; it contains a diorama depicting the Battle of Murten in 1476, when the Swiss defeated Charles the Bold, Duke of Burgundy.

■ **TOURING TIPS** Hotels and restaurants are located in the center of town and on a terrace overlooking the lake. From May through September, you can take boat trips on the lake, or circular tours of the three lakes—Neuchatel, Biel (Bienne), and Murten—which are linked by canals through the marshes.

Hallstatt

Wachau, Danube Valley,
page 88

Melk, page 89

Salzburg's Lake
District, page 86

Map, page 86

● Melk

Vienna ●

Map,
page 88

Vienna Woods,
page 88

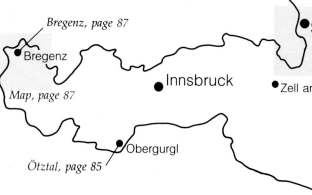

Bregenz, page 87

● Bregenz

● Salzburg

● Hallstatt

A U S T R I A

● Innsbruck

● Zell am See

Hallstatt,
page 87

Map, page 87

Piber ● ● Graz

● Obergurgl

Ötztal, page 85

Durnstein

Bregenz

AUSTRIA

Leisurely exploration in Austria can take you from dramatic mountain valleys to the shores of the Danube, from relaxing lakeside towns to footpaths in the Vienna Woods.

Excursions lead to the Bodensee resort of Bregenz and into Tyrolean mountain valleys. In the lake district near Salzburg, you can visit Austria's oldest settlement, tour one of several salt mines, or take a lake cruise or a train ride on a mountain railway.

A cruise or drive through the scenic Wachau section of the Danube Valley offers the chance to detour into delightful riverside towns or tour the magnificent abbey at Melk. In the Vienna Woods surrounding that city, you'll discover marked hiking trails and rustic village inns where you can sample locally-made wine.

UP THE ÖTZTAL TO OBERGURGL

See map page 84

You probably won't arrive in Obergurgl by stratospheric balloon, as Auguste Piccard did one day in 1931, but the dramatic mountain road winding up Austria's beautiful Ötz Valley (Ötztal) is an excellent alternative. You pass through a number of attractive Tyrolean mountain villages along the route to Obergurgl, tucked into a valley high in the sparkling clear air of the Tyrolean Alps—the highest village in Austria, and a popular winter sports and summer mountaineering center.

From Innsbruck, it's a comfortable day trip to Obergurgl. Head west up the Inn River Valley about 30 miles/50 km. Near Silz the road up the Ötztal branches south, rising in a series of natural steps to the alpine glaciers surrounding Obergurgl. The road closely follows the cascading river and passes through a number of inviting villages, each with a sprinkling of Tyrolean chalets. Peach and apricot orchards, surprising in this region, owe their existence to the *Föhn*—the dry, hot wind that sweeps down valleys north of the Alps.

The tiny village of Obergurgl sits high in the mountains, surrounded by the ice-covered peaks of the Ötztaler Alps. A favorite mountaineering center, Obergurgl is the starting point for high-country climbs and tours.

A two-section chair lift takes visitors from Obergurgl to the summit of the Hohe Mutt spur for a panoramic view. In midsummer, after the snow has melted, walking and hiking trails let you penetrate deep into the Alps without pack gear. However, you will need stout boots and warm, windproof clothing.

■ **TOURING TIPS** Hikers and mountaineers can obtain detailed information from the Austrian National Tourist Office (address on page 128); if you plan to do much hiking, consider joining the Austrian Alpine Club. Mountain guides can be hired in the village for tours across the glaciers to the high peaks. Food and lodging are available at several Alpine Club huts within a 3- or 4-hour hike from Obergurgl.

St. Wolfgang streets invite strolling; you can also cruise on the lake or ride a cogwheel train up the Schafberg.

gen and Strobl at opposite ends of the lake, and St. Wolfgang on the northern shore. In keeping with the holiday atmosphere, you can travel by boat from the southern shore to St. Wolfgang.

Sitting on a rocky spur, St. Wolfgang's church is known for its artistic altar, but don't miss the arcaded cloisters high above the water and the glimpses of the lake they offer you. You'll also want to stroll along the shore to the Weisses Rössl, the famed White Horse Inn that once inspired an operetta. From mid-May through September, an old-fashioned cogwheel train leaves St. Wolfgang to chug up the slopes of the Schafberg. On a clear day you can see more than a dozen of the Salz-kammergut lakes from the summit.

Franz Josef made the spa of Bad Ischl his summer residence. From May through September, you can visit the Hapsburg imperial villa in the landscaped Kaiserpark north of town. A photography museum is housed in the Marmorschlossl, Empress Elisabeth's tea house. You can also visit the villa of composer Franz Lehár, whose oper-ettas are performed here in summer.

Surrounded by wooded hills, the resort clusters within a river bend at the confluence of the Traun and Ischl streams. You'll enjoy Bad Ischl's relaxed 19th-century ambience on a stroll along the shop-lined Pfarr-gasse or upstream from Elisabeth Bridge along the Traun River.

■ **TOURING TIPS** In Salzburg you can board a postal bus for St. Gilgen, St. Wolfgang, Bad Ischl, and other Salzkammergut towns. From Bad Ischl, trains depart for Obertraun/Hallstatt. In summer, day excursions operate from Salzburg to various Salzkammergut destinations. Don't forget to take a raincoat, even in summer; during warm weather it rains often in the lake district.

SALZBURG'S LAKE DISTRICT

From the mid-19th century to the outbreak of World War I, the lake-dotted Salzkammergut was the fashionable summer retreat of Europe's royal families and leading personalities in the theater, music, and art worlds. Em-peror Franz Josef presided over the light-hearted group as they waltzed to the melodies of Johann Strauss and hummed songs from Franz Lehár operettas.

One of the Salzkammergut's gems is the St. Wolf-gangsee. Sailboats flit across the water between St. Gil-

SALT MINE TOURS

Salt mining has played an important role in the Salzburg district since prehistoric days. The syl-lable salz *or* hall *(meaning "salt") is part of many place names. Mines are still worked, and adven-turous travelers can tour several of them.*

Before you begin a typical mine tour, you'll check your hand luggage and dress in coveralls. Then you'll follow the guide into a dimly lighted mountain tunnel. You'll proceed through mine gal-leries on foot and by mine train, occasionally tak-ing tobogganlike slides down steep slopes or cross-ing illuminated underground lakes by barge.

Most tours are conducted in German, but some student guides speak English. The trip is not suitable for children under 6 or persons not in good physical condition.

Tours operate year round in Berchtesgaden, Germany, and from late April or early May to October in the Austrian towns of Hallein, Hall-statt, Bad Ischl, and Altaussee.

BREGENZ ON THE BODENSEE

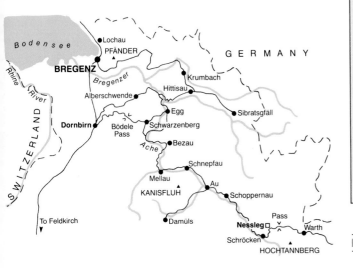

Climbing the wooded slopes at the east end of the Bodensee (Lake Constance), Bregenz overlooks a panorama spanning three countries. It lies within minutes of the German and Swiss borders. A busy lakeside resort, Bregenz offers water sports, a summer music festival, and nearby hiking trails in the Bregenzerwald.

The site of present-day Bregenz was colonized by the Celts about 400 B.C., and the Romans established a lakeside trading camp here about 15 B.C. An impressive gateway marks the entrance to the fortified medieval town, built on high ground overlooking the lake. Quiet streets and weathered buildings lend a storybook air. In the ancient Martinsturm, chapel frescoes date from the 14th century; attic skylights offer glimpses of the lake.

The city's shopping district clusters below the old town. You can learn about regional history and culture at the Vorarlberger Landesmuseum (closed Monday) on the Kornmarktplatz and purchase regional handicrafts at Heimatwerk-Voralberger, Montfortstrasse 4. A landscaped 5-mile/8-km promenade rims the lake shore, providing a place for strollers to watch activity on the lake. During the Bregenz Festival in July and August, operas are presented outdoors on a stage built over the water.

From town, the Pfänderbahn cable car climbs in 6 minutes to a superb viewpoint overlooking parts of three countries and the entire length of the shimmering lake. A network of mountain trails traverses the Pfänder; hikers can follow paths downhill to Bregenz.

From Bregenz, a scenic road climbs southeast through gentle foothills, ending dramatically at Warth in the high Alpine regions of the Hochtannberg. The Bregenzerwald covers a wide area of densely wooded highlands, green valleys, and lush meadows set against the majestic Alps.

■ **TOURING TIPS**   Boat trips to towns bordering the Bodensee depart from Bregenz from spring to early autumn. You can explore the Bregenzerwald on the narrow-gauge Bregenz Forest Railway, which links villages between Bregenz and Bezau, a village set amid fruit trees.

SCENIC ALPINE ROAD

One of the most spectacular routes into the Alps is the Grossglockner High Alpine Highway, a magnificent mountain road that climbs into the Alps south of Zell am See. This scenic toll road is usually open from mid-May through October; you can make the trip by automobile or by bus from Salzburg or Zell am See.

Highest in the Alps, the road follows an old Roman route to the Franz-Josefs-Höhe, where you can have lunch. From its terrace, you view a panorama of the Pasterze Glacier and the Grossglockner itself, towering 12,457 feet /3,797 meters high.

AUSTRIA'S OLDEST SETTLEMENT

See map page 86

Hallstatt's scenic lakeside setting gives few clues to its remarkable past. Balconied houses cling precariously to a wooded slope above the deep blue waters of the Hallstättersee. Narrow, curving streets follow the contours of the steep hillside, into which Celtic tribesmen dug for salt a thousand years before Christ. Above the town rise the sheer granite walls of the Dachstein.

Archeologists have discovered more than a thousand graves of these prehistoric lake dwellers, who built their homes on pilings above the water. Because of these important discoveries, the early part of the Iron Age was named the "Hallstatt Period." Objects discovered during the excavations, including miners' clothing and tools from 2,500 years ago, are displayed in a museum.

Climb the steep covered stairway to the large parish church for a look at its handsome carved altar, then walk through Hallstatt's small cemetery.

Visitors can rent rowboats or arrange for a ride in one of Hallstatt's long, flat-bottomed gondolalike boats. Swimmers find pleasant beaches on the lake's eastern shore near Obertraun. Summer evenings are usually warm enough for diners to linger over dinner in outdoor lakeside restaurants.

Across the lake from Hallstatt at Obertraun, cable cars take visitors up to the famous Dachstein ice cave, continuing on to the summit of the Krippenstein, an impressive viewpoint overlooking the Dachstein plateau. Lights illuminate the subterranean caverns of the ice caves, where hanging icicles and ice draperies create a fairy-tale scene. In the Mammoth's Cave, you follow the guide through a labyrinth of passages into a majestic cavern over 130 feet/40 meters high.

■ **TOURING TIPS**   Allow at least half a day for the full trip and tour of the ice caves (open May to mid-October). In summer, an early start will help you avoid midday crowds. Don't forget a warm wrap, for the temperature inside the caves stays near freezing even in midsummer.

THE HISTORIC DANUBE

Europe's longest river, the Danube crosses or borders eight countries on its 1,754-mile/2,826-km course from the Black Forest region of Germany to the Black Sea.

Through the centuries, the Danube Valley has been a strategic route between Europe and the East. Romans, Huns, and Crusaders traveled this gray-brown river highway; later the Turks, followed by the Swedes during the Thirty Years' War; after them came Napoleon. Local rulers built castles on crags high above the river. Along its banks, they constructed fortified villages to collect taxes from passing ships carrying salt, iron, and wine.

From May to September, passenger boats cruise the Danube between Passau, Germany, and Vienna, continuing downstream to the Black Sea. Day excursions travel from Vienna upstream through the Wachau section of the river to Linz, docking briefly at small riverside towns.

A DAY IN THE VIENNA WOODS

See map this page

The thickly wooded, rolling hills of the Wienerwald stretch out from Vienna's suburbs to the north, west, and south. Crisscrossed by country roads and footpaths, they are a magnet for Austrian families. Quiet villages and towns nestle in the valleys. You can stop for lunch or refreshment in an inn or wine garden *(Heuriger),* where you'll sample the locally made wine in a rustic atmosphere.

Hiking trails.   You'll discover a hiker's paradise on the astonishingly rural outskirts of the cultured Hapsburg capital. Marked day-hike trails wind through the scenic woodlands, hillside vineyards, pastoral meadows, and rural hamlets. Eight trails have been mapped; two well-marked routes lead through vineyard districts, while the others cover both vineyards and woods. Each walk takes a leisurely 3 to 5 hours.

Wine gardens.   No visit to Vienna is complete without at least one stop at a wine garden or country inn where you can sample chilled mugs of the local white wine in a relaxed setting.

You'll find wine gardens in several Viennese suburbs—Grinzing, Sievering, and Nussdorf—and in wine-producing villages of the Wienerwald such as Gumpoldskirchen, Mödling, and Perchtoldsdorf. Look for a branch of greenery hanging over the door; it signifies that the current year's vintage is being served inside. You'll sit at wooden tables beneath shady trees, or inside in rustic surroundings.

If you wish to convert wine tasting into a meal, you'll find light foods available. In the late afternoon and evening, the atmosphere becomes more festive as musicians entertain with traditional *Schrammelmusik.*

■ **TOURING TIP** Maps showing walking routes in the Vienna Woods are available from the information desk at Vienna's *Rathaus* (city hall) on the Rathausplatz; ask for *Stadtwanderweg* maps. Though they are printed in German, they have pictorial legends. The maps show how to reach the starting point by streetcar or bus. They also mark inns and taverns along the routes, where you can sample hearty country food and local wine.

CRUISING THROUGH THE WACHAU

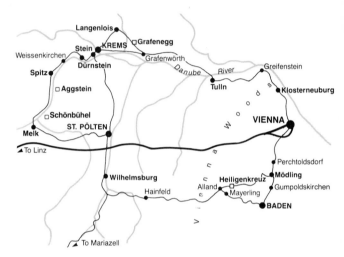

The most scenic section of Austria's Danube Valley, called the Wachau, begins at Melk and extends some 22 miles/35 km downstream to Krems. Delightful villages nestle along the sunny north bank of the river. Terraced vineyards, fruit orchards, and cultivated fields cover slopes above the water. Castle ruins perch on lofty crags, and churches with bulbous spires add a whimsical note.

Many of the small towns along the Danube were founded in the 9th and 10th centuries. Almost every one has its quiet square and old houses, dominated by a lovely Gothic church. Many of the churches contain beautiful paintings or carved wooden statues.

From Melk, follow the north bank of the Danube downstream; you can see Schönbühel Castle on the opposite shore. Farther downstream, the ruins of Aggstein mark the site of one of the most formidable medieval fortresses in the heart of the Wachau.

The village of Spitz lies off the main road, hidden behind fruit trees at the foot of terraced vineyards. Arcades and balconies enhance its old houses. The 15th-century parish church is worth a visit. Above, the ruins of Hinterhaus Castle stand out against forested slopes.

Continuing downstream, you'll pass the fortified church of St. Michael. Built about 1500, the Gothic-style church is flanked by a big round tower.

In the charming medieval market town of Weissenkirchen, a covered wooden stairway leads up to the fortified parish church. In the 16th century, villagers surrounded the church with a wall to protect it from invading Turks. The Wachau Museum is located in the Teisenhofer-Hof, a fortified 16th-century dwelling with an attractive arcaded courtyard. It is open daily except Monday from April through October.

One of the prettiest Wachau towns is Dürnstein, which overlooks the Danube from a rocky ridge. The ruins of Dürnstein Castle tower above it. Walls were built up from the river to surround the village. An ancient fortified gateway marks the south end of the Hauptstrasse, the town's main street. Attractive old houses and inns line the narrow streets. Don't miss the village church, notable for its baroque tower and interior decoration. A rocky path leads to the castle ruins where, according to legend, King Richard the Lion-Hearted was imprisoned in 1193 while returning from the Crusades.

Krems, a delightful old town at the foot of terraced hills, marks the eastern end of the Wachau. You can visit its parish church and a wine museum showing items connected with the vineyards of the Danube Valley. The town of Stein, on the opposite shore of the river, has some interesting old houses ornamented with oriel windows and turrets.

■ **TOURING TIPS** Excellent white wines with a delicate bouquet come from the Wachau towns of Spitz, Dürnstein, Weissenkirchen, and Krems. You can enjoy the current year's vintage in wine gardens and inns. The wine museum in Krems is open from April through October (closed Sunday and holiday afternoons and all day Monday); it offers a comprehensive introduction to wine production in the region.

BAROQUE SPLENDOR AT MELK

See map page 88

The magnificent Abbey of Melk overlooks the Danube River from a high bluff on the south bank about 52 miles/84 km west of Vienna. Rising above the town nestled at is base, the abbey's domes and symmetrical towers stand out against the sky. One of Austria's most beautiful baroque churches, the existing abbey was built in the early 18th century.

Melk occupies the site of a Roman stronghold and, later, a castle of the ruling Babenberg family. Late in the 11th century the Babenbergs transferred their Melk castle to members of the Benedictine order, who converted it into a fortified abbey. It flourished as an important spiritual and intellectual force in the region until the spread of the Reformation. The original abbey was gutted by fire in 1683 during the Turkish invasion; rebuilding began in 1702. During his successful campaign against Austria in 1805–06, Napoleon I established his headquarters in the abbey.

Many artistic treasures have been preserved on the premises, which visitors can see during a guided tour. Groups visit the Marble Hall, noted for its strong design and lavish decoration; on the ceiling, an allegorical painting shows Reason guiding Humanity out of dark oblivion into the light of civilization. The Terrace links the symmetrical buildings; from it you'll enjoy a fine view

Bulbous-domed belfry rises high above Schönbühel Castle, built on a rock above the Danube downstream from Melk.

over the Danube Valley and the façade of the abbey church. Two stories high, the Library contains approximately 80,000 books and 2,000 manuscripts; it has a painted ceiling and gilded wood statues.

Dominating the complex is the Abbey Church, recognizable by its towers and octagonal dome. Marble, frescoes, and gold ornamentation lavishly decorate its interior; many windows add an impression of lightness.

■ **TOURING TIPS** Trains run west from Vienna to Melk; you can also visit the abbey on guided day trips from Vienna. Abbey tours take about 1 hour; ask for the English-language brochure.

LIPIZZANER STUD FARM

The famous Lipizzaner stallions perform at the Spanish Riding School in Vienna. Bred in the Styrian village of Piber near Köflach, west of Graz, the horses are descendants of ancient Iberian stock. The horses were brought to Piber at the end of World War I from the former stud farm at Lipizza near Trieste, at that time located in Austrian territory.

The stud farm is open to visitors from mid-April to mid-October, except when closed for breeding. Afternoon tours include a visit to the stables and a walk in the fields, where you watch the horses at close range. Born black or bay-colored, they don't get their white coats until they are several years old.

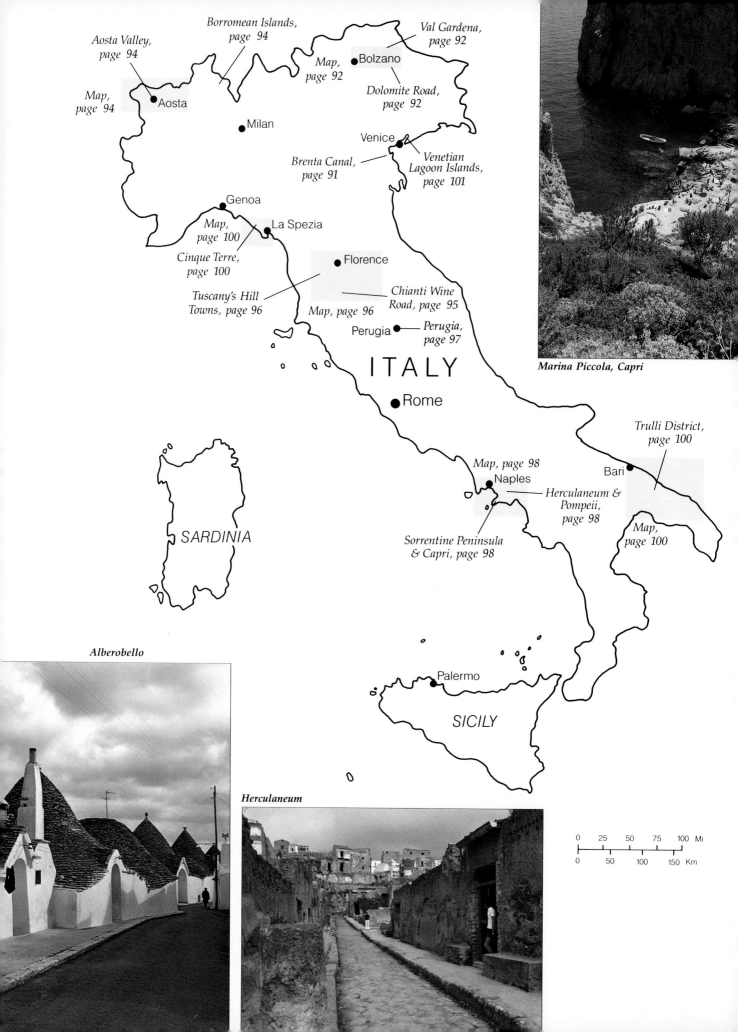

Aosta Valley,
page 94

Borromean Islands,
page 94

Val Gardena,
page 92

Map,
page 92

Bolzano

Map,
page 94

Aosta

Dolomite Road,
page 92

Milan

Venice

Brenta Canal,
page 91

Venetian
Lagoon Islands,
page 101

Genoa

Map,
page 100

La Spezia

Cinque Terre,
page 100

Florence

Tuscany's Hill
Towns, page 96

Map, page 96

Chianti Wine
Road, page 95

Perugia

Perugia,
page 97

Marina Piccola, Capri

ITALY

Rome

Trulli District,
page 100

SARDINIA

Map, page 98

Naples

Bari

Herculaneum &
Pompeii,
page 98

Map,
page 100

Sorrentine Peninsula
& Capri, page 98

Alberobello

Palermo

SICILY

Herculaneum

0   25   50   75   100 Mi

0   50   100   150 Km

ITALY

Roam this rich land to discover new pleasures: the secluded Aosta Valley, fascinating islands in the Venetian Lagoon, an Alpine meadow high above the Val Gardena, ancient hill towns in the heartland, and the unusual trulli district deep in the heel of Italy's boot.

You can explore Lake Maggiore's lush islands, or take a boat ride on the Brenta Canal. Learn more about Italian wines in Tuscany's Chianti district. Along the Italian Riviera, you can follow a seaside path from village to village. The spectacular route across the Dolomites is a favorite of those who love the mountains. Or you may prefer to settle into a cliffside inn and explore the Amalfi Coast.

THE BRENTA CANAL BY BOAT

See map page 90

During the 17th and 18th centuries, wealthy Venetians built splendid villas along the quiet Brenta Canal, where they retreated each summer to escape the city's sultry heat. Evening gatherings were lighted by flickering lanterns, and hidden orchestras played softly.

During this era, the luxurious *Il Burchiello* canal boat transported its titled passengers between Venice and Padua, over the Venetian Lagoon and through a network of rivers and canals. Horses towed the narrow boat through the waterway.

Modern travelers now cruise the classic waterway between Venice and Padua on a new motorized 200-passenger canal boat *Il Burchiello*. From the tree-lined waterway, you'll enjoy views of more than 70 villas and make brief stops at several.

Loveliest and most important of the country houses is Palladio's Villa Foscari at Malcontenta; most impressive is the Villa Pisani at Stra, surrounded by its park. Largest of the towns along the canal is Mira, where the English poet Byron wrote part of *Childe Harold* in the Palazzo Foscarini, now the post office. The boat stops at Oriago to let passengers lunch in a canalside restaurant. A multilingual hostess on board offers commentary and assistance.

On arrival at Padua, passengers can explore the city for several hours before returning to the starting point by motor coach.

Motorists can obtain glimpses of the grand old houses by following the Venice-Padua route, which passes through Mira and Stra.

■ **TOURING TIPS** From mid-March to October, the *Il Burchiello* makes daily trips between Venice and Padua. Additional information about the excursion is available from your travel agent or from the Italian Government Tourist Office (address on page 128).

BOAT EXCURSIONS

Steamers and hydrofoils transport travelers from Italy's mainland ports to Elba, Capri, Ischia, Procida, Sardinia, Sicily, and many small islands along the Italian coast. In the Italian lake district, steamers and hydrofoils operate on lakes Como, Garda, and Maggiore.

For information on steamer, car ferry, and hydrofoil services, write to the Italian Government Travel Office (address on page 128).

THE VAL GARDENA

Best known as one of Europe's fashionable Alpine ski areas, the Val Gardena is isolated high in the Dolomite Mountains near Italy's northern border. Opened to visitors only a century ago, it is the home of the Ladini, descendants of Roman soldiers sent here centuries ago to conquer the area.

Some traditional customs are still observed. The Val Gardena is noted as one of the major European centers of wood-carving, a family industry passed down from fathers to sons since the 17th century. Nearly every family has at least one skilled member carving traditional toys and statuettes.

One of the most characteristic Dolomite valleys, the Val Gardena offers the visitor incomparable mountain vistas, an abundance of woods and open meadows, and a wide choice of excursions, walks, and climbs. The verdant valley widens and narrows by turns, its slopes covered by forests, cascading streams, and mountain dwellings.

Valley towns. Three Ladin communities—Selva in Val Gardena, Santa Cristina, and Ortisei—sit astride the road that winds through the Val Gardena; all have a delightful Alpine flavor. Ortisei is the valley's main town. Though known primarily as ski centers, the three towns are also summer resorts.

Life moves at a relaxed pace, particularly in the spur valleys. People speak the Ladin-Romansch dialect and some occasionally wear regional costumes to church and at weddings and other celebrations.

In winter, numerous lifts and cableways transport skiers to vast snowfields on the high slopes, where powdery snow lasts until spring.

Alpe di Siusi. From Ortisei, you can take a cableway to the snowfields—or summer flowers—on the Alpe di Siusi. From this viewpoint, you'll have breathtaking vistas over the Val Gardena and nearby Dolomite peaks. In late spring and early summer, this great open mountain pasture is an enchanting place—an idyllic sea of Alpine wildflowers, including many not found at lower elevations.

You can also reach this beautiful Alpine meadow by road from the west. The road veers southeast from Ponte Gardena; about 1 mile/1½ km north of the village of Siusi, take the side road that leads uphill to the east to reach the alp.

■ **TOURING TIPS** From Bolzano, there's daily bus service to Val Gardena towns. You can arrange to see some of the region's wood-carvers at work in their shops and homes; inquire in local tourist information offices or at your hotel to learn which carvers welcome visitors. If you're planning a hiking or mountaineering holiday, you can use Siusi as a base for fine Alpine walks or climbing excursions.

ACROSS THE DOLOMITES

See map this page

Many fast-moving travelers speed south from Austria toward the heart of Italy, bypassing the spectacular mountain region just a few miles east of the Brenner Highway. Here the craggy peaks of the Dolomites jut skyward behind sun-bathed valleys and flower-filled meadows.

Best known for their excellent winter sports facilities, the rugged Dolomites make a delightful detour in any season. When skiers and skaters depart, the mountaineers arrive for some of the best climbing on the Continent. Hikers follow well-marked trails through the valleys and across the slopes.

Springtime visitors enjoy green hillsides and valley fruit trees in full bloom. In early summer, dwarf pink rhododendrons, blue gentians, and other Alpine wildflowers brighten the high meadows. Late-season travelers appreciate the cool, clean mountain air. Most valleys in the Dolomites are protected by high mountains from the fierce northern winds, while receiving the southern sun.

Originally part of Austria, the South Tyrol was annexed to Italy following World War I but retained its autonomy in language and education. The blending of Italian and Austrian influences is evident in the food, the architecture, and even the signs, which identify streets in both German and Italian.

Bolzano. Capital of the mountainous South Tyrol district, Bolzano is an old commercial city that retains much of its medieval charm. It borders the Brenner Pass route, the main traffic artery linking the Germanic north with the Latin south for more than 2,000 years.

In Bolzano's old district, high-gabled houses line narrow streets. Stroll down the Via dei Portici, the arcaded main commercial street, to the Piazza delle Erbe, where a weekly fruit market takes place. At the center of town is the Piazza Walther; facing it is the cathedral, built in Romanesque Gothic style with a tall, open belfry.

The Dolomite Road. Cutting a spectacular route through the mountains, the Dolomite Road twists through high peaks for a thrilling 68 miles/110 km, linking Bolzano and Cortina d'Ampezzo. For much of the way, it follows a historic route once used by Renaissance merchants traveling between Venice and Germany.

Dramatic scenery is dominated by rugged limestone rocks that are pinkish in color but change with the light. Wind and rain have eroded the high peaks into ragged towers and rough domes with sides too steep for glaciers. At their bases lie gentler slopes, covered with open pastures, evergreen forests, or cultivated land.

Southeast of Bolzano, the Dolomite Road angles between high cliffs into the narrow Val d'Ega gorge. High above on a cliff, Cornedo Castle guards the gorge and its turbulent little river. You climb slowly past small villages to tiny Lake Carezza; a small blue jewel edged by dark green conifers, it reflects the jagged peaks of the Catinaccio and Latemar massifs.

Here you begin to sense the Alpine grandeur of the Dolomites. Long ago these coral-tinted rocks thrust above an ancient sea. Glaciers covered them during the Ice Age. Later, wind and rain eroded them into weird towers and spires, and sculptured the wall faces.

Cross the Costalunga Pass, then descend the winding road to Canazei, a busy summer and winter sports resort deep in the mountains. Climbers use the town as a base for summer mountaineering excursions into the Marmolada range to the south.

If you continue east on the Dolomite Road, you'll cross the high and desolate Pordoi and Falzarego passes. Pause and absorb the view before making the awe-inspiring descent to the elegant mountain resort of Cortina d'Ampezzo, site of the 1956 winter Olympics.

To loop back toward the Brenner Highway, turn north off the Dolomite Road above Canazei toward the Sella Pass. Its extensive panorama encompasses the mountain massifs of Sasso Lungo to the west, Marmolada to the south, and Sella to the east. Your route leads northeast through the Val Gardena (see page 92).

■ **TOURING TIPS** You can drive between Bolzano and Cortina d'Ampezzo in about 3 hours, but you may prefer to travel by bus or chauffeured car so you can give full attention to the landscape. Daily bus service links the two cities. If you like, shop for picnic supplies before you depart.

Rugged peaks of Dolomites are stunning counterpoint to plump haystacks drying in meadow. Mountain highway offers views of eroded crags and leads to mountaineering and winter sports resorts.

THE BORROMEAN ISLANDS

See map page 90

Ancient glaciers gouged out the jewel-like lakes that adorn Italy's northern border. One of the loveliest is island-dotted Lake Maggiore, a 40-mile/65-km ribbon of beauty connecting the Swiss Alps with the plains of Lombardy.

Villas and terraced gardens climb the hillsides above the lake, and lush subtropical vegetation rims the shore: orange and lemon trees, pomegranates, palms, cedars and myrtles, oleanders, magnolias, camellias, rhododendrons, and azaleas.

No visitor should leave Lake Maggiore without visiting the delightful Borromean Islands, a tiny archipelago of three wooded isles scattered across the short northwestern arm of the lake. Since the 12th century they have belonged to the aristocratic Borromeo family.

Regular boat trips on the lake travel from Arona to Locarno, Switzerland, with stops at resorts along the lake's western shore. You can take a boat to the islands from Stresa, Baveno, or Pallanza. Between April and October, day return tickets allow you to stop at each of the islands.

Isola Bella (Beautiful Island). Most visited and best known of the three islands, this one is renowned for its terraced gardens in the Italian style. They rise from the water to provide a lush setting for the baroque Palazzo Borromeo.

The richly furnished and decorated palace was built in the 17th century by Count Vitaliano Borromeo; it contains a fine art collection. From the palace terrace you'll enjoy a memorable view of the lake and the other islands. A profusion of exotic plants surrounds you, and aromatic shrubs perfume the air. Guided tours are available from April through October.

Isola dei Pescatori (Fishermen's Island). Sometimes called Isola Superiore (Upper Island), this tiny isle retains a miniature fishing village with the atmosphere of a bygone day. Like many artists and writers, you'll probably be captivated by the village's quaint charm as you wander through its alleys and along its esplanade and port.

Isola Madre (Mother Island). A quiet place, this island has an 18th-century palace and gardens of subtropical plants even more luxuriant than those of Isola Bella. Outstanding plant specimens include the tallest palm trees in Italy, a venerable cypress, and a massive wisteria plant. White peacocks strut through the lush gardens. You can visit the palace and enjoy superb views over the lake.

■ **TOURING TIPS** The lake region enjoys a mild climate and a long tourist season—from April through October. You'll find the countryside at its most beautiful in May and June, and in the autumn. The most pleasant way to enjoy the lake is by boat, for traffic along the lakeside is often heavy, and views of the water are often hidden by villas and trees. A car ferry links Verbania-Intra and Laveno.

OPERA & MUSIC FESTIVALS

Opera began in Italy in the 16th century, and it has flourished ever since. The Grand Opera season opens late in the year, usually in December, and runs through May or June. The concert, theater, and ballet seasons extend from September through June.

Most famous of Italy's opera houses are Teatro alla Scala in Milan, Teatro dell'Opera in Rome, Teatro la Fenice in Venice, Teatro Massimo in Palermo, and Teatro di San Carlo in Naples, but other Italian towns also have performances during the season.

From May through September, operas, concerts, and ballets are performed outdoors in many Italian cities. Classic Greek and Roman dramas are presented in open-air theaters throughout the country.

For more information on scheduled performing arts events and festivals in Italy, and on how visitors can obtain tickets for performances, write to the Italian Government Travel Office (address on page 128).

AOSTA VALLEY: ALPINE VACATIONLAND

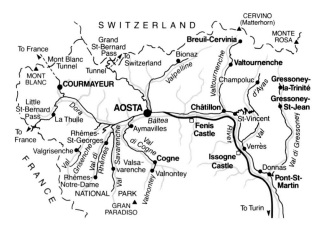

High in Italy's northwestern corner, the snowy Alpine peaks and famous resorts of the Aosta Valley signal good skiing to winter sports fans. Summer visitors walk in the woods and Alpine pastures, go mountain climbing, watch summer skiing at Courmayeur and Breuil-Cervinia, and explore the historic valley towns and Roman ruins.

This is Italy with a French accent, a bilingual region spiced with the rustic zest of the mountains. Qualities of neighboring France and Switzerland blend with the Italian heritage to create a regional mountain identity in food, customs, and architecture.

Invaders, too, have left their marks: Celtic tribes, barbarian hordes, Roman legions, Hannibal and his elephants, Napoleon's armies. The French feudal House of Savoy ruled the region for centuries. In the high valleys, you'll find villagers still clinging to the French language and their pastoral customs.

Valley towns. The main route through the valley angles north and west from Pont-St-Martin along the Dora Báltea River. Feudal castles command the entrances to the tributary valleys. You can visit two of the castles, Issogne and Fénis, daily except Monday.

Scattered remnants of the Roman occupation still remain: bridges at Pont-St-Martin and Châtillon, an archway and portions of the Roman road at Donnas, large waterworks at Aymavilles.

The largest concentration of ruins is located in Aosta, "the Rome of the Alps," where city walls and streets are laid out on the rectangular plan of a Roman military camp. Here you'll see the great arch and gateway, sections of the Roman wall, a bridge, and the remains of the theater.

Alpine excursions. The high peaks of the Alps—Mont Blanc, Monte Rosa, Cervino (known as the Matterhorn in Switzerland), and the Gran Paradiso—fan out along the north, west, and south boundaries of the valley. Major resorts are at Courmayeur, against the bulwark of lofty Mont Blanc, highest mountain in Europe; Breuil-Cervínia and Valtournenche, below Cervino; and the Gressoney settlements, which provide access to the Monte Rosa peaks.

A memorable trip by aerial trams links Courmayeur with the French Alpine resort of Chamonix. You'll change cars several times along the tram route, which glides high over the glaciers of the Mont Blanc massif. Cable cars offer close-up views of the high mountains from Aosta, Breuil-Cervínia, and other resorts.

Southwest of Aosta, roads lead up wild ravines into the mountains that form the border with France. Unspoiled villages, some hundreds of years old, border the mountain streams.

Rare ibex still roam the high mountains of the Gran Paradiso National Park. The road up the wild Val Savarenche penetrates the heart of the park. In Rhêmes-Notre-Dame on the park's western boundary, a small museum and park information center is open during July and August.

Along the park's northeast border, the Cogne Valley has well-developed visitor facilities and is the starting point for many climbing excursions into the high peaks. Rare high mountain plants have been collected in the Paradisia garden of Alpine plants at Valnontey (open from June to September).

■ **TOURING TIPS** The Valle d'Aosta is linked with Switzerland by the Grand St-Bernard Pass and Tunnel, and with France by the Little St-Bernard Pass and the Mont Blanc Tunnel. You can travel by train to Aosta, where buses fan out into the side valleys. Make your headquarters in Aosta or in one of the resort towns.

During autumn harvest in Tuscany's Chianti vineyards, pickers fill large woven baskets with juicy wine grapes.

CHIANTI COUNTRY WINE ROUTE

See map page 96

Vineyards frequently cover the rolling hills between Florence and Siena. This is Chianti Classico country, a lovely and historic region where Chianti wine has been produced since the 13th century. Wines from this area that meet government standards are labeled Chianti Classico and proudly wear the famous *gallo nero* (black rooster) trademark.

Tuscany's traditional wine route is the Chiantigiana (Route 222) winding south from Florence through the towns of Greve and Castellina in Chianti in the heart of the vineyards. Black rooster signs mark the Chianti country roads. Some 800 wineries repose in centuries-old villas, farmhouses, castles, and abbeys. Their historic roots go deep into the green fields and into the gentle hillsides quilted with vineyards.

If you'd like information about touring the area and perhaps visiting a winery or two, write or visit the Chianti Classico Wine Consortium, Via dei Serragli 146, Florence. The Consortium has published a detailed, liberally illustrated, 340-page guide to the Chianti region, which describes in detail each of the areas, its wineries, and other attractions. The paperback book can be purchased at the office in Florence.

■ **TOURING TIPS** You can taste wine at some of the larger wineries, but don't count on a tour unless you've made an appointment through the Chianti Classico office in Florence or the tourist office in Greve. Some winery tour leaders speak English, but most workers do not. Along the main routes, look for signs illustrated with a black rooster that point the way to Chianti wineries off on country roads. Many wineries are closed on Sunday.

TUSCANY'S HILL TOWNS

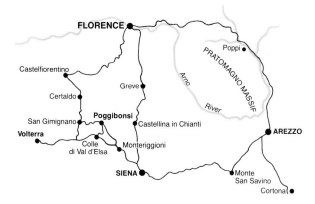

Beyond Florence, the Tuscan landscape is a delight of earthy colors and changing patterns—verdant fields, silvery gray groves of rounded olive trees, leafy vineyards alternating with great rectangles of ripening corn, tawny haystacks drying in the sun, dark green cypress trees etched against a pale blue sky. Fortified towns crown the strategic hills, remnants of medieval conflicts between Florence and Siena. Tucked back in valleys or perched atop hills are towns and villages little changed in appearance since the Middle Ages.

Probably no other region in Italy contains such a wealth of art as Tuscany, despite damage wrought by time, nature, and man. Here in central Italy, the mysterious ancient race of Etruscans left their Greek-influenced art and fortified ruins scattered across the fertile valleys and hills. Many of the hill towns contain art treasures ranging from Etruscan urns to medieval frescoes and Renaissance paintings.

Arezzo.　In the beautiful Etruscan hill town of Arezzo, travelers converge on the Church of San Francesco to view the magnificent frescoes painted by Piero della Francesca during the mid-15th century. In understated tones of blue, gray, and reddish brown, the frescoes depict the story of the Holy Cross. Their facial expressiveness and subdued use of light mark a departure from the work of earlier artists. Don't miss the splendid stained glass window of Saint Francis offering roses to the Pope; it was created by master French glass stainer Guillaume de Marcillat, who settled in Arezzo after working at the Vatican with painters Raphael and Michelangelo.

Medieval houses and palaces surround Arezzo's Piazza Grande. To get the flavor of the town, explore the narrow side streets south and east of this great square lined with old houses, small churches, and palaces.

Cortona.　About 20 miles/30 km south of Arezzo, Cortona clings to a steep slope above the broad plain. Girdled in ramparts, this silent town has changed little since the Renaissance. Its steep, narrow streets paved with flagstones open onto irregularly shaped squares bordered with buildings and arcades.

Artists have come to this remote hillside town to paint since the 14th century. Rich collections, including works by Fra Angelico, will be found in the Diocesan Museum.

Siena.　Best preserved of the art towns is Siena, an enchanting treasure trove of medieval art and architecture. In the Middle Ages, Siena was Italy's financial capital, rivaling Florence in wealth and importance before finally bowing to that city's powerful Medicis.

Eleven streets lead into the striking, fan-shaped Piazza del Campo, where the famous Palio festival is held each July 2 and August 16. Dominating the square is the graceful Town Hall, one of Italy's most handsome public buildings. If you're feeling energetic, you can climb to the top of the bell tower—some 287 feet/88 meters. In late afternoon, pause at an outdoor café at the edge of the piazza and enjoy the animated scene while sipping a Campari or espresso.

Siena is a city made for strolling. Patrician houses built by the town's wealthy merchants line the lively streets just above the piazza, and intriguing alleyways and side streets invite you to explore off the main route.

You'll find many of Siena's art treasures near the Piazza del Duomo. Inside the cathedral, notice the unique mosaic paving that depicts allegories and scenes from the Bible. Nearby is the Piccolomini Library with its famed Pinturicchio frescoes. The city's art gallery is one of Italy's finest, highlighted by an extensive collection of paintings from the 13th to 16th centuries.

Monteriggioni.　North of Siena, you can detour off the main road to the medieval village of Monteriggioni, mentioned by Dante in his *Inferno* and a bastion in Siena's continuing battles with Florence. You'll find the town's walls and towers intact. A single street skirts the thick 13th-century walls, offering glimpses of private gardens. Farm families still use the 12th-century church and the cistern in the piazza.

Colle di Val d'Elsa.　This hill town appears suddenly, sitting high on a ridge above the Volterra road. You enter its massive fortified gate through a stone arch wide enough for only a single car. Handsome old medieval houses and *palazzi* line the town's long single street; narrow alleys occasionally angle off. Once a Renaissance palace, the town hall bears a Medici insignia over its door. An Etruscan archeological museum contains exhibits dating from the 4th century B.C.

Volterra.　Ancient gray Volterra, many of its buildings dating from the 13th century, commands an austere countryside. You can see works of Tuscan painters in the art gallery and Etruscan funeral urns in the local museum. From the Porta all'Arco, the town's only remaining Etruscan gate, walk uphill and left along the Via Fornelli. Through open doorways you'll see men and boys at work making alabaster objects.

San Gimignano.　In the 13th century, dozens of square stone towers jutted above the walled town of San Gimignano; today 14 remain, mellowed by the centuries.

Popular San Gimignano is best visited on a weekday out of season. Hours pass quickly as you amble along the narrow streets of this beautiful little national monument. At noontime the sound of bells fills the town, reverberating from the town walls.

Square stone towers jutting above red tile rooftops add drama to skyline of ancient San Gimignano, an inhabited town preserved as a national monument. At noon, bells resound from several belfries.

You'll want to linger in the Piazza Cisterna, characterized by a patterned brick pavement and 13th-century octagonal well faced with travertine (a type of limestone); towers and patrician houses face the piazza. From the rooms and terraces of the Albergo Cisterna, you'll see laundry hanging in the sun and garden patios where children study in the open air.

■ **TOURING TIPS** **You'll find the hill towns most pleasant to visit in spring and autumn, for temperatures soar in central Italy during the summer months. From Florence you can travel by train in 1 to 2 hours to Arezzo, Poggibonsi (where you transfer to a bus for San Gimignano), or Siena. SITA buses (a national line) and various tours also serve the historic Tuscan towns.**

PERUGIA, UMBRIA'S CAPITAL

See map page 90

Deep in Umbria, the old Etruscan stronghold of Perugia commands a hilltop site overlooking the gentle green valley of the Tiber River. Beginning about the 8th century B.C., the powerful Etruscan empire extended its control throughout central Italy. In Perugia you can trace part of the route of the ancient city wall and see arched gateways dating from the Etruscan era. Romans occupied the settlement in later centuries.

Partially encircled by medieval ramparts, Perugia is a town that invites exploration on foot. Narrow lanes and alleys curve through the old quarter, lined with centuries-old buildings. Viewpoints offer panoramic vistas of the city and countryside.

The heart of the city is the Piazza 4 Novembre, where you'll find the main buildings: the impressive

Palazzo dei Priori and the Cathedral. Here also is the Fontana Maggiore, an impressive round fountain handsomely decorated with sculptures and carved panels around its basin. The city's main thoroughfare, the Corso Vannucci, leads from the piazza.

On the top floor of the palace, the National Gallery of Umbria contains many paintings by artists of the Tuscan and Umbria schools, including outstanding works by Pintoricchio and Perugino.

From Perugia you can make day excursions to many nearby Umbria towns, most of them built of stone on hilly sites and enclosed by ramparts. Their streets and buildings have changed little over the centuries. Some towns have monuments dating from the Etruscan or Roman eras.

Northeast of Perugia is Gubbio, noted for its dramatic site and picturesque old quarter. To the southeast is Assisi, the city of St. Francis; and charming Spello, built on hillside terraces. Driving south of Perugia you'll come to Torgiano, in the middle of vineyards; and Deruta, noted for its ceramics. Farther south is Todi, another attractive hill town, with city walls dating from the Etruscan and Roman eras.

An intriguing town for strolling, Spoleto is noted for its summer music festival. Orvieto is located southwest of Perugia near the Florence-Rome highway; it is noted both for its handsomely decorated Cathedral and for its excellent white wine.

■ **TOURING TIPS** **You'll find driving the most enjoyable way to tour Umbria. Most towns have visitor parking areas just outside the town walls. Train travelers will find the rail stations are located in the valleys; you can take a bus or taxi to reach the town atop the hill. Streets in the older parts of most hill towns are often cobbled or rough, so wear sturdy walking shoes. A good guidebook and a modest knowledge of Italian art and history will increase your appreciation of these old towns.**

BURIED BY A VOLCANO'S FURY

See map this page

Mount Vesuvius suddenly looms up southeast of Naples, a beautiful yet menacing vision dominating the countryside.

On an August day in A.D. 79, Vesuvius erupted spectacularly, spewing superheated mud, lava, and cinders over several Roman towns and luxurious villas facing the Bay of Naples. Among the towns buried in the volcanic rubble were Herculaneum and Pompeii. In recent centuries both towns have been rediscovered and excavated.

Pompeii usually receives top billing for its varied and striking ruins. Herculaneum, northwest of its more famous neighbor, is noted for the outstanding preservation of its private homes. Silent streets offer glimpses of both the simple and grand ways of Roman life, catastrophically preserved for later discovery. Many valuable relics have been moved from the excavated buildings to the National Museum in Naples.

Herculaneum. Until its destruction, Herculaneum was a popular country resort on the Bay of Naples. Buried by mud and lava, it was better preserved and more carefully excavated than Pompeii, and it offers a fascinating look at life in a 1st-century Roman provincial town.

You explore along three main streets, each lined by houses up to three stories high. Furniture is often intact. A bakery contains an oven, flour mills, and even jars for storing grain. A wooden clothespress stands in a dyer's shop. Frescoes and other works of art ornament the House of the Stags, a mansion featuring a central garden and a sun porch overlooking the sea.

Pompeii. When Vesuvius erupted, this town of 20,000 people was interred in more than 20 feet/6 meters of cinders and ashes. Though only 2 miles/3 km in circumference, Pompeii has too many attractions to see thoroughly in a single day. At the museum, castings, models, and excavated objects introduce you to Pompeii's daily life and grim fate.

As you explore Pompeii's cobbled streets, you'll see ruts etched by the wheels of Roman chariots. Highlights include the Forum, center of Pompeii's political, social, and religious life; the public bathhouses; and the open-air theaters and stadium where actors, musicians, dancers, and athletes entertained the citizens. Large patrician villas such as the House of the Vettii provide a look at the sybaritic life of wealthy Romans.

■ TOURING TIPS You can reach Pompeii by train from Naples (Circumvesuviana Station); Herculaneum lies just off the *autostrada* (highway) between Naples and Pompeii. Day excursions from Naples also visit the excavated sites. If you're touring independently, purchase a well-illustrated, English-language guidebook to help you understand the highlights of the town. If you prefer, you can hire an English-speaking guide and perhaps team up with a few other visitors. Many of the interesting buildings are protected behind locked gates; you can usually find a courteous guard who will unlock the door.

Afternoon pause in Umbrian wine town of Torgiano provides a chance to relax and catch up on the day's news.

NEAPOLITAN JEWELS: SORRENTO, CAPRI & THE AMALFI COAST

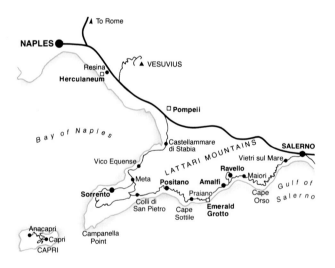

Few regions offer the exhilarating beauty of southern Italy's Sorrentine Peninsula, which juts westward into the Bay of Naples. Dipping and climbing along steep cliffs above the sea is the twisting Amalfi Drive, the corniche road linking Sorrento and Salerno.

Across a 10-mile/16-km channel from Sorrento is Capri, an island jewel in the crown of Neapolitan attractions. Granite cliffs honeycombed with grottoes shoot up from the deep blue sea to a pair of suspended, flower-decked towns. Numerous villas peek out from subtropical greenery.

It's possible to make day trips south from Naples to explore this scenic region, but many travelers prefer to establish a suburban base in Sorrento or in one of the towns along the Amalfi Coast. The best time to visit is from mid-October through May, when summer crowds are absent. It's a favorite winter destination for British and northern European visitors, who come here seeking Italy's warm sunshine.

Sorrento. Praised by poets and musicians, Sorrento overlooks the Bay of Naples from cliffs that drop straight to the clear blue sea. Off season, the town has an almost quiet air.

You can use Sorrento as headquarters for sightseeing, shopping, or sunbathing. Life centers around several small squares, each with its statue surrounded by flowers and greenery. Numerous short piers, used solely by sunbathers, extend from shore. At night, fishermen sail out in their small boats, lighted lanterns gleaming like stars to attract the fish.

Capri. Buses and taxis link the small island's two harbors—Marina Grande and Marina Piccola—with the towns of Capri and Anacapri. However, the most charming way to get around the island is by horse-drawn *carrozzelle*.

Capri is a town of small squares and rustic alleyways. Pedestrians follow narrow stone walks that wind among shops, houses, and walled gardens.

A road carved into the cliffside provides breathtaking views as you climb to delightful Anacapri. A chair lift transports you even higher to the summit of Monte Solaro, 1951 feet/594 meters above the sea.

From Marina Grande, motorboats take visitors to the entrance of the Blue Grotto, where you transfer to a small rowboat to enter the cave. Inside, you are suddenly floating on a shimmering blue sea as refracted sunlight illuminates the large cavern to dazzling brightness.

Amalfi Coast. Dipping and climbing along steep cliffs above the sea, the twisting Amalfi Drive passes terraced vineyards and vegetable gardens, small cliffside resorts, and fishing villages nested beside curving bays. Belvederes offer magnificent vistas. Pine trees, citrus blossoms, and flowers perfume the sea air.

From Sorrento the road climbs through citrus orchards, then descends steeply toward the south coast of the Sorrentine Peninsula. Through the trees you glimpse the sea far below.

Sheltered on each side by hills, the fishing village of Positano spills down the mountainside. Small shops tucked in narrow lanes offer an array of merchandise ranging from local crafts to chic Italian wares. Living like cliff dwellers, Positano's residents descend steep stone stairways to reach the pebbly beach.

The twisting road climbs around Cape Sottile and passes through the small resort and fishing village of Praiano. You reach the Emerald Grotto by elevator from the road.

Amalfi's site is spectacular; its tall, white houses rise from rocky slopes overlooking a blue bay. It prospered as a 9th-century trading town, and by the 11th century it regulated all Mediterranean navigation under the world's oldest maritime code. The cathedral, begun in the 11th century, blends oriental splendor and Romanesque austerity. Walkers join the promenade along the oleander-lined Corso Flavio Gioia or take the path up the Mulini Valley.

East of Amalfi, a winding mountain road climbs through vineyards to Ravello, which hangs like a balcony suspended between sky and sea. Cool and peaceful, Ravello is a town of small squares, covered passageways, and gardened stairways. Everything is within strolling distance of the central piazza. Dating from the 11th century are the cathedral, with Byzantine mosaics in its nave, and the Villa Rufolo, residence of several popes and other illustrious guests. Gardens of the Villa Cimbrone extend to a viewpoint overlooking the sea.

■ **TOURING TIPS** From Naples, trains depart for Sorrento from Circumvesuviana Station; trains for Salerno depart from Central Station. Driving the narrow coastal road can be difficult; take a local bus and enjoy the views. Steamers and hydrofoils provide year-round service from Naples and Sorrento to the isle of Capri; small boats also serve peninsula ports.

ISCHIA—A GREEN RETREAT

A less crowded alternative to Capri and the popular resorts of the Amalfi Coast is the island of Ischia, the largest of the Neapolitan islands. Rising above a translucent sea, Ischia is known as the Green Island because of its pine woods, vineyards, citrus groves, and subtropical vegetation. Hot mineral springs at the thermal resort of Casamicciola draw many visitors. Mount Epomeo rises in the center of the island.

Hydrofoils transport travelers from Napoli Mergallina or Beverello Wharf in Naples to the island in about 40 minutes; car ferries also link Ischia with Naples and Pozzuoli (60 to 80 minutes).

The Greeks colonized Ischia in the 5th century B.C. Many others—Syracusans, Romans, Visigoths, Vandals, Ostrogoths, Normans, Angevins, Spaniards, Austrians, French, and finally Italians—also left their marks on the island. Ruins at Lacco Ameno date back to Greek, Latin, and early Christian periods. The port town of Ischia and the major thermal centers get most of the visitors.

To get away from the crowds, take the island loop road and visit some of the smaller villages: Forio, on a promontory on the west coast; Sant'Angelo, an attractive fishing village on the southern shore; or the towns of Serrara Fontana or Barano on the slopes above the sea. All have accommodations. You can swim, skin-dive, or stretch out on the sand.

The winding road along the southern slope of Mount Epomeo provides many fine views over the island and coast. If you've brought along a picnic, you can enjoy lunch beneath the pines.

THE TRULLI DISTRICT

Few American travelers venture deep into the sundrenched Apulia region, which stretches along southern Italy's Adriatic shore between the ports of Bari and Brindisi. In the heel of Italy's boot, you'll discover fantasy villages where each whitewashed dwelling is topped by a conical dome, and hex signs are painted on stone roof tiles to ward off evil spirits.

Groups of the sparkling white, cone-topped houses, called *trulli,* rise above the ocher-and-green plain of the Itria Valley, where vineyards and olive orchards abound. You'll have good views from the rounded hills between the towns of Monopoli and Martina Franca, particularly near Selva di Fasano and from the Locorotondo–Martina Franca road.

A strange dry-stone structure built on a square plan, the *trullo* is the typical peasant house of the region. Its mortarless walls are plastered dazzling white and crowned with a pointed roof tiled with concentric slabs of smooth gray limestone; each roof is topped by a slender finial. Astrological and religious symbols decorate some houses. The origin of this primitive dwelling is obscure, but the edifices show traces of prehistoric Greek and early Christian civilizations.

The best display of the bright white trulli structures is found in the small town of Alberobello. More than a thousand of the unusual buildings climb the side of a wooded hill, their stone-tiled domes pointing skyward like a fanciful garden city. Alberobello is located about 35 miles/56 km south of the city of Bari.

Alberobello's most characteristic quarter lies on a wooded slope to the south, beyond a mall. As you walk along the town's narrow, flagstone streets, you'll pass dark-garbed women sitting in front of their white houses, weaving mats and shawls from threads hung on nails.

Structures in the Monti and Aia Piccola areas of the town's old quarter date from 1070 and lie in picturesque disorder on the slope of the hill; largest of these buildings is the two-story Trullo Sovrano in the Piazza Sacra-

mento. In the upper part of Alberobello's old quarter, you'll see the trullo-topped Church of Sant'Antonio.

■ **TOURING TIPS** Rental cars are available in both Bari and Brindisi. You'll find accommodations in Alberobello and other nearby towns. The region is most pleasant in the spring, when everything is in bloom, and during the mild fall months. Weather extremes make summer and winter uncomfortable. Nearby are the Castellana Grottoes, Italy's largest and most spectacular caverns.

CLIFFSIDE PATH ABOVE THE SEA

A world apart from the crowded resorts of the Riviera, five unspoiled Ligurian fishing villages of the Cinque Terre (Five Lands) cling to a steep section of the Mediterranean coast north of La Spezia. Terraced vineyards climb the ridges above the rugged shore. Until recent years these cliffside villages were isolated, accessible only by rail and water and linked only by paths above the sea.

You catch glimpses of the villages—Riomaggiore, Manarola, Corniglia, Vernazza, and Monterosso al Mare—on a train ride between La Spezia and Genoa. But for a memorable interlude in your trip, leave the train and walk the footpaths that lead from village to village. A seaside pathway cuts across cliffs above the Mediterranean, and an upper track threads through the vineyards and wooded areas. If you visit during the autumn grape harvest, you'll find the upper path is crowded with vineyard workers carrying great baskets of grapes to the villages below.

To sample this steep, dramatic stretch of coast, leave the train at Riomaggiore at the southern end of the string. Crowded into a narrow valley, its old houses climb slopes on either side. It's about a 20-minute walk north to Manarola along a section of path known as the Via dell'Amore (Lovers' Walk). A guardrail bounds the seaward side of the level flagstone path.

Most rugged of the five villages, Manarola perches precariously just out of reach of the crashing waves, its

Riomaggiore's colorful buildings cling to cliff above the sea. Coastal path links the Cinque Terre villages.

colorful houses clinging to the slope above the dock. You can decide whether to continue your walk or wait in the village for the next train. If you walk farther, you'll find the trail to Corniglia unpaved, slightly more rugged, and often littered with fallen rocks. The trip takes about an hour.

Corniglia has tall houses carved from the rock along very narrow streets. Its Romanesque church has an elegant rose window. The steepest part of the trail is between Corniglia and Vernazza; allow 1½ hours for this section.

High on a rocky promontory, Vernazza has a breathtaking view of the sea. Narrow streets lined with colorful old houses radiate from a small square in the center of town, and a fort—built to repel invading Saracens—overlooks the village. Fishing boats bob in the tiny harbor cove. It's a steep 4-mile/6-km descent from Vernazza to Monterosso al Mare; walkers enjoy sweeping views during the 1½-hour jaunt.

Monterosso al Mare, largest of the towns, has a swimming beach and good resort hotels.

■ **TOURING TIPS** All five villages can be reached by train. Local trains between Genoa and La Spezia stop in each village; some direct trains stop at Monterosso al Mare. In summer, excursion boats cruise to the Cinque Terre from Portofino, Levanto, and other ports. Hillside erosion may make passage difficult on some parts of the paths.

EXPLORING THE VENETIAN LAGOON

See map page 90

About 40 islands, many of them unpopulated, dot the Venetian Lagoon. Three of them—Torcello, Burano, and Murano—offer attractions that lure visitors from Venice.

Torcello. Called the Mother of Venice, Torcello was settled between the 5th and 7th centuries and became a prosperous lagoon community and the bishop's seat. The growth of Venice brought about its decline, and now only a few dozen people live on the island. Torcello's main sights are a short walk from the boat dock.

Facing a grassy piazza, the island's cathedral was built in the 7th century and substantially rebuilt in the 9th and 11th centuries. In front of its entrance you'll see the remains of the 7th-century baptistry. Notable interior features include the 11th-century mosaic pavement, handsome Greek marble columns with Byzantine decoration, and bas-reliefs and paintings, including a large mosaic of the Last Judgment.

Standing beside the cathedral is the little church of Santa Fosca, built in Romanesque style by Greek workers in the 11th century. Opposite the cathedral, a museum contains archeological materials and exhibits from the churches. The museum is open daily except Monday.

Burano. Cheerful Burano looks like a stage set for an Italian opera. Brightly painted houses adorn its streets and small bridges arch across its canals. Seafood restaurants line the main thoroughfare. Fishing, boat building, and lacemaking are the island's principal industries.

Burano first won renown for its fine lace in the 16th century; the skilled craft died out for a period but was revived in the late 19th century. Though much of the inexpensive lace and crochet work displayed in local shops is imported from the Orient, you can see traditional lacemaking at the Scuola dei Merletti, the lace school, at Piazza B. Galuppi.

Murano. Glassware has been made on Murano since the late 13th century, when furnaces were banned from Venice as a precaution against fire. In the 16th century, Murano had nearly 40 glass factories, and glassmakers were privileged craftsmen who closely guarded their techniques. Today, the larger factories are located along the Fondamenta dei Vetrai, where you can have glassware made to order and shipped to your home.

If you'd like to see some remarkable pieces by master glassmakers, visit the Museo dell'Arte Vetraria on Fondamenta Giustinian. Housed in a 17th-century palace, its collection consists of some 4,000 pieces dating from the 15th century to the present. The museum is open daily except Wednesdays and Sunday afternoons.

■ **TOURING TIPS** Waterbus 12 makes regular trips to the three islands from Venice, departing from Fondamenta Nuove; in summer, there's also service from the Riva degli Schiavoni. From the city it's a 10-minute trip to Murano, about 35 minutes to Burano, or 45 minutes to Torcello. Many travelers visit Torcello to dine at the Locanda Cipriani, one of the gastronomic institutions of the Venice region.

Galicia's coast,
page 105

Santillana del Mar,
page 106

Santander

Bilbao

Ordesa National Park,
page 107

Santiago de Compostela,
page 105

Map, page 105

Zaragosa

Barcelona

Segovia, page 109

Montserrat, page 104

Segovia

Avila, page 103

Avila

Madrid, page 104

Cuenca, page 109

Madrid

Toledo

Cuenca

Toledo, page 108

Valencia

Map, page 108

SPAIN

Córdoba, page 107

Córdoba

Seville

Ronda, page 106

Malaga

Map, page 107

0   50   100 Mi

0   100   200 Km

Cathedral, Santiago de Compostela

Plaza del Zocodover, Toledo

Roman aqueduct, Segovia

SPAIN

Several civilizations and religions have left enduring imprints on Spain. Moorish and medieval fortress cities hint at the country's turbulent history. Animal paintings on cave walls attest to the skill of ancient artists.

Our trips explore Córdoba, the city of the Moorish caliphs, and the wonderful old strongholds of Castile—Ávila, Toledo, and Segovia. You can follow the pilgrims' route to Santiago de Compostela or stroll through a medieval Cantabrian farming village. Other destinations include the legendary monastery of Montserrat, an Andalusian mountain stronghold, Galicia's fjordlike coast, and a tiny park high in the Pyrenees.

ÁVILA, A MEDIEVAL FORTRESS

See map page 102

Impressive walls completely enclose Ávila, renowned as one of Europe's most complete medieval fortifications. Begun about 1090, the fortress commands a high plateau between the Gredos and Guadarrama mountain ranges. The town is a monument to Saint Theresa, founder of many of Spain's religious institutions, who was born here in 1515.

The walls contain eight arched gateways and 88 towers and extend more than 1½ miles/2½ km around the town. For the best view, stop at Cuatro Postes viewpoint on the road to Salamanca, just beyond the river.

Ávila's unspoiled medieval character is its primary attraction. Begin your explorations with a walk atop the ramparts that enclose the city. Dominating the town's low skyline is the square-towered cathedral, which is attached to the eastern part of the wall. A walk through the town's narrow streets leads to handsome and historic churches, convents, and fortified mansions.

Southwest of Ávila, the Sierra de Gredos range has much to offer sports enthusiasts: mountain climbing, horseback riding, fishing, and hunting.

Near the main route to Madrid, you can stop at El Escorial, which recalls the grim days of the Inquisition. Built by Philip II in the late 16th century as a palace, monastery, and mausoleum, El Escorial was a bulwark against heresy, proclaiming the absolutism of the monarch and the Church. You can also stop at the Valley of the Fallen (Valle de los Caídos), a monument to Spanish Civil War dead. A cathedral built inside the mountain houses the tomb of Francisco Franco.

■ **TOURING TIPS** Accommodations inside Ávila's ramparts include the parador Raimundo de Borgona, with its lovely gardens, and the Palacio de Valderrabanos, converted to a hotel from a 15th-century palace. Spring and autumn are the best seasons to visit. Harsh sun bakes the land in summer, and biting winds sweep across the dry plateau in winter.

A LEISURELY STROLL IN MADRID

See map page 102

One way to enjoy life in Madrid is to join the *madrileños* on a predinner stroll. Each evening from about 8 until dinner time, it's customary to saunter through the heart of the city, stopping at various bars and cafes for an aperitif and savory tidbits. Ask for a *chato* (a small glass of red or white wine), and sample the tempting array of *pinchos* or *tapas*—tidbits of fried or marinated fish, prawns, meat morsels, cheese, mussels, or sausage.

You can roam the old-world Madrid of the Spanish writer Benito Pérez Galdós, sometimes called the Spanish Dickens, along the Calle de Postas, San Cristóbal, and the little streets around the Plaza Mayor. You'll find numerous taverns in the square itself, and under the steps leading down to the Arco de Cuchilleros.

Another lively tavern district, crowded in the evenings, centers around the Calle de Echegaray and the Travesía de Fernández y González.

A third option takes you to the bullfighters' taverns on the Calle de la Victoria, and on Espoz y Mina, Cruz, Núñez de Arce, and other quaint little streets such as San Ricardo, Cádiz, del Pozo, and Álvarez Gato.

■ **TOURING TIP** Meals are habitually taken much later in Spain than in other European countries. In Madrid, 3 P.M. is considered a normal hour for lunch, and dinner is usually served between 10 and 11 P.M.

LEGENDARY MONTSERRAT

See map page 102

For more than a thousand years, pilgrims have come to pay homage at the Monastery of Montserrat, about 33 miles/53 km northwest of Barcelona. Standing on the edge of a deep ravine, the Benedictine monastery is dwarfed by the grandeur of its setting. Strangely gnarled granite pillars loom above the huge mountain mass like scupltured stone figures, dominating the sawtoothed skyline as you approach from any direction.

One of Montserrat's legends inspired Richard Wagner's opera *Parsifal*, perpetuating the theme that Montserrat was the home of the Holy Grail.

Another legend recounts how shepherds found an image of a black Virgin—supposedly carved by St. Luke and brought to Spain by St. Peter—deep in a cave on the mountainside where it had been hidden during the Moorish occupation. You can see the ancient wooden statue—known as the Black Madonna—encased in glass in a high niche behind the altar of the monastery cathedral. Miracles have been attributed to the statue.

For natives of Catalonia, a visit to Montserrat is like a holiday. Families come here on feast days, anniversaries, and school holidays. Church services, conducted in the local Catalan language, are rich in pageantry. The famous boys' choir, founded in the 13th century, sings daily at 1 P.M.

Gnarled granite pillars loom behind Benedictine monastery of Montserrat, a destination of pilgrims near Barcelona.

Footpaths wind across the slopes. On a quiet path near the monastery, you'll come upon a statue of cellist Pablo Casals, a Catalán who achieved worldwide fame.

Montserrat has several funiculars and *teleféricos* (a type of cable car) that transport visitors up the heights— more than 4,000 feet/1,300 meters above sea level—and down into the valleys. When the weather is favorable, views from the top are magnificent—extending to the eastern Pyrenees and the Balearic Islands.

■ **TOURING TIPS** You can reach Montserrat easily from Barcelona by bus, rental car, or group excursion. Try to arrive early in the morning. Crowds peak about midday, but you can still find solitude away from the center of activity. Tranquility descends in the evening. If you stay overnight at one of the village's two central hotels, you can enjoy evening vespers and listen as church bells ring out each quarter hour.

REGIONAL HANDICRAFTS

Travelers with an eye for locally made handicrafts will find some fine examples in Spanish shops and regional markets. Each provincial center has an official Artespaña handicraft shop, carrying the work of Spanish craftspeople. You'll find leatherwork, jewelry, ceramics and pottery, embroidery and lace, and metalwork. Regional tourist information offices can direct you to the best craft outlets.

PILGRIMS' ROUTE TO SANTIAGO

For more than a thousand years, Santiago de Compostela has been the goal of religious pilgrims who travel long distances to visit the tomb of St. James the Apostle, patron saint of Spain. Beginning in the 9th century they came—a few at first, later by the hundreds of thousands—following a historic trail across northern Spain to pay homage at his shrine.

The city's medieval district is virtually intact, a labyrinth of cobbled lanes leading into the impressive central plaza. The ancient streets retain a mystical air, yet this university city also has its lively side. In late July, the streets fill with celebrants who mark the feast day of St. James (July 25) with a week-long festival.

The Way of St. James. You can make your own pilgrimage, following "Camino de Santiago" signs. Much of the route follows rural roads through countryside little changed from medieval days. You can linger in cities such as Burgos and León; visit magnificent urban cathedrals and remote shrines; and explore intriguing fortresses and walled villages atop hills along the way.

The historic road passes south of Lugo, a provincial capital completely encircled by Roman walls. Small squares, historic lanes, arcades, and noble houses add atmosphere to this old city.

Santiago de Compostela. Soaring above Santiago's rooftops are the baroque towers of the cathedral, marking the pilgrims' goal. Built between the 11th and 13th centuries with later additions, it ranks among the most richly detailed European cathedrals. Its ornately carved main façade was completed about 1750. The triple-arched inner portal—the Door of Glory—is a masterpiece of carved granite.

Just inside the main door, press your fingertips into grooves worn in the central pillar, a gesture traditionally made by pilgrims over the centuries to acknowledge a safe arrival. The cathedral's cool, dark interior is largely Romanesque, dominated by thick columns and an ornamented high altar. Behind it, stairs lead down to the crypt.

Diagonally opposite the church is the Hotel de los Reyes Católicos, founded by King Ferdinand and Queen Isabella as a pilgrims' inn and hospital; now a parador, it is one of Spain's most beautiful and luxurious hotels.

Narrow arcaded streets (called *rúas*) twist and turn through the district. Tall houses from the 15th century,

palaces, and old churches line the routes. Small plazas surround fountains and statues. Near the large Plaza de la Quintana, the streets teem with university students.

On a hill southwest of the city center, the Paseo de la Herradura (Blacksmith's Walk) loops through Alameda Park, providing views of the city's soaring cathedral towers and red-tile roofs.

■ **TOURING TIPS** Before you start out, obtain a copy of the booklet "The Way to Santiago" from the National Tourist Office of Spain (address on page 128). You'll find a pair of distinctive paradors on this route: the Hotel San Marcos in León, formerly a 16th-century monastery and still filled with art treasures; and the magnificent Hotel de los Reyes Católicos in Santiago de Compostela, which has been host to pilgrims for more than 400 years.

GALICIA'S UNSPOILED COAST

See map this page

Far from most of the country's tourist centers, narrow fjordlike estuaries cut deeply into the Atlantic coastline of Spain's northwestern corner. The four inlets known as the Rías Bajas carve out a spectacular array of harbors and coves, promontories and beaches. Offshore waters still conceal the remains of Spanish galleons—loaded with gold, silver, rare woods, and other treasures from the New World—scuttled here in 1702 during battles with the English fleet.

The unspoiled Galician coast is a delightful choice for a relaxing holiday. Modern towns and scattered villages border the *rías*. You'll find seafarers' hamlets to explore and plenty of swimming beaches and picnic sites beneath pine trees. Inland, the countryside is etched by numerous rivers and sprinkled with lovely old country houses, barns on pilings, and ancient megalithic monuments.

Few towns have a more beautiful setting than Vigo, which Sir Francis Drake plundered in 1589. Its busy harbor is a regular port of call for ocean liners. Though a modern city, Vigo's old section holds special charm, particularly the El Berbes quarter with its flavor of the sea.

Pontevedra exudes a meditative and aristocratic air; the old city dates back to Roman times. To the northwest, a corniche road passes Poyo's monastery and follows the shore to the island resort of La Toja. Pine trees cover the island.

Bayona's *parador* occupies a striking site facing the mouth of the Vigo inlet. Julius Caesar reputedly stopped at this port in 62 B.C. on his way to Britain. In 1493 the caravel *Pinta* sailed into port, and Bayona became the first settlement to learn of the discovery of the New World by Christopher Columbus.

■ **TOURING TIPS** Pontevedra and Vigo are the main stopping points on the northwestern coast; several fine hotels are located on the resort island of La Toja. Paradores are located in Bayona, overlooking the water, and in Pontevedra, in a 16th-century Galician baronial manor in the heart of town. Rail and bus routes link the region's main towns, but you'll see more of the countryside if you have a car. Visitors without transportation will find Vigo the best center.

PREHISTORIC CAVE ART

Preserved on the walls and ceilings of numerous caverns in northern Spain are paintings, drawings, and engravings created by primitive artists during the Paleolithic Age, approximately 25,000 to 12,000 B.C.

Most famous is the painted cave of Altamira, southwest of Santander near Santillana del Mar, now virtually closed to the public (only five visitors daily are permitted). Its outstanding frescoes show bison and other animals in motion; the Ice Age artists used the ridges and cavities of the rock wall to enhance muscular bulges and hollows in the animals' bodies.

El Castillo and Las Monedas caves, both near Puente Viesgo southwest of Santander, and other caves are open to the public. More than 130 pictures of bison, deer, wild horses, and bulls are scattered through El Castillo's cavern amid petrified cascades, forests of stalagmites, and shimmering limestone draperies.

Santander's Museum of Prehistory and Archeology, located in the Diputación (the local government seat), contains a rich collection of prehistoric objects excavated from caves in the province.

MEDIEVAL SANTILLANA DEL MAR

See map page 105

Many Europeans spend their summer holidays in lively Cantabrian resort towns along Spain's northern coast, seeking to escape the inland heat. Yet only a few miles away you may see oxen drawing wooden-wheeled farm carts, donkeys plodding along country roads, and farmers tilling and harvesting with simple tools, as their families have for generations.

If you pause awhile in the farming village of Santillana del Mar, southwest of Santander, you may feel you've stepped back into a medieval farming village. In the quiet plaza near the church, you may see a herdsman water his cows at an ancient stone trough beside the public pool where women kneel to scrub laundry. An ox-drawn cart rumbles toward you over the stones of the narrow street—so narrow that you must step aside into the protection of a doorway.

Handsome stone mansions, once the town houses of noble families, line the village streets. The town's architectural treasure is the Church of Santillana; though not large, it is classed as one of the best Romanesque structures in Spain.

To preserve its medieval character, Santillana del Mar has been declared a national historic monument. Its appeal lies in its lack of pretension: it remains a small community inhabited by farm workers, who return each evening with their animals up the village's main street.

Stone houses from the 15th to 17th centuries line the cobbled alleys off the main roads. Their rough façades are ornamented with half-timbered supports, balconies, balustrades, and heraldic crests of the noble families. Some are open to visitors or occupied by shops.

■ **TOURING TIP** Hotels in Santillana del Mar also evoke an earlier era. The Spanish government has renovated a 16th-century palace into the 28-room Parador Gil Blas. Its furniture is old Spanish provincial; in the bedrooms, heavy shuttered doors—set in thick walls—open onto wrought-iron balconies.

RONDA, A REMOTE STRONGHOLD

See map page 107

One of Spain's oldest towns, Ronda occupies a spectacular site inland from the Costa del Sol, perched atop high cliffs above the Guadalevín River gorge. Over the centuries, the town has gained renown as a stronghold of Andalusian bandits, as the site of the final Moorish uprising against Ferdinand and Isabella, and as the birthplace of classical bullfighting. Ronda has long been a favorite of artists and writers, including Goya and Hemingway.

To fully appreciate Ronda's setting, stop at the viewpoint near the Puente Nuevo (New Bridge) spanning the river; you'll have an awesome vista of El Tajo, the deep chasm dividing the town, and two other bridges.

The old town, called La Ciudad, clusters around the church south of the gorge. Whitewashed houses ornamented with ironwork line the quarter's narrow alleys and huddle behind walls remaining from the Moorish occupation. Near the church is Mondragon Palace, summer home of several early Spanish kings. Overlooking the Tajo near the old Roman bridge are several distinctive houses, including the 11th-century residence of the settlement's Moorish ruler.

In the newer (15th- and 16th-century) part of Ronda, called the Mercadillo, you'll find the town hall and Ronda's famous 200-year-old bullring. One of Spain's oldest, it was built in 1785 and is distinguished by an elegant entrance and slender arcades.

Ronda was the birthplace of Francisco Romero, who defined the rules of bullfighting and introduced the cape and *muleta* (small red cloth attached to a stick, used in the fight's final phase).

About 16 miles/27 km west of Ronda, a rugged unpaved road leads to Pileta Caves. Inside the cavern are black and red drawings painted by cave dwellers more than 25,000 years ago, predating those of Altamira. Be sure to check in Ronda regarding road conditions and visiting arrangements before you make the trip.

■ **TOURING TIPS** You can reach Ronda on several lonely roads. Shortest of the routes is the one from San Pedro de Alcántara; it climbs steeply from the Costa del Sol to reach a high corniche road overlooking the deeply eroded Serranía de Ronda. If you prefer not to drive, take one of the scheduled day excursions to Ronda departing from Costa del Sol resorts.

Ponds with splashing fountains add a cooling touch to the lush, manicured gardens of the Alcázar in Córdoba.

CÓRDOBA, CITY OF THE CALIPHS

A Moorish aura and spirit linger in Córdoba, the ancient city of the caliphs in the heart of Andalusia. Built along the Guadalquivir River, it is one of Spain's oldest cities.

Three different civilizations—Romans, Visigoths, and Moors—and religions left early imprints on Córdoba, but the city blossomed under Arab rule. Between the 8th and 11th centuries, it flourished as the capital of Islamic Spain and a center of science, philosophy, and the arts. In 1236, during the Spanish Reconquest, Ferdinand III of Castile added the city to his kingdom.

The most lasting monument of the Moorish dynasty is the Great Mosque, an 8th-century masterpiece built on the foundation of a Visigothic church. The mosque was converted into a Christian cathedral in the 16th century. Its airy forest of 850 marble columns supports a double canopy of red-and-white-striped stone arches. The Mih-

rab Chapel features a spectacular jewellike inlaid dome and a rich array of mosaic work.

You'll discover the essence of old Córdoba as you stroll its *callejas,* narrow alleys lined with whitewashed buildings roofed in red tile. The lanes wind through some of the city's most characteristic quarters. One of the loveliest sections is the Judería, the old Jewish quarter north of the cathedral.

Motor traffic crosses the Guadalquivir on a Roman bridge built in the 2nd century. At one end is a triumphal arch, the Gate of El Puente; La Calahorra fortress guards the far side.

Near the mosque and bridge is the Alcázar, the 14th-century palace-fortress of the Christian kings. Its gardens, pools, and fountains alone are worth a visit.

Most of Córdoba's beautiful old churches face onto charming plazas such as the Capuchinos, Los Dolores, Flores Square, and Plaza del Potro. Plaza de Colón and its old park face the old Convent of La Merced. Spacious 17th-century arcades surround the Corredera, queen of Córdoba's plazas and site of the open-air market. Modern Córdoba centers around the Plaza de José Antonio.

Art lovers will find two excellent collections—the Fine Arts Museum and the Julio Romero de Torres Museum—facing the Plaza del Potro. The Córdoban crafts of silverwork and embossed leatherwork are featured, along with bullfight memorabilia, in the Municipal Museum on the Plaza de Maimónides. Nearby you'll see Córdoba's 14th-century synagogue, and the *zoco* (souk) where craftsmen work around a large patio.

■ **TOURING TIPS** Córdoba is at its best in spring, when the city resembles one vast flower garden; during May fiestas, flamenco singers, dancers, and guitar players add spirit to the merrymaking. Autumn visitors enjoy soft, balmy weather, and winters are relatively mild; however, in midsummer, the torrid sun beats relentlessly on this inland city.

ORDESA NATIONAL PARK

See map page 102

Hikers and others who love the mountains will enjoy a detour to small but awesome Ordesa National Park, high in the Pyrenees in Huesca Province. It contains some of Spain's most spectacular mountain scenery.

Reddish sandstone escarpments rise some 3,200 feet/1,000 meters above the Ordesa Valley. A turbulent stream tumbles along the valley floor, and a hiking trail loops upstream past waterfalls. You'll find a pleasing mix of woods, mountains, wildflowers, rushing streams, and mountain wildlife. The park is open from May to September; snow makes it inaccessible by car in winter.

To reach the park, drive north from Zaragoza, on the Madrid–Barcelona highway, to Huesca; continue north on route C138 to Torla. You can also reach the park by driving east from Pamplona.

■ **TOURING TIPS** Inside the park, you'll find an information center (maps and literature), a modest restaurant, and a small store. Accommodations and a campground are located just outside the park in the small town of Torla.

TOLEDO, A LIVING MUSEUM

From its hilly site overlooking the Tajo River, Toledo spreads like a vast and complex mosaic. Dominating the skyline is the Alcázar, a medieval fortress restored to its 16th-century appearance.

A national monument, Toledo is a treasure house of art and Mudéjar (Spanish-Moorish) architecture, reflecting the grandeur of Spanish civilization and the varied influences contributing to it.

Settled by the Romans, Toledo underwent long occupations by the Visigoths and Moors before Alfonso VI reconquered the city in 1085. For nearly 500 years it was the capital of the monarchy and the heart and soul of Spain. Toledo became a leading center of medieval learning and a rich commercial and industrial city. Art and architecture flourished there as well.

A maze of narrow, cobbled alleyways, often steep and twisting, Toledo invites walkers to explore a city virtually unchanged in the last 400 years. Its architecture and art reflect the various cultures—Roman, Visigothic, Moorish, Jewish, and Christian—that have developed and shaped this unique city. Many of the houses in Toledo have been built in traditional Moorish style around attractive patios; windowless walls and barred gates screen garden and household activity from passersby.

Toledo on foot. A good place to begin your explorations is the Plaza del Zocodover, Toledo's traditional market square and formerly the site of public executions. Time has mellowed its buildings, constructed centuries ago by skilled artisans, whose work reflects their pride and imagination. You'll find many talented craftspeople still practice in Toledo; the most distinctive of regional handicrafts is damascene work (steel inlaid with gold), which you'll see in local shops.

Spanish influences enhance Toledo's magnificent 13th-century Gothic cathedral. Richly ornamented both inside and out, the immense church contains many priceless works of art. Other churches also reflect the city's medieval wealth.

You can also visit the Alcázar, first governed in the 11th century by El Cid, Spain's great national hero; in the 16th century, it was converted to a royal residence by Charles V.

Nearby, the Alcántara Bridge spans the Tagus River between high cliffs. First built by the Romans, the bridge was rebuilt in 1259.

Rich artistic legacy. Painter Domenico Theotokopoulos (El Greco) found inspiration in Toledo, where he lived for nearly 30 years until his death in 1614. His house is open to the public; from its garden you have a view overlooking the city and the river. Some of his paintings may be seen in a nearby museum; others are on view in the Santo Tomé Church and in Toledo's art museums.

More of Toledo's artistic legacy can be seen in a pair of historic buildings that have been converted into museums. Exquisite paintings by El Greco, Titian, and Ribera hang in the Hospital de Tavera, a museum housed in a 16th-century feudal mansion. The former Hospital de Santa Cruz is now Toledo's municipal museum; it features 16th- and 17th-century paintings, including 22 by El Greco.

To view the city's striking site from a variety of perspectives, drive around Toledo on the Carretera de Circunvalación, a route that is especially enjoyable when traveled at dusk.

■ **TOURING TIPS** Excursions from Madrid offer an easy way to visit Toledo, but the city contains more treasures than you can possibly absorb in a single day. You can hire open carriages and taxis to get around the city, but many fascinating corners can be explored only on foot. Daytime crowds depart around sunset, and the city reverts to the *toledaños* and the mood of an earlier era. A parador, built in traditional Toledo style, offers modern accommodations with dramatic views of the city and countryside.

YOUR CASTLE IN SPAIN

Among Europe's most enjoyable accommodations are Spain's paradores, a network of more than 80 government-operated hotels scattered across the countryside.

Many occupy historic buildings—renovated castles, palaces, monasteries, convents, and aristocratic homes—which are now equipped with private baths and central heating. Other paradores are newly built in areas with limited accommodations. Parador restaurants feature regional food specialties.

The government also operates other tourist establishments: albergues de carretera *(wayside inns) located along major highways;* hosterias *(restaurants decorated in regional folk style); and* refugios *(mountain shelters) providing accommodations in mountain sports areas.*

For more information and a listing of paradores throughout the country, contact the National Tourist Office of Spain (address on page 128). Your travel agent can make parador reservations for you.

Balconied houses in Cuenca hang on side of precipitous cliff. Spectacular setting enhances town's old quarter.

CUENCA'S HANGING HOUSES

See map page 102

Situated in the center of a hilly, boulder-strewn region southeast of Madrid, the town of Cuenca enjoys a striking setting. Its old quarter commands a cliff top, surrounded on three sides by a precipice. Exceptionally tall, slender houses line its narrow streets. Some, known as the *Casa Colgada* (hanging houses), project outwards from the rock face, appearing to defy gravity.

To discover Cuenca's unique appeal, stroll from the Plaza Mayor de Pío XII through the curving alleys of the old quarter. Its heart is the cathedral, Gothic in design, Renaissance in decoration. Near the hanging houses you'll find the Museum of Abstract Art, which displays works by Spanish painters.

During Holy Week, dramatic processions wind through the steep alleys of the old quarter.

▦ **TOURING TIP** For a close view of the hanging houses, walk along the cathedral's south wall and through an arched passage beside the *mesón* (inn); it leads to the San Pablo footpath, from which you can see the houses. For another view, take the road paralleling the Huécar River at the base of the rock.

ELEGANT SEGOVIA

See map page 108

The atmosphere of medieval Spain pervades Segovia. Soft, clear light washes over the town's ocher-colored buildings and red-tile roofs. Romanesque churches and small houses decorated with ironwork and colorful flowers are scattered along the narrow streets and small squares.

You'll enjoy roaming around this relatively small and compact hill town. Many of its crooked, crowded streets are too narrow for cars. Facing the cathedral is the Plaza de Franco, Segovia's main square, with side streets radiating from it.

Three historic structures reflect aspects of Segovia's past: the great Roman aqueduct, the Alcázar, and the cathedral.

Built of huge, uncemented blocks of granite, the majestic arches of the Roman aqueduct have towered over Segovia for more than 2,000 years. Its 148 arches stretch some 1,800 feet/600 meters in length, rising in a graceful double tier high above the Plaza Azoguejo to join two hills in the center of the city. The aqueduct supports a conduit that still brings water to Segovia from hills more than 10 miles/16 km away.

One of medieval Spain's great fortress-castles, the romantic Alcázar crowns a rocky spur high above converging river valleys. Before you cross the drawbridge over the moat, walk along the curving terrace and gaze over the valley. Look up at the castle's pointed turrets with the battlemented central tower rising above. In 1474 Isabella was proclaimed Queen of Castile in the castle's throne room, and in 1505 Christopher Columbus made his will here, with King Ferdinand acting as a witness.

Segovia has many beautiful churches, most built in Romanesque style during the 12th and 13th centuries. The elegant 16th-century cathedral occupies a place of honor above the town. Splendid stained-glass windows, carved choir stalls, wrought-iron chapel gates, and tapestries distinguish the interior. Don't miss the Gothic cloisters and the museum.

You can walk on the ramparts near the aqueduct and visit the three city gates that remain of the original seven: San Cebrian, set in the oldest section of the walls; Santiago, built in Mudéjar style; and the recently restored San Andreas, leading into the Jewish quarter. The city walls were built as a defense during the battles to reconquer Spain from the Moors.

On a trip from Madrid to Segovia, you cross the pine-covered Guadarrama Mountains. *Madrileños* come here for climbing in summer and skiing in winter. The royal hunting lodge of La Granja, one of Spain's showplaces, was built by the homesick Bourbon King Philip V to remind him of Versailles; formal gardens with fountains surround the castle.

▦ **TOURING TIPS** You can visit Segovia on a day trip from Madrid. If you'd like to stay longer, you'll enjoy Segovia's 80-room parador, built on a hillside overlooking town, or one of the traditional hotels in the city's old quarter. The best view of the Alcázar is from the Vera Cruz church, a Knights Templar church consecrated in 1208, just outside town.

Sintra

Pousada dos Loios, Evora

Obidos

Costa Verde,
page 112

● Viana do Costelo

● Braga

Douro Valley,
page 113

● Porto

Map, page 112

● Coimbra

PORTUGAL

Central Coast,
page 114

● Obidos

● Portalegre

Alentejo,
page 115

Sintra,
page 111

● Lisbon

● Evora

Sesimbra,
page 113

Map, page 115

● Beja

Map, page 114

● Portimao

Faro ●

Algarve, page 114

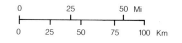

PORTUGAL

The traveler in Portugal has a delightful array of choices. Our destinations include some of the best.

Along the varied coast, you can relax in resorts or stop in lively ports where you can attend a fish auction on the beach. For a restful interlude, stop in the walled town of Óbidos.

Other routes lead inland to towns noted for traditional handicrafts, and to the port-producing vineyards of the Douro Valley. You'll also find traditional Portugal on a loop through the sun-drenched Alentejo Plain.

Easy day excursions include a walking tour through Lisbon's Alfama district, a visit to mountain palaces once used as royal retreats, and a trip to a lively deep-sea sport and commercial fishing port south of the capital.

SINTRA, LOFTY ROYAL RETREAT

See map page 115

Tucked against the slope of densely wooded mountains northwest of Lisbon, lofty Sintra was the favorite summer refuge of Portugal's kings for six centuries. Today you can enjoy the fresh, cool mountain climate and enchanting scenery that attracted Portuguese royalty and inspired writers and poets.

One of Portugal's oldest and most beautiful towns, Sintra perches high in verdant hills. Red-roofed villas and palace towers peek out above luxuriant vegetation.

Distinctive twin conical chimneys mark the Palácio National, formerly the summer residence of the kings of Portugal. Originally built in the late 14th century, the palace was enlarged and embellished in the early 16th century.

The road climbs south in a series of hairpin curves to the old Moorish castle, built in the 7th and 8th centuries. Towers guard its perimeter wall. A wild and lonely place, it rises from a rocky spur and provides sweeping views from Sintra to the sea.

Crowning one of the highest peaks in the Sintra Mountains is Pena Palace, built by King Ferdinand II in the 19th century. Combining a Gothic tower, Moorish minarets, and an odd mixture of architectural details, the building is enhanced by its lonely setting. A large botanical park surrounds the palace, and period furnishings decorate its interior. From atop the tower you have an awesome view of the region.

Nearby, the botanically fascinating Gardens of Monserrate contain some 3,000 species of trees and plants from around the world, many brought here as seedlings aboard sailing ships.

■ **TOURING TIPS** Frequent suburban trains make the 17-mile/28-km run between Lisbon (Rossio Station) and Sintra. Guided excursions also depart from Lisbon for Sintra and the Costa do Sol. In Sintra, horse-drawn carriages transport visitors up the hills to nearby attractions.

111

ALONG PORTUGAL'S COSTA VERDE

Steeped in history and tradition, Portugal's remote northwest corner is considered the birthplace of the nation. In fishing villages and small inland towns, rural families still follow many customs and practices passed down from earlier generations.

At outdoor markets you can purchase regional handicrafts made in the time-honored ways. Here you'll find lace and embroidery, handwoven fabrics, pottery and ceramics, cane and rush articles, carved wood objects, and decorative metalwork. Energetic dancing and singing are highlights of many local celebrations.

Coastal settlements. Along the coast, deep pine forests edge peaceful beaches. Seaside resorts alternate with simple villages where the day's highlight is the return of the fishing boats.

Shuttle lacemaking is the traditional craft at Vila do Conde, a resort amid pines at the mouth of the Ave River. The lacemakers' procession is the highlight of a celebration held around June 23.

Part fishing port and part elegant resort, Póvoa de Varzim borders a magnificent golden-sand beach. At its southern end you'll find the fishermen's quarter, where family members keep busy working on boats, mending nets, preparing fresh fish to dry in the sun, or assembling piles of seaweed for later use as fertilizer. Fish auctions on the beach are a weekday highlight.

Beyond the fishing village of Apúlia stretches the long, sandy beach of Ofir-Esposende, a relaxing coastal resort on the Cávado River.

Viana do Castelo flourished during the 16th century, when it developed a prosperous fishing trade with the Hanseatic cities. Handsome buildings from that era dot the old town, and gardens border the Lima River. The region's most famous folk celebration occurs here in mid-August.

Inland craft towns. You can return to Porto through several towns noted for handicrafts. If possible, time your visit to coincide with market day activity. Religious festivals in Braga on June 23 and 24, and in Guimarães in early August, feature processions, folk dancing, and fireworks.

Braga, the capital of Minho province, is surrounded by mountains. Founded by the Romans, it is known for its strong religious tradition, for its lively Tuesday market, and for the awesome baroque stairway at Bom Jesus do Monte.

Thursday is the day to visit Barcelos, a busy agricultural town on the Cávado River; its center becomes a vast outdoor marketplace where you'll see regional crafts in abundance: pottery (depicting the cockerel, a national symbol), handmade rugs, crochet work, and wood carvings. Later, you can stroll around the town's old quarter; take a look at the open-air archeological museum in the ruins of the Ducal Palace and see local pottery in the ceramics museum.

Founded in the 10th century, Guimarães is a prosperous commercial center known for fine embroidery on locally made linen. It also has historic buildings in an attractive old quarter.

Craftswomen in the village of Trofa make articles of net and lace; you may see their wares displayed beside the road.

■ **Touring Tips** Rail and bus services link the main towns. From Porto, trains travel north to the coastal towns of Póvoa de Varzim and Viana do Castelo, and inland to Braga and Guimarães. Hotels and inns are located in the main towns; pousadas (see page 133) are located in Viana do Castelo and Guimarães.

Smiling vendor weighs fruit in outdoor market. You'll find festive bazaars in country towns throughout Portugal.

DOURO VALLEY WINE TOURING

See map page 112

Portugal's wine country comes alive in autumn, when families from remote mountain villages make their way to the terraced vineyards above the Douro Valley for the annual grape harvest. The country's finest wine region lies east of Porto in northern Portugal.

During the annual harvest, women cut grape bunches from the vines, filling large baskets that men carry on their backs down the slopes. Musicians often accompany the workers to the vineyards and during nighttime partying.

A good road follows the Douro upriver from Porto, winding among undulating hills. White houses and villages stand out against the green slopes. Beneath family grape arbors, corn and beans grow. As you progress farther east, vineyards appear between the terraced olive orchards and cornfields. Near Entre-os-Rios, the Tâmega River angles northwest toward Amarante. Commercial center for the light and sparkling *vinho verde* (green wine) is Sinfães. Port-producing vineyards begin near Régua and extend eastward along the Douro.

Vila Real and Amarante are busy small towns with attractive Renaissance houses. Look in Vila Real shops for examples of the region's distinctive black pottery. Just outside town is the elegant Mateus manor, where Mateus rosé wine is produced.

Amarante's houses ascend a slope above the tree-shaded Tâmega River. Amarante plays host to one of Portugal's most colorful fairs on the first Saturday in June. In the town hall, a small museum displays works by local Cubist painter Amadeu de Sousa Cardoso.

■ **TOURING TIP** Accommodations are limited in the small towns, but you'll find pousadas in Alijó in the vineyard district and at São Gonçalo, east of Amarante.

VISIT A PORT LODGE

From hilly vineyards above the Douro River east of Porto, casks of new port wine are shipped downriver by rail each spring. Traditionally, they were transported aboard rabelos, *high-prowed, flat-bottomed, square-rigged Douro riverboats steered with poles and rudder.*

Brought to the dimly lit warehouses (called port lodges) of Vila Nova de Gaia on the south bank of the river, the wine is stored in enormous barrels, and later in bottles, until it is ready for shipping. On weekdays, visitors are welcome at the old lodges to learn how port is made and to sample the final product.

Cruises up the Douro River depart daily except Monday from the quay at Ribeira Square in Porto.

Brightly painted fishing boats are pulled up on shore at Sesimbra, busy port for a sport-fishing and commercial fleet.

FISHING ACTIVITY IN SESIMBRA

See map page 115

South of Lisbon, the bustling fishing village of Sesimbra nestles below rugged hills along the southern coast of the Setúbal Peninsula. A center for deep-sea sportfishing, Sesimbra also is home port for a commercial fleet.

After you've explored the old town, take one of the steep, narrow streets descending to the beach. Often along the way you'll pass fishermen mending nets or townspeople exchanging the day's news. Each afternoon, the brightly painted boats return home and the catch is auctioned on the beach.

Above the port are the ruins of Sesimbra Castle, originally a Moorish fortress. Inside its crenelated walls, a small museum displays archeological artifacts.

Inland, you may want to stop at Azeitão, where you can visit the José Maria da Fonseca winery (home of Lancers wine) on weekdays year round. A short stroll will take you past the town's fine old houses, 16th-century church, and carved stone fountain. Azeitão is also noted for its *queijo fresco*, a creamy white cheese made from ewes' milk. On the first Sunday of each month, Azeitão is the scene of a boisterous open market.

On weekdays, visitors are welcome at the Bacalhoa *quinta*, a large country estate near the Lisbon–Setúbal road (open weekdays from 1 to 5 P.M.). Built in the 15th century, the manor house shows Moorish and Florentine influences rather than the more typical Manueline style. You'll see arcaded chambers lined with pictorial glazed tiles (*azulejos*) and enjoy strolling through the gardens.

■ **TOURING TIPS** You can visit Sesimbra on a half-day excursion from Lisbon. Buses for Sesimbra depart from Lisbon and Cacilhas. Motorists will find hotel accommodations in Sesimbra, but may prefer nearby pousadas at renovated castles in Palmela and Setúbal.

Nazaré fishermen mend nets along wide beach. Since town has no harbor, boats are pulled high onto the sand.

ÓBIDOS & THE CENTRAL COAST

See map page 115

Silhouetted against the sky, crenelated walls encircle the enchanting medieval town of Óbidos, about 58 km/94 miles north of Lisbon. Its weather-beaten castle and sturdy towers have guarded the town since the Moorish era. Behind the walls, compact whitewashed houses gleam in the sun.

Donkeys and pedestrians have the right of way in streets barely wide enough for a single car. As you walk along the twisting route, you may see artisans weaving cotton carpets. Churches are everywhere, decorated with painted ceilings and walls of colored tile. Ancient stairways lead up to the path atop the city wall.

West of Óbidos, the fishing port of Peniche comes to life each afternoon when the boats unload their catch.

Nazaré, north of Óbidos, is known for its wide, sandy beach and the colorful traditions of its fisherfolk. On this harborless coast, boats are pulled up on the sand. Fish are sorted and sold on the beach, or dried on racks. When tourists overwhelm the village, you can escape by cable car (along with most of the local folk) to the peaceful village of Sítio on the cliff above.

■ **TOURING TIPS** Day excursions from Lisbon offer an easy way to visit Óbidos and other attractions; you can also reach the town by train. You'll find a selection of cozy inns at Óbidos; part of the medieval castle now houses a small pousada.

THE ALGARVE'S MOORISH HERITAGE

An exotic Moorish flavor lingers in the Algarve, Portugal's subtropical southern coast. Separated by hills from the dry Alentejo plain, this region is one vast garden.

The Algarve's main resorts lie west of Faro. If you head east toward the Spanish border, you'll find small towns so Moorish in appearance that you could easily imagine yourself in North Africa.

Visitors are drawn to the fishing port of Olhão by its busy fish market, as well as by its white, cube-shaped houses separated by narrow alleys. Nearby Fuzeta, similar in appearance to Olhão, has a good beach.

Encircled by gray stone ramparts, Tavira rises at the foot of a hill facing an estuary of the Asseca River. One of the coast's oldest and most attractive towns, Tavira has a bridge dating from Roman times. From the castle, you gaze over Tavira's peaked roofs and many churches.

One of the largest Algarve ports, Vila Real de Santo António borders the west bank of the Guadiana River. Black-and-white mosaic paving radiates from the main square, and gardens line the riverbank. Ferries cross the river to the Spanish town of Ayamonte.

From the ancient fortified castle of Castro Marim, you look across the Guadiana River and its border towns to the ocher-colored Spanish plain.

■ **TOURING TIP** From Lisbon it's a 35-minute flight or a 4- to 5-hour drive to Faro. Express trains link the capital and the Algarve coast in about 6 hours. Local trains serve large coastal towns from Lagos east to Vila Real de Santo António. A pousada is located inland at São Brás de Alportel.

SAGRES PENINSULA

Southwest of Lagos, the bleak and lonely Sagres Peninsula is haunted by the spirit of Henry the Navigator, the Portuguese prince who settled here in 1418. He established a school of navigation and an observatory, became a patron of voyagers and explorers, and dreamed of finding a sea route to the riches of India. Vasco da Gama, Ferdinand Magellan, and Christopher Columbus learned their skills here. The school still stands within the walls of the rebuilt fortress. A movie in English tracing the era of maritime discovery is shown daily at 3:45 P.M.

ON FOOT IN LISBON'S ALFAMA

Oldest and most picturesque of Lisbon's bairros is the Alfama, a maze of twisting streets lined with venerable mansions and attractive churches. Eight centuries of history is distilled in this delightful old quarter, which survived the 1755 earthquake.

Walk these cobbled lanes in early morning when the fish market is open on Rua de São Pedro, or in late afternoon when everyone is outside on the streets and square.

THE SUN-DRENCHED ALENTEJO

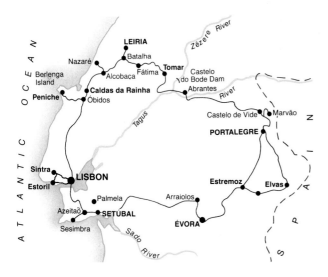

For centuries Portugal's broad inland plain was a vast battlefield, first filled with Moorish invaders, later with the Spaniards. Fortified towns still mark the plain, but today the sunny Alentejo—the land "beyond the Tagus"— is Portugal's granary.

The northern Alentejo is a land of undulating hills and fast-flowing streams. Portalegre, its major city, gained wealth and fame through its tapestries, woven here since the 16th century. On weekdays you can visit the tapestry workshop, located in the former monastery, to see handwoven tapestries made and displayed.

Access to Marvão is difficult, but you'll be glad you made the effort. Anchored to a granite peak near the Spanish border, the town is a delight. From atop the still-intact ramparts of the fortress above it, you can gaze down on the town's narrow alleys, across to Spain's jagged mountains, and over the Alentejo plain.

Another delightful town is Castelo de Vide. Whitewashed houses with handsome doorways and unusual chimneys line the narrow streets; you'll absorb the town's gracious ambience as you make your way up to the castle.

Stretching southward is the flat, sunburnt plain, its vast wheat fields occasionally broken by groves of cork oak or olive trees or a flock of grazing sheep.

A hilltop castle juts against the blue sky at Estremoz, encircled by a network of narrow, winding streets and guarded by medieval fortifications. A well-known pottery center, Estremoz bustles during its Saturday market, when handmade ceramics and many other wares are displayed on the main square. Visit the small museum here to learn more about the Alentejo and its people.

Detour east through Borba—notable for its marble and its excellent wine—to Elvas. Here elaborate 17th-century fortifications still guard the dazzling white town. Stroll about the town to see its impressive defenses, Manueline cathedral, and attractive squares. A 15th-century aqueduct still brings water to the town.

Another hilltop town dominated by its castle, Arraiolos is known for its brilliantly colored wool carpets executed in simple designs; you're welcome to visit the workshops.

Allow at least a full day to explore Évora, one of Portugal's most interesting cities and the market center of the Alentejo. A walled town since the Roman era, Évora faded under the Visigoths and in 715 was occupied by the Moors. Dazzling white houses, balconies, hanging gardens, and arched alleyways reflect its Moorish character. From a rich past, it retains a 2nd-century Roman temple and many handsome medieval and Renaissance buildings.

▪ **TOURING TIPS**   The Alentejo is best in spring; in summer, the sun parches the land as temperatures soar. Pousadas in Marvão, Estremoz, Elvas, and Évora reflect the architecture, food specialties, and crafts of the region.

Handmade ceramic dishes are spread on ground to entice passing shoppers at outdoor market in Estremoz.

Julian Alps,
page 118

● Ljubljana

● Zagreb

Rijeka

Istrian
Peninsula,
page 120

Adriatic Islands,
page 118

Plitvice Lakes,
page 119

Danube Cruise,
page 121

Belgrade ●

Map, page 118

Zadar

Y U G O S L A V I A

Map, page 121

● Sarajevo

Trogir, page 117

Split

Mostar, page 120

Niš

Trogir marketplace

Map, page 120

Dubrovnik

Titograd ●

● Skopje

0	25	50	75	100 Mi
0	50		100	150 Km

Boskoviceva Street, Dubrovnik

Mostar

YUGOSLAVIA

Yugoslavia's long Adriatic coastline offers a tempting array of touring possibilities—both in mainland towns and on islands scattered offshore. Our suggestions include port towns along the Istrian Peninsula, several island hideaways where you can relax and soak up the sun, and the tiny medieval fortress of Trogir.

In the country's northwest corner you can enjoy lakeside resorts in the foothills of the Julian Alps. Plitvice, the country's best-known national park, is a wonderland of lakes, streams, and waterfalls. Inland you'll find Mostar, an intriguing city that retains mosques and minarets from the era when the Ottomans ruled Yugoslavia. From Belgrade you can take a memorable cruise on the Danube River to the renowned Iron Gate section of the gorge.

TROGIR, AN ISLAND FORTRESS

See map page 120

Fortified medieval port towns stud the Adriatic coast and islands, recalling centuries of military conflict and foreign occupation. One of the most unspoiled is tiny Trogir, a 30-minute drive northwest of Split. Situated on a small island just offshore, the compact town is connected to the mainland by a bridge.

Colonized by Greeks about 385 B.C., the settlement somehow escaped the raiding barbarians who sacked the nearby Roman city of Salona (Solin). Occupied in turn by Byzantines, Croats, Venetians, French, and Austrians, Trogir existed in relative isolation for centuries. An impressive number of medieval buildings reflect the architectural styles of different cultures.

Passing through its narrow Renaissance gate and cramped streets, you'll feel transported to another era. Near the Porta Civitatis is the attractive Renaissance loggia, once the civic center of Trogir. Just beyond, you enter the small town square, distinguished by its Venetian-inspired town hall and 15th-century clock tower. The 9th-century Church of St. Barbara is decorated in early Croatian style.

Trogir's most notable building—and one of Yugoslavia's best examples of medieval architecture—is the 13th-century Cathedral of St. Lawrence, designed in the form of a Romanesque basilica. Opposite the cathedral is the 15th-century Cipiko Palace, adorned with a decorative Venetian Gothic façade.

Other splendid monuments in Trogir include churches and convents, palaces built by noble families during the Middle Ages, and the 15th-century Kaštel-Kamerlengo fortress facing the nearby island of Čiovo.

■ **TOURING TIPS** Spring is the prettiest time to visit the Adriatic coast. Knowledgeable travelers arrive before or after the summer crowds, who pack the beaches from mid-June to mid-September. Warm, sunny days linger into November; even in midwinter you'll often enjoy brilliant sunshine.

EXPLORING THE POSTOJNA CAVES

Impressive, illuminated limestone formations lie deep within a vast subterranean maze of caverns and passageways at Postojna Caves, located midway between Ljubljana and Opatija in northwestern Yugoslavia (see map below).

You board an open, narrow-gauge electric train for a 10-minute ride into the caves, then take a guided group tour through the complex. It's chilly down in the caves (42°F/6°C all year), but you can rent a warm cape.

During World War II, Nazi troops stored thousands of tons of aviation fuel in the caves. Yugoslav partisans sneaked in through a secret entrance, planted time bombs, and destroyed the fuel in a blaze that lasted for days. The tunnels are still smoke blackened near the entrance.

YUGOSLAVIA'S ALPINE CORNER

Austrians ruled Slovenia for centuries until 1918. In Yugoslavia's northwest corner, both the Alpine countryside and way of life share traits with Austria, the northern neighbor.

Tucked into the foothills of the Julian Alps are a pair of lovely tree-rimmed lakes, Bled and Bohinj. Generations of European vacationers have come here in both summer and winter, but only in recent years has this scenic mountain region been discovered by many American visitors.

In summer, climbers and mountaineers arrive, and hikers find challenging trails in a nearby wilderness area. Boating, fishing, and lake swimming draw water sports enthusiasts; golfers head for the golf course just east of Bled, above the Sava River gorge.

Winter visitors enjoy cross-country trails near Bled and Bohinj, and downhill skiing at the resort town of Kranjska Gora. Other activities include skating and curling on frozen lakes, sledding and horse-drawn sleigh rides over the snow, and indoor swimming in Bled's thermally heated pool.

Bled. A favorite of 19th-century Austro-Hungarian aristocrats, Bled retains the charm of an old-world spa. Wooded hills frame the lake, whose quiet waters reflect a small island in the middle and a castle looming on a high crag. Village shops and hotels border one shore. You can stroll along the lakeside promenade or board a horse-drawn carriage for a ride around the lake. On summer Sundays, a band often performs at the bandstand.

You can hike a steep path or drive up to the 11th-century castle topping a sheer bluff above the lake. From the terrace you'll gaze over a panorama of village, lake, and mountains. The castle contains a small museum.

To explore the island, board one of the small gondolalike boats that transport visitors across Lake Bled. Rising above the foliage is an interesting 900-year-old church, built over a graveyard. Skeletons of early Slavs can be seen through a glass panel in the floor.

Bohinj. Beneath some of the country's highest peaks, the road to Lake Bohinj winds 17 miles/27 km west from Bled through the Sava Bohinjska River valley.

Less developed than Bled, Bohinj offers relaxation in a scenic setting. You can board a cable car that climbs to a viewpoint high above the long, finger-shaped lake. A 20-minute trek along a wooded trail leads to the 195-foot/65-meter Savica waterfall.

Kranjska Gora. Slovenia's liveliest winter sports center is located just minutes from the Italian and Austrian borders. Relatively uncrowded, Kranjska Gora is an international resort with challenging trails and lively après-ski activity.

■ **TOURING TIPS** Trains link Ljubljana with Bled and the Austrian border; you'll board buses to reach smaller towns. In Slovenia, cuisine also reveals an Austro-Hungarian influence. Slovenian wines are among the best in the country.

ADRIATIC ISLAND HIDEAWAYS

See map this page

Scattered like jewels on the blue Adriatic waters are dozens of islands, each with its coves and bays that attract those who love the sun and sea. Among the most popular are the islands south of Opatija and Rijeka—Krk, Rab, Cres, and Lošinj; they offer delightful possibilities for short excursions or prolonged relaxation. The port towns are popular with yachters, and many nudists come to these islands to soak up the sun.

Island scenery is wild and majestic—luxuriant with subtropical plants and pine woods descending the western slopes, more arid and rocky bordering the eastern shores. Each island offers charming ports, swimming coves, and hideaway accommodations.

Largest of the Adriatic islands, Krk is linked by bridge with the mainland. The town of Krk has Roman monuments and mosaics as well as medieval fortifications. Malinska, on the lush west coast, offers shady walks by the sea and excursions by donkey as well. On the east coast is Vrbnik, an old and picturesque fortified village, encircled by walls and built on a rock rising above the sea. Its 15th-century church contains art treasures, and the town is known for its wines and cheese. Baška, a charming seaside resort on Krk's southeast coast, has a fascinating old quarter that lures many painters.

Rab's wooded mountain chain protects it from cold winds that sweep down from the north and east. The town of Rab, a popular resort, retains a medieval appearance with city walls, churches, and palaces dating from the 13th century.

Cres, in the middle of Kvarner Bay, is linked by bridge to Lošinj to the south. Facing a bay, the town of Cres has a well-preserved core with town gate, defensive towers, town hall, churches, and belfry. The tiny settlement of Osor occupies the isthmus between the islands.

Lošinj has long been a favorite of travelers; the Romans established summer homes here. Today's visitors enjoy its very mild climate, luxuriant vegetation, and modern amenities. Mali Lošinj, the main resort, draws many winter visitors; it's a popular stop for boaters. Just south is Veli Lošinj, a small maritime town with fine old buildings and lush parks.

■ **TOURING TIPS** Ferries link mainland ports with the islands, though you can also reach Krk across a new bridge. Ferry service links the island of Krk with the mainland towns of Crikvenica and Senj; the island of Rab with Senj and Jablanac (or with Baska on Krk); the island of Cres with Rijeka or Brestova; and the island of Lošinj with Pula or Zadar. Ferries also depart from Mali Lošinj to Rimini and Venice. The island towns of Rab and Mali Lošinj are the largest tourist resorts and main excursion centers.

PLITVICE'S LAKES & WATERFALLS

See map page 118

The country's best-known national park, Plitvice is one of Europe's gems. Thick forest rims a magnificent complex of 16 lakes, linked like a necklace of watery jewels by numerous waterfalls and cascades. The park is cut into the mountains of northwest Yugoslavia some 50 miles/80 km inland from the sea.

Driving inland from the coastal town of Senj, you become aware of the mountains only after climbing high above the sea to a fertile plain. Here you enjoy the peaceful scenes of the countryside—farmers plowing fields or pitching hay into bulbous stacks, village women wrapped in dark shawls exchanging the day's news,

Wooden walkways invite visitors to enjoy Plitvice's sparkling waterfalls, tumbling streams, and tree-rimmed lakes.

youngsters and their dogs herding animals in from the fields.

Many travelers regard the Plitvice lakes district as one of the most beautiful regions in Europe. The scenic park is lovely in any season. In spring, melting Balkan snows feed the lakes and thundering waterfalls. Lush greenery frames the blue-green lakes in summer. Autumn is a tranquil time, when still waters mirror their spectacular surroundings. Winter brings a white mantle of snow to the mountainous park.

From Lake Prošće, highest of the Plitvice lakes at some 2,000 feet/600 meters above sea level, water flows into a second lake, and from it spills over into a third. Filmy waterfalls and foaming cascades tumble over rocky ledges to connect the 16 lakes, which step down a total of several hundred feet.

Miles of paths wind through the park, edging some of the lakes and offering close views of certain waterfalls. Here and there, rough steps chiseled into the rock lead to a cave. From viewing terraces you can take in the broad scene of greenery-rimmed water, or you may prefer to find your own spot to linger, watching the play of light on water.

Water from the lowest lake flows northward as the Korana River. It offers excellent kayaking and fishing in lovely wooded country.

Several modern hotels serve park visitors. In restaurants you can enjoy trout or salmon from local lakes and rivers, or fresh crayfish caught near the upper end of Lake Kozjak, largest of the lakes.

■ **TOURING TIPS** Plitvice lies midway between Zagreb and Zadar, a 2- to 3-hour drive on asphalt roads from the Adriatic. If you're driving, plan ahead; rural villages have few tourist services. Coach excursions depart for the park from Zagreb and several Adriatic resorts.

ENCHANTING MOSTAR

From the first glimpse, Mostar has an exotic air. Against a dramatic backdrop of rugged purplish mountains, slim minarets jut skyward and rounded domes add an oriental note. They provide a visual reminder that for more than four centuries much of Yugoslavia was part of the Ottoman Empire.

Turkish forces occupied the region in 1463, and Eastern influences filtered into the architecture, religion, food, and other aspects of local life until the late 19th century.

Mostar's pride is its famous humpbacked stone bridge, built over the turquoise-colored Neretva River by the Turks in 1566. Pedestrians stream across the bridge—housewives carrying wicker baskets of produce, farmers guiding mule carts, workers toting wine barrels. Local boys consider it a test of courage to dive from the arch of the bridge 70 feet/21 meters into the chilly water. On the west bank of the river, a path winds down to a small sandy beach.

Stone houses and copper-domed mosques cluster upstream from the bridge. Along narrow lanes in the old section of Mostar, sloping stone roofs overhang houses whose high-walled courtyards once shielded Moslem women from the outside world.

A village bazaar atmosphere prevails in the restored Kujundžiluk (Goldsmiths' Street), where metalsmiths and other craftspeople work in the doorways of brightly painted shops facing a cobbled lane. You can visit the Karadžoz Beg mosque, notable for its graceful architecture and lavish interior decoration.

Mostar's rather stark business district dates from the Austrian occupation. On a slope above town is a memorial to World War II dead.

About 20 miles/32 km south of Mostar, Počitelj is a centuries-old Turkish frontier post on the banks of the Neretva River. The charming little fortified village has been carefully restored.

■ **TOURING TIPS** The most pleasant time to visit is in spring or early autumn; summer can be hot inland. From the Adriatic town of Kardeljevo (Ploče), road and railway head inland up the Neretva Valley through Mostar to Sarajevo; a network of buses also serves the region. Life proceeds at a leisurely place in the inland provinces, so allow ample time if you plan to tour the area. Yugoslavia's best white wine, made from Žilavaka grapes, comes from the village of Blagaj southeast of Mostar.

BOATING ON THE DRINA RIVER

Marking the frontier between Bosnia and Serbia, the Drina River is a favorite of boaters. In summer, groups raft downstream from Foča through relatively placid waters to Goražde, then continue through more turbulent rapids to Višegrad. Kayakers and canoeists also paddle through the moderately easy but exciting rapids. For information on river trips, contact the Yugoslav National Tourist Office (see page 128).

ALONG THE ISTRIAN COAST

See map page 118

Popular with European vacationers, the Istrian Peninsula offers a rocky coastline marked by small tree-rimmed bays and attractive coastal towns. Most travelers head for the lively activity of busy Adriatic resorts such as Portorož and Pula, or Opatija facing Kvarner Bay. However, you can also settle in smaller towns and explore at your leisure. Architecture is a delightful mix, frequently reflecting the eras of Venetian and Austro-Hungarian rule as well the more solid Yugoslavian style.

On the northwest coast, Piran perches on a rocky headland above a colorful harbor. Narrow streets and Venetian-inspired buildings are part of the old town's charm. Take a look at the remains of Piran's medieval walls, climb the cathedral belfry for a sweeping view, then enjoy refreshment at an outdoor restaurant.

Sheltered by hills, fashionable Portorož (Port of Roses) is known for its broad seaside promenades bordered with palm trees and roses. It also offers a good beach, numerous parks, luxury hillside hotels, and sophisticated after-dark entertainment.

Farther south, Poreč and Rovinj attract many artists. Founded by the Romans, Poreč contains ruins of ancient temples and the old city walls. However, its most important monument is the 6th-century basilica.

Rovinj, a lovely old seaside town, has an intriguing central district that is a labyrinth of crooked streets and brightly painted houses bordering a small harbor.

Near the peninsula's southern tip, busy Pula takes pride in its Roman arena. Today, the oval amphitheater is used for outdoor concerts, operatic performances, and an annual film festival. You'll also enjoy Pula's other Roman and medieval buildings, its archeological museum, and the bustling, colorful harbor.

Southeast coastal towns face island-studded Kvarner Bay. Largest of the resorts is Opatija, a delightfully old-fashioned resort that was a turn-of-the-century playground for Hapsburg aristocrats. Subtropical plants thrive in a balmy climate; the town is also noted for fine beaches and evening entertainment.

Attractive little towns dot the southeast coast. From the village of Volosko, in the suburbs of Opatija, you can

Swimmers, snorkelers, and sunbathers enjoy clear waters and sandy shore at Icici Beach on Istrian Peninsula.

walk along the coast to Lovran, an old town with luxuriant gardens and a 12th-century church and tower. The port of Rabac is one of the largest and most popular of the Kvarner coastal resorts.

■ **TOURING TIPS** Most visitors come here between May and October, but the Kvarner Bay resorts enjoy a mild winter climate that makes an off-season stopover enjoyable. Bus service connects the coastal towns. Motorboat excursions operate from the larger resorts. Ferry and hydrofoil services transport travelers to Rab, Krk, and other islands.

DANUBE CRUISE TO IRON GATE

East of Belgrade, the Danube River broadens impressively as it flows through the fertile Serbian plain, then becomes the border between Yugoslavia and Romania. More than a mile wide at Golubac, the river dramatically narrows through the awesome 90-mile/145-km Djerdap Gorge between Golubac and Kladovo. The most spectacular section of the river, known as the Iron Gate, is the deepest gorge in Europe. Best viewed from the river

itself, the gorge is accessible by hydrofoil on day trips from Belgrade between April and September.

Downstream from Belgrade, the Danube flows leisurely past scattered low islands, along banks planted in wine grapes, and past the impressive military fortress of Smederevo, built about 1420.

Farther downstream, near the Romanian border, you'll pass the 15th-century Turkish fortress of Ram and the ancient Golubac stronghold, which once defended the entrance to the gorge.

A spur of the Carpathian Mountains forces the mile-wide Danube into a narrow, rocky channel as it flows through the "Little" Djerdap Gorge. As the river drops more than 80 feet/24 meters in a series of rapids, ships bypass the white water in a navigation canal. You'll pass Lepenski Vir, where archeologists in 1965 discovered the site of a Danube fishing settlement dating from about 6000 B.C.

Continuing downstream past Donji Milanovac, the river enters the *Kazan*, or cauldron, the gorge of the "Great" Djerdap. Trapped between sheer rock walls rising to a height of 2,600 feet/1,800 meters, the Danube is channeled into a narrow torrent. The renowned Iron Gate section of the gorge, about 2 miles/3 km in length, encompasses a series of cataracts bypassed by another canal.

Now underwater on the Yugoslav side of the river is an old Roman road, cut into a rock wall over the water some 2,000 years ago. It once connected Golubac with Orsova. Above the river's narrowest point—433 feet/132 meters wide—a Roman tablet commemorates this astounding achievement.

The river widens as it approaches Kladovo, site of the massive Djerdap Hydroelectric Dam, a joint Yugoslav-Romanian project. In the Roman era, a bridge spanned the Danube near the site of Kladovo; the Emperor Trajan led his legions over it in quest of victory over Dacia (Romania).

■ **TOURING TIPS** From April through September, hydrofoil boats travel from Belgrade to Kladovo, departing about 6 A.M. and returning to Belgrade the same evening. You can make reservations through your Belgrade hotel or local travel agencies. It's a good idea to take snacks along to fortify you until the lunch stopover at Kladovo.

YUGOSLAV ARTS & CRAFTS

Yugoslavian handicrafts bear the imprint of the country's rich folklore. You'll find them in regional markets and in Narodna Radinost (folk crafts) shops and other stores located in larger towns and resorts.

Look for hand-embroidered articles with regional motifs, lace, national costumes, wood carvings, leather articles, cloth, handmade carpets, filigree jewelry, ceramics, tapestries, and paintings by Yugoslav artists.

Corfu, page 125

Méteóra, page 126

Corfu

G R E E C E

Kavala

Salonika

Thassos

Delphi, page 127

Cephalonia

Hios

Patras

Athens

Corinth

Cyclades Islands,
page 125

Map, page 126

Saronic Gulf
Islands, page 124

Cyclades

Greek Islands by Yacht,
page 123

Map, page 124

Dodecanese

Rhodes

Map, page 127

Heraklion

Samaria Gorge,
page 127

Crete

Corfu

Temple of Athena, Delphi

Naxos, Cyclades Islands

GREECE

What better way to enjoy Greece's unique appeal than on a leisurely island-hopping cruise through the Ionian and Aegean seas? Design your own trip by hydrofoil or interisland ferry, or if you prefer, concentrate on a single island such as Corfu.

To immerse yourself in the world of ancient Greece, travel to Delphi, where pilgrims came to consult the famed oracle. To learn more about Greek drama, attend a performance under the stars in one of the ageless open-air amphitheaters.

For a change of pace, seek out the medieval monasteries built atop rock pillars at Metéora. One of the country's natural wonders is the awesome Samaria Gorge on Crete.

THE GREEK ISLANDS BY YACHT

See map page 122

Round up a few friends, choose your islands, and board a yacht for an exciting and memorable Greek holiday. You can charter your own boat or, if you prefer, join a regularly scheduled tour on a motor yacht carrying 14 to 40 passengers.

Cruising through the islands, you can forget about hotels and restaurants, schedules, and constant repacking. Passengers sleep on board and eat both on the yacht and ashore. Yachts cruise to well-known islands but also pause at smaller isles off the cruise-ship routes.

On most boats, passengers sleep in narrow bunks, usually two to four to a compartment, with a small porthole. Bathing facilities are cramped. There's little cabin storage for clothes or purchases. Dress is casual (but bring appropriate attire for churches). Activities may include sunbathing, board games, and fishing. Most days you'll pause for swimming or snorkeling. You'll go ashore for shopping, sightseeing, and dinner at island restaurants.

Most charter yachts are based in the marinas of the Athens–Piraeus area, but others sail from Corfu, Rhodes, Thessaloníki, and other major ports. You can charter yachts of various sizes, with crew or without; or you can join a flotilla of small yachts, which are guided along a preplanned cruise route by a lead boat.

From April through early October, scheduled motor-yacht cruises depart weekly from Piraeus. A ferry often takes passengers out to the first island on the itinerary or back from the last one. For information on these trips, check with your travel agent. Write to the Greek National Tourist Organization (address on page 128) for trip-planning information.

■ **TOURING TIP** Peak-season rates for yacht charters apply from June through September; reduced rates may be obtained in other months. Some travel agents offer yacht-charter packages that include air travel, provisions, and cruise planning.

Along Hydra's busy waterfront you'll see interisland ferries, loaded donkeys, fishing and pleasure craft of all sizes.

DAY TRIPS TO THE SARONIC ISLANDS

Speedy hydrofoils dart back and forth between Athens's port of Piraeus and the islands of the Saronic Gulf, offering delightful opportunities for day trips.

In only 35 minutes you can be visiting Aegina, with its waterfront *tavernas,* white-sand beaches, and well-preserved Temple of Aphaia. In just over an hour you can be on rocky Hydra, where terraces of colorful villas hover above the harbor. If you prefer, you can head for Poros or Spetses, or one of the Peloponnesian port towns.

Hydrofoils are most popular with Athenians who own or lease beach houses on the islands near the city, but visitors also can use the boats to get to these busy retreats.

Aegina. Monuments dating from the 6th century B.C. dot the island, though most visitors come to enjoy its fine beaches and balmy climate. Relatively flat, Aegina is a favorite with cyclists; you can also get around by bus, taxi, and horse-drawn carriage.

From the port, you can travel south to the fishing village of Perdika, to the sandy beach at Agia Marina on the east coast, or along the northern shore to a country chapel at Kipseli and the waterfront village of Souvala.

Poros. South of Aegina, thickly wooded Poros has a lively port bordered by cafes and bars. Small boats ferry passengers to the island beaches of Askeli and Neorio, or to the mainland port of Galatas. Other island excursions include the monastery of Calavria and the sanctuary of Poseidon, traditional haven for shipwrecked mariners.

Hydra. The lively port and traditional architecture of cosmopolitan Hydra have inspired many painters. Windmills line the island's high mountain ridges, and several monasteries perch on bare knolls. Gleaming white houses and steeply terraced alleys climb the lower slopes.

Visitors can stroll along waterside paths, relax on splendid beaches, cruise around the island, enjoy the island's active night life, or travel by boat to mainland ports.

Spetses. Southernmost of the islands, Spetses offers a relaxed atmosphere, good beaches, and lush natural beauty. You'll want to visit Dappia Square, the open-air social center, and beaches around the island's rim. Colorful pebble mosaics ornament the town's narrow alleys. Several museums recall the island's maritime history. Small boats link the island port with the mainland village of Porto Heli.

■ **TOURING TIPS** Hydrofoils depart several times daily from Zea port in Piraeus to the Saronic Gulf islands and other destinations. The trip to Aegina takes only 35 minutes, while the excursion to Spetses takes 1 hour, 50 minutes. Reservations are advised, especially from May through September. Your travel agent can handle this, or you can contact the booking office at 8 Themistokleous Street in Piraeus. There are small hotels on all four islands.

DRAMA UNDER THE STARS

During the summer, ancient Greek dramas are performed in outdoor theaters in Athens; at Epidaurus, south of Corinth; at Dodoni, south of Ioannina in northwestern Greece; at Philippi, near Kavala in Macedonia; and on the island of Thassos.

From spring to autumn, sound-and-light shows retelling ancient history are presented in several languages in Athens, Corfu, and Rhodes.

Information and tickets are available from the Festivals Box Office, 4 Stadiou Street (in the Arcade), Athens; telephone 322-1459 or 322-3111, extension 240.

ISLAND-HOPPING IN THE CYCLADES

See map page 124

You could spend a lifetime traveling among the 1,400 Greek islands and never visit them all. Each has its distinct identity. Some are lush and green, others arid and rocky. Some have resort hotels and lively night life; many are relatively untouched by modern influence.

Typifying this variety is the Cyclades group, a few dozen islands in the central Aegean. Here you'll find whitewashed fishing villages rimmed by a deep blue sea, small chapels tucked in the folds of the hills, ancient monuments, and a history stretching back 5,000 years.

Ferry travel. If you have time and want to take an independent tour, you can sail aboard public ferries to islands off the main tourist routes, stopping as they pick up and discharge passengers, autos, and cargo.

Major islands—Mykonos, Naxos, Paros, Siros, Thera (Santorini), and Tinos—usually have daily ferry service from Piraeus. In summer, additional service links the islands. From Piraeus, it's a 5- to 6-hour trip to Mykonos or Paros, about 13 hours to Thera. Ferries call several times a week at other populated islands. Budget travelers usually book deck space; a second class ticket entitles you to a seat in the salon.

Which islands for you? Each island has its special appeal and atmosphere, but all share sunshine, beaches, hospitable residents—and numerous summer visitors. Accommodations are ample on Andros, Mykonos, Naxos, Paros, Siros, Thera (Santorini), and Tinos; smaller islands offer a slimmer selection. Most of the better hotels and restaurants close during the winter.

Travelers who enjoy activity and night life head for Mykonos. The sacred isle of Delos draws those interested in the monuments of antiquity. Paros and Naxos offer attractive towns, good beaches, and island excursions without large crowds. On Thera, travelers can climb onto donkeys for the journey to its main town, high on the slope of a volcanic crater.

Lesser-known islands offer small waterside villages, chapels and monasteries, quiet beaches, and a leisurely atmosphere. Distinctive windmills can be found on Serifos, Kea, and Sifnos. Many wealthy shipowners live on Andros, also known for its good swimming beaches and ruins of an ancient city at Palaiopolis. Mountainous Tinos has traces of Venetian architecture, numerous chapels, and the enormous Church of the Blessed Virgin.

Siros's shipbuilding industry gives it a different atmosphere than those of its fishing- and agriculture-based neighbors. Ios has a beautiful bay cutting into olive-clad hills; Amorgos is known for great orange limestone cliffs; Milos is volcanic in origin. The white, "cubist" architecture of the Cyclades is best seen on the remote islands of Sifnos and Folegandros.

■ **TOURING TIP** Rough seas can make crossings unpleasant when the strong north wind called the *meltémi* blows, from mid-July to mid-September. Three to six days of wind are followed by a similar period of calm. Winds are strongest from sunrise to noon; their force abates in afternoon and evening.

LUSH & COSMOPOLITAN CORFU

See map page 122

Travelers accustomed to the austere barrenness of the Aegean islands delight in the greenery and mild climate of Corfu (Kérkira), a verdant oasis in the Ionian Sea.

Corfu has a cosmopolitan legacy. Protected by the Venetians for more than 400 years, it reveals Italian touches in its main town and the ancient harbor fortresses. French troops occupied Corfu during the Napoleonic era, followed by British rule until 1864.

Corfu town. Located on the east coast, the island's largest town blends architectural styles. Tree-lined avenues sweep through the modern sector, contrasting with a maze of pedestrian lanes in the old town. From atop the medieval harbor fortifications, you'll enjoy broad vistas.

A favorite place for people-watching is the Spianada, largest of the town's squares. Along one side, you can relax at cafe tables in the shade of arcades, a reminder of the French era. At the north end of the Spianada is Saints Michael and George Palace, once the residence for British high commissioners.

West of the Spianada, you'll discover the old Venetian section, a labyrinth of cobbled walkways lined by multistoried houses. Shutters and ironwork balconies frame vertical windows. Along Spiridon Street or Dousmani Street you can shop for *flokati* rugs, worry beads, and other souvenirs. The entire island shuts down for a 3-hour midday meal and siesta.

The Church of Saint Spiridon, honoring the town's patron saint, stands in the middle of the marketplace. A splendid example of Venetian architecture is the town hall, built in 1663. Other buildings reflect the French influence in their arches and colonnades, and the Georgian style popular in 19th-century England.

(Continued on next page)

Streetside cafe in Corfu offers a shady place to pause for refreshment, converse with friends, or watch passersby.

Exploring the island. Roads follow the coast through a succession of small fishing ports and beaches, climbing to whitewashed villages tucked into the green hills. Buses depart from Neo Frourio Square and San Rocco Square in Corfu for other parts of the island; you can also arrange sightseeing by rental car, taxi, or motor bike.

South of town, swimmers find a good public beach at Mon Repos. You'll want to stop at Kanoni viewpoint, where you gaze down on two island monasteries.

Gastouri is the site of Achilleion Palace, built in 1890 as a retreat for Empress Elisabeth of Austria. Daytime visitors enjoy its terraced gardens above the sea; at night the building becomes a casino.

Weathered cliffs and white-sand beaches rim the rugged west coast. Most visitors head for Paleokastritsa, renowned for its clear waters, good fishing, and seafood restaurants. If you prefer less-crowded coves for swimming and sunning, try Glifada or Agios Gordis beaches.

■ **TOURING TIPS** You can fly to Corfu from Athens, or travel by ferry from the Greek towns of Igomenitsa or Patras or the Italian port of Brindisi. Horse-drawn carriages transport passengers around the central district, but you should plan to explore the old town on foot. You'll find the cooler hours of early evening (between 5 and 8) best for unhurried shopping.

Medieval monastery buildings top rocky pillars at Metéora, near Kalambaka. Visitors must climb steps cut into rock.

ANCIENT REFUGES OF METÉORA

Looming above the fertile plain of Thessaly in central Greece is an awesome sight: a strange grouping of gigantic rock pillars rising up to 1,800 feet/550 meters in height. Topping some of the pinnacles are the medieval monasteries of Metéora. These ancient refuges symbolize a way of life that is almost extinct: an austere regimen of infinite labor, discomfort, and self-denial.

Located 6 miles/9 km northwest of Kalambaka, the monasteries were originally refuges from medieval warfare. Ancient hermits sought solitude in the rifts and caves of the pillars, but the first monasteries were not built until the 14th century. While Serbians and Byzantines battled for control of the Thessalian plain, the hermits could meditate, undisturbed by fighting below.

After the first monastery was founded on the Great Meteoron, other hermitages evolved into monasteries. By the late 16th century, 24 rose atop the black pillars. Women were excluded, and inhabitants lived an austere life. For centuries the sole access was by rope ladder or by net basket, which the monks hoisted by windlass. Today, some of the monasteries are historical monuments; only four are still inhabited.

A road winds near the bases of the pillars, and visitors climb steps cut into the rock to reach the buildings. To visit the next monastery, you must descend from one pinnacle and climb another. Though some of the stone stairways are long and steep, they're not dangerous to climb. Women are expected to wear skirts, and apparel should also cover their shoulders.

Oldest and most important of the monasteries is the Monastery of the Transfiguration, built about 1350. Perched atop the Great Meteoron, an almost perpendicular cliff, it is reached by a strenuous climb. Its chapel contains an unusual 12-sided dome and several beautiful frescoes.

A drawbridge connects the monastery of Ayios Stefanos to the main cliff. Old, treasured wood carvings and icons have been preserved here. Ayias Trias tops a particularly forbidding pinnacle; to reach it you climb a steep flight of steps cut into the rocky face.

Largest of the retreats is fortresslike Varlaam, notable for its restored frescoes in the chapel and a small museum containing ecclesiastical treasures. Ayias Roussani, now a convent, is located on the lowest rock and is less difficult to reach than most of the monasteries.

■ **TOURING TIPS** Guided bus tours depart from Athens for Metéora, or you can hire a car with a driver-guide. If you drive, you'll find the road good, but narrow and winding the last few miles. Many road signs are in English as well as Greek, but be sure to get detailed directions before you start out. Spring is the best season for traveling in this part of Greece.

SEEKING THE SPIRIT OF DELPHI

See map page 126

To the ancient Greeks, Delphi was the center of the world, the point where earth touched heaven. Pilgrims journeyed to the Delphic oracle to learn of the future. Today, travelers visit these ruins in search of the past.

Located about 110 miles/180 km northwest of Athens, Delphi is a 3- to 4-hour trip by car or bus from Athens, through Thebes and Levadia. You can travel independently or join a group.

On the tree-covered southern slope of Mount Parnassus, the land forms a natural amphitheater facing the Gulf of Corinth. Sheltered at its base is the sanctuary of Apollo, antiquity's leading pilgrimage destination for many centuries. Visitors climbed difficult mountain paths to reach the shrine and seek the oracle's advice. Delphi lay buried for 15 centuries, until French archeologists began excavations in the late 19th century.

If you're touring independently, take along an illustrated English-language guidebook as you seek the spirit of Delphi, a site important in Greek legends.

Begin your walk at the sanctuary of Athena Pronaia, below the road on a narrow terrace surrounded by olive trees. Known as Marmaria (The Marbles), it includes the 4th-century B.C. Tholos, or rotunda, one of Delphi's finest Doric monuments. Beyond are the gymnasium and other facilities where athletes trained.

Along the roadside, a sign identifies the Castalian Spring, where priests and pilgrims cleansed themselves before presenting their questions to the oracle.

Ruins of ancient treasuries (small temples containing offerings), arcades, and monuments commemorating great military victories flank the Sacred Way, the traditional route followed by Greek pilgrims nearly 3,000 years ago.

From the southeastern side, a flagstone path winds uphill to the Temple of Apollo, a large Doric temple dominating the site. Ancient philosophers once inscribed maxims—such as "Know thyself" and "Avoid excess"—on these walls. Here the oracle Pythia pronounced her prophecies, which were interpreted and written down by priests and presented to visitors as advice from the gods.

At the end of the Sacred Way is the open-air theater, built of white marble with space for 5,000 spectators. It overlooks the Temple of Apollo and a spectacular panorama. Higher on the slope, rimmed by pine trees, is the 7,000-seat stadium, once the site of musical and athletic competitions.

Statues, friezes, altars, and other treasures from ancient Delphi, dating from the 6th century B.C., can be seen in the modern museum.

■ **TOURING TIPS** Greeks consider May and September the best months for touring; in midsummer the country is crowded, and searing sun beats down on the old ruins. Delphi is most spellbinding during the serene hours of early morning or early evening. From April to mid-October, gates to the sacred city are open weekdays from 7:30 A.M. to 7:30 P.M., Sundays and holidays from 10 to 6. Hours are shortened during the winter.

HIKING CRETE'S SAMARIA GORGE

Largest of the Greek islands, Crete was the birthplace of Minoan culture, Europe's oldest civilization. The island's archeological treasures draw many travelers, but this ancient island has scenic treasures as well.

Near the island's western end is the remarkable Samaria Gorge, where hikers can enjoy a majestic 12-mile/19-km nature walk through wild landscape. You can hike on your own or join a group.

From Haniá on the northwest coast, you travel south to the plateau surrounding the village of Omalos. A steep, zigzag path descends about 2,500 feet/800 meters into the tremendous gorge, which splits the cliffs for about 8 miles/12 km down to the sea.

Awesome in its grandeur and wild beauty, the gorge sometimes narrows to less than 15 feet/5 meters. Sheer walls rise high to hide the sunlight. A clear mountain stream rushes past. Trees cling to the rocks, birds swoop overhead, and seasonal wildflowers abound.

From the gorge entrance, it takes casual hikers 4 to 5 hours to reach the sea at the small port of Aghia Rouméli. After refreshments at the cafe or snack bar, you'll have time to relax on the beach or go for a swim before returning by boat and bus to Haniá.

■ **TOURING TIPS** From Piraeus, it's a 12-hour trip by ferry to Crete; boats dock at Heráklion or Haniá. Local tourist offices organize guided trips to Samaria Gorge. Hikers are transported from Haniá to the gorge entrance; in late afternoon, a boat arrives at Aghia Rouméli to take hikers to Sfakia, where they board a waiting bus for Haniá.

GREEK HANDICRAFTS

A permanent showroom of Greek handicrafts is located in Athens at 9 Mitropoleos Street, near Syntagma Square. Organized by the National Association of Greek Handicrafts, the exhibit displays examples of all types of Greek popular art, including handwoven textiles, embroidery, carpets and rugs, pottery, metalwork, and woodwork. The exhibit offers an overview of Greek handicrafts and direct contact with craftspeople. Other showrooms are located in cities throughout the country.

GOVERNMENT TOURIST OFFICES IN THE UNITED STATES

Below are addresses of European government tourist offices in the United States. Contact the regional representative nearest you for information on tourist travel within the country.

Addresses are updated each printing (see page 2) but offices do shift locations. We suggest you re-check addresses before writing if possible.

Austrian National Tourist Office

New York, NY 11010: 500 Fifth Avenue, Suite 2009-2022
Chicago, IL 60611: 500 North Michigan Avenue, Suite 544
Houston, TX 77056: 4800 San Felipe, Suite 500
Los Angeles, CA 90025: 11601 Wilshire Boulevard, Suite 2480

Belgian Tourist Office

New York, NY 10151: 745 Fifth Avenue, Suite 714

British Tourist Authority

New York, NY 10019: 40 West 57th Street, Suite 320
Chicago, IL 60611: John Hancock Center, Suite 3320, 875 North Michigan Avenue
Dallas, TX 75201-1814: Cedar Maple Plaza, 2305 Cedar Springs Road
Los Angeles, CA 90071: World Trade Center, Suite 450, 350 South Figueroa

Danish Tourist Board

New York, NY 10017: 655 Third Avenue

Finnish Tourist Board

New York, NY 10017: 655 Third Avenue

French Government Tourist Office

New York, NY 10020: 610 Fifth Avenue
Beverly Hills, CA 90212: 9454 Wilshire Boulevard, Suite 303
Chicago, IL 60611: 645 North Michigan Avenue
Dallas, TX 75258: P.O. Box 58610, 2050 Stemmons Freeway
San Francisco, CA 94102: 1 Hallidie Plaza, Suite 250

German National Tourist Office

New York, NY 10017: 747 Third Avenue, 33rd Floor
Los Angeles, CA 90071-2997: 444 South Flower Street, Suite 2230

Greek National Tourist Organization

New York, NY 10022: 645 Fifth Avenue
Chicago, IL 60601: 168 North Michigan Avenue
Los Angeles, CA 90017: 611 West Sixth Street, Suite 1998

Iceland Tourist Board

New York, NY 10017: 655 Third Avenue

Irish Tourist Board

New York, NY 10017: 757 Third Avenue, 19th Floor

Italian Government Travel Office—E.N.I.T.

New York, NY 10111: 630 Fifth Avenue, Suite 1565
Chicago, IL 60611: 500 North Michigan Avenue, Suite 1046
San Francisco, CA 94108: 360 Post Street, Suite 801

Luxembourg National Tourist Office

New York, NY 10017: 801 Second Avenue, 13th Floor

Netherlands Board of Tourism

New York, NY 10017: 355 Lexington Avenue, 21st Floor
Chicago, IL 60601: 225 North Michigan Avenue, Suite 326
San Francisco, CA 94105: 90 New Montgomery Street, Suite 305

Norwegian Tourist Board

New York, NY 10017: 655 Third Avenue

Portuguese National Tourist Office

New York, NY 10036-4704: 590 Fifth Avenue

National Tourist Office of Spain

New York, NY 10022: 665 Fifth Avenue
Beverly Hills, CA 90211: 8383 Wilshire Boulevard, Suite 9960
Chicago, IL 60611: 845 North Michigan Avenue

Swedish Tourist Board

New York, NY 10017: 655 Third Avenue

Swiss National Tourist Office

New York, NY 10020: 608 Fifth Avenue
San Francisco, CA 94108: 250 Stockton Street

Yugoslav National Tourist Office

New York, NY 10111: 630 Fifth Avenue, Suite 280

EXPANDING YOUR EUROPEAN ADVENTURES

Transportation ▪ *Accommodations* ▪ *Special Interests*

For those travelers who maintain that half the fun is in the planning, we've added this special section to spark your imagination. In these pages we suggest ways to perk up your journey and to tailor the trip to your personal interests and hobbies. Have a great trip!

TRAVEL INFORMATION

If you enjoy trip planning, you'll spend many pleasant hours collecting ideas from books and magazines, newspaper articles, travel newsletters, and well-traveled friends with similar tastes.

Each European government has tourist representatives in the United States to promote travel to its country (see page 128). These offices can provide maps; city and regional brochures; hotel and restaurant listings in various price categories; information on special events, sports and entertainment, and special-interest touring; and details about obtaining rail passes and other travel bargains.

If you have one or two specific hobbies or activities in mind, be sure to mention them in your request for information.

The British and Netherlands tourist offices also offer detailed maps, guides, and booklets on specific subjects at moderate cost.

Once you are in Europe, you'll find at least one tourist information office in nearly every city and town of any size. Often the office is located in or near the railway station, town hall, or market square. Check with this office for information about local attractions and excursions, accommodations, and events.

TRANSPORTATION TIPS

Whether you rent a car for independent touring or use trains, buses, and other public transportation, planning can help you obtain maximum enjoyment and value as you travel.

Exploring by rental car

Driving in Europe gives you a delightful sense of freedom. You can explore any road you fancy, stop where you want, and set your own pace without worrying about schedules. You become an adventurer, probing out-of-the-way places that public transportation doesn't reach.

Making arrangements. The cost of rental cars has soared in recent years, making it more important than ever to plan your trip if you want to gain maximum value for your money. Short-term rentals are usually more expensive per day than those for a week or longer.

Most car rental companies offer two plans: you can pay a basic daily charge plus a specified add-on amount per kilometer driven, or a higher flat rate with unlimited mileage. Expect extra charges for optional insurance, taxes, and gasoline. Talk to your travel agent about fly/drive trips; these offer flexibility at fixed rates.

The nation in which you rent a car can make a difference in costs. Charges vary from country to country, as do Value Added Taxes (VAT). Arranging credit card payment when you reserve your car saves problems about making a deposit or settling your final bill. Some companies offer prepayment plans.

Most large cities have car rental offices, but you can avoid the anxieties of city driving by taking delivery of your car at the airport or in a suburban or regional town.

Before you start out. When you pick up your car, be sure it has a "green card" (it indicates third-party insurance, and may need to be shown when crossing national borders) and a parking disk (for use in city restricted parking zones). Before you leave the rental agency, be sure you know how to operate the headlights and dimmers, windshield wipers, turn signals, and horn.

Don't try to drive without a good guidebook and detailed road maps that show route numbers, distances, and towns along the way. Be aware of national motoring regulations and

customs. Seat belts are mandatory in some countries. Drunk drivers face severe penalties—even imprisonment—in Scandinavia.

Drive defensively. On country roads you'll meet hay wagons, cyclists, and even meandering cows and sheep.

International road signs. Graphic symbols on international road signs minimize confusion from language barriers. The signs are simple in design and based on geometric shapes. Familiarize yourself with the signs so you can recognize them quickly.

Traveling by train

Europeans ride the railways everywhere. When you join them, you watch the countryside unfold. At the same time, you can rest, read up on the next destination, or converse with fellow passengers.

More than 100,000 miles/160,000 km of track crisscross Western Europe. High-speed trains, such as the TEE (Trans-Europe-Express), IC (InterCity) and EC (EuroCity) express trains, and the TGV in France, link the larger cities and vie with each other in speed and service. Many of the fastest express trains are first-class, reserved seating only.

Trains depart and arrive in the heart of the city. Many services are available in large city rail stations. Often there's a tourist information office where you can book local lodgings. Signs with symbols direct travelers to various services.

Eurailpasses. If you plan extensive travel over long distances, the Eurailpass can be a remarkable bargain. It is valid in 16 countries for unlimited first-class rail travel—and some ferry, steamer, and bus transportation. You need a separate BritRail Pass for British trains.

You can buy a Eurailpass for periods of 15 or 21 days, or 1, 2, or 3 months. Travelers under 26 years of age can purchase a 2nd class Eurail Youthpass for 1 or 2 months. Your pass lets you avoid standing in ticket lines; just show it to the conductor along with your passport. You still must stand in line for seat reservations and TEE reservations. The Eurailpass eliminates the TEE surcharge but not the seat booking charge.

National travel passes. If you plan to visit just one or two countries, a national or regional transportation pass may be the most economical option. Nearly every country in Western Europe has its own transportation pass; contact the appropriate tourist office for information. Some offer discounted rates to senior travelers.

A Swiss Holiday Card, for example, can be purchased for first or second class travel for 4, 8, or 15 days, or 1 month; it covers travel on trains, postal coaches, lake steamers, most private railroads, and streetcars and buses in many Swiss cities.

If you're traveling extensively in Scandinavia, you can purchase a Scandinavian Rail Pass for either first or second class rail travel and limited ferry travel within the four countries; the pass also entitles the holder to a 50% discount on other routes.

Among the French National Railroads plans is Train + Auto service, which combines long-distance train travel with car rental.

Travelers who plan extensive rail travel may want to obtain a copy of the Thomas Cook *International Timetable*, which lists schedules for most European routes. National railways also issue rail schedules.

Day excursions. You can also use the train for short day excursions from the main cities to countryside destinations. Netherlands Railways, for example, has day excursion tickets to popular destinations in all parts of the country; the price includes admission fees.

Narrow-gauge and cogwheel railways wind through the mountain valleys and into the high peaks in Switzerland and Austria. Britain is proud of many small 19th-century railways that have been preserved and are now operated for tourists.

Board the local bus

Regional and local buses allow you to travel to many towns and suburban destinations where trains do not go. Regional buses usually depart near the train station. Local buses may depart from the station, or near the town hall or main square. Often you'll find a tourist information office nearby where you can learn about interesting destinations accessible by public transportation.

Europe from the water

One of the most pleasant ways to enjoy the European countryside is from the water—sailing along rivers and canals, through farm land and forest, past waterside villages and sturdy castles. You'll see farmers working in the fields and anglers fishing.

Hotel boats. Informal "hotel boats" cruise the inland waterways of Britain and northern Europe. Onboard accommodations allow you to relax as you glide along scenic rivers and canals. Your travel agent or the appropriate tourist office can provide information on many trips.

You can cruise along the River Thames in England, the Shannon in Ireland, and the Rhine and Danube rivers on the Continent.

Trips by canal boat or barge offer intimate glimpses of rural life. Among the routes available are Holland's bulb fields, France's wine country, and Sweden's Göta Canal.

If you want a look at magnificent coastal scenery, board the informal Norwegian coastal steamer that cruises north from Bergen along the scenic fjord coast; it stops at more than 30 northern ports to deliver passengers, mail, and cargo.

In the Greek isles, large yachts cruise the island-dotted waters, stopping for sightseeing, shopping, or swimming at islands in the Cyclades, Dodecanese, or Ionian groups.

Self-drive rental boats. If you're happiest handling the wheel yourself, why not rent a boat for a holiday afloat? You can arrange for cabin cruisers, narrow canal boats, or yachts by the week and sail Europe's inland waterways. Boats vary in size, with berths for 2 to 8 people. If you prefer, charter a boat with crew.

In Britain, you can rent boats to cruise along the River Thames or penetrate the maze of waterways in the Norfolk Broads. In Ireland, rental boats cruise along the River Shannon and the Grand Canal.

You'll see boats everywhere in Holland; you can hire cruisers and yachts for sailing on Dutch lakes, canals, and estuaries.

Scenic districts that are popular with boaters in France include Burgundy's rivers and canals, Brittany, and the Canal du Midi in southwestern France.

Summer trips by canoe, kayak, or river raft are another way to enjoy the European countryside from the water. Participants stay in riverside hotels or camp along the waterway. Among the organized excursions are trips on Sweden's canals and paddling trips on France's Dordogne and Vézère rivers; write to tourist offices to learn about additional excursions.

Day excursions. Most of Europe's larger towns began as ports, and you'll usually find at least one boat trip where you can see the city's harbor, river, lake, or canals from a watery perspective.

Horse-drawn wagons

Another way to get acquainted with the rural countryside at a leisurely pace is in a horse-drawn wagon. Though certainly not for every traveler, these wagons offer a delightful family holiday and opportunities to meet local people.

Although you must harness and drive the horse yourself, you don't have to be an accomplished equestrian. Before you start out, the operator will instruct you on the care of your horse and the operation of your wagon equipment. He'll suggest good travel routes and places where you can stop along the way.

Ireland is one of the best countries for traveling in this style, because there's no language barrier. Operators of horse-drawn "gypsy caravan" trips are based in counties Cork, Kerry, and Wicklow. At vari-

ous times, operators have offered similar excursions in France, Austria, Germany, Switzerland, and Denmark. If this type of holiday appeals to you, inquire from tourist offices if such trips are currently available.

Cycling excursions

You'll need an adventurous spirit, a bit of energy, and ample time—but if you have all three, consider making part of your European tour by bicycle. In countries like Holland and Denmark, you'll see cyclists everywhere, pedaling to work, school, and market. For more on cycling, see page 137.

Other ways to get around

If you're an active traveler, you can combine a love of the outdoors with more energetic pursuits. If you enjoy horses, inquire about equestrian holidays. Many Europeans enjoy horseback touring and riding holidays, and equestrian packages are available in some countries.

Hiking is a popular pastime in Europe, and you'll find hikes and walks to suit any level of proficiency and amount of time. For more ideas on hikes and walks, see page 136.

In the mountains, cable cars and teleferics allow you to reach the high peaks and pastures with minimum effort.

LODGINGS WITH ATMOSPHERE

During your travels in Europe, you can live in regal comfort in an elegant castle hotel, snuggle down in a cozy country inn, stay with a farm family, or rent your own chalet or cottage as a base for nearby sightseeing. European accommodations offer some enjoyable options that can add extra pleasure to your visit. Government tourist offices (addresses on page 128) can provide specific information on some of their distinctive hostelries.

Castles & châteaux

As you travel in the European countryside, you'll discover many ancient castles, baronial mansions, and old monasteries that have been trans-

formed into delightful hotels. When you cross the narrow bridge over the old moat to reach a castle's inner courtyard, you enter another era. Your imagination is quickly captured by the fairy-tale aura of these buildings, where you dine and rest in settings once reserved for nobility. From your tower room, you can gaze in a lordly fashion over villages, fields, and vineyards.

Castle hotels and stately homes have diverse charms, but they reflect a certain style in appointments and way of living. Some serve their guests fish or game from the estate or wine made from grapes grown in the castle vineyards. Frequently your host is also the owner; some buildings have housed members of a single family for many generations.

Not all castle accommodations are grandiose; some lodgings are relatively intimate. Rates vary, from surprisingly reasonable at some hotels to expensive at those offering elegant appointments and cuisine.

Country inns

When you venture off the well-trodden routes, you'll discover charming country inns and hotels where individuality is the key. Many are family owned and operated hostelries

whose proprietors take a personal interest in serving their guests in an informal atmosphere.

You can choose among thatch-roofed pubs, timbered inns, mountain chalets, and country villas. Most inns have only a modest number of rooms, which may be decorated in regional style. Some country hotels offer praiseworthy cuisine; in small inns, the owner may also be the chef.

A sampling of offerings

Each country offers accommodations with special appeal. The brief descriptions below can only hint at your options.

Austria. Palaces and imperial residences that once housed Austrian nobility have been converted into gracious hotels with the charm and elegance of an earlier era.

In the country, you'll find mountain inns serving Alpine hikers, charming hotels overlooking the Danube, or lakeside inns for enjoying sailing and swimming. Information on Austrian hotels may be obtained from the Austrian National Tourist Office.

Belgium. Belgian country hotels range from elegant country estates to family-operated inns. Some occupy historic buildings or offer riverside or mountain settings. Many take pride in their cuisine. Information on Belgian hotels of special interest is available from the Belgium Tourist Office.

Hotel reservations throughout the country can be made through Belgium Tourist Reservations at P.B. 41, 1000 Brussels 23.

Britain. It's easy to return to the days of chivalry in Britain. Historic strongholds there are marvelous settings for imaginary medieval living. You may pass a knight's armor in the hall on your way to your canopied bed. If you'd like to spend a weekend as a guest at a British country estate with the marquess or duke as your host, it can be arranged discreetly and courteously by a London agency—for a hefty price. You'll get acquainted with your host over tea, take a tour of the house and grounds, dress for dinner and partake with the family and other guests, and spend the night in a room furnished with antiques.

Or consider the great Victorian and Edwardian hotels built in the mid-19th century. Spacious and uncrowded, they echo with memories of a more leisurely age.

You really haven't seen the English countryside until you sample some of the delightful country inns and pubs along the rural byways. Here, hospitality comes with a thatched roof, a resident ghost, or a tale of smugglers.

For information on castle hotels, overnight visits to stately homes, country inns, and other hotels with special appeal, write to the British Tourist Authority.

France. Travelers who relish the luxurious life enjoy France's châteaux hotels. These renowned establishments can be found in all parts of the country—perched atop cliffs, commanding valleys and rivers, surrounded by manicured fields. Each has its own personality.

Other elegant country hotels occupy former abbeys, coaching inns, mills, and manor houses. You'll also find country hospitality in a simple, family-run *auberge* or a charming *relais,* where your room may be furnished in provincial style and overlook a garden, a vineyard, or a placidly flowing river.

Many French country hotels and inns pride themselves on their cuisine and wine cellars; others provide a pleasant springboard for great eating at notable restaurants in the area.

Some of these hotels belong to an international association—Relais de Campagne, Châteaux-Hotels, and Relais Gourmands. Other excellent country hotels and inns belong to the Logis de France federation, the Petits Nids de France, or other groups. For more information, contact the French Government Tourist Office.

Germany. Many of the fine old castles of Central Europe date from the Middle Ages, when they were built as defensive fortresses. Feudal rulers often collected tolls from passing travelers. Later castles were built as country residences or retreats. About 50 German castle hotels belong to an association called Gast im Schloss (Guest in a Castle).

Country hotels in Germany occupy old coaching inns, renovated farmhouses and breweries, cozy forest hideaways, country guest houses, and hotels near thermal springs. Some are furnished with regional antiques. Many belong to the Romantik Hotels association. Numerous family-run hostelries belong to Ringhotels, an association of individually operated hotels. For information, write to the German National Tourist Office.

Greece. In eight Greek villages, the National Tourist Organization of Greece is restoring and conserving traditional buildings to house visitors. They offer a taste of Greek village life with modern amenities. Several are located on islands, others in mountain or country settings. For information, contact the Greek National Tourist Organization.

Ireland. Castles in Ireland were built for strength rather than beauty. Dating from the 12th century, they evoke memories of the country's colorful families and tempestuous history. Several now operate as hotels, offering warm hospitality amid luxurious furnishings.

Charming country hotels are scattered across the Irish countryside—overlooking the sea, beside lakes and rivers, on wooded estates, in the hills. Many are family owned and operated. Some are small and elegant; many are informal. Some feature Continental cuisine, but most serve traditional Irish country fare. More information is available from the Irish Tourist Board.

In Ireland, the Irish Tourist Board operates a Central Reservations Service at 14 Upper O'Connell Street, Dublin 1, where you can book all types of accommodations throughout the country (using MasterCard and VISA credit cards only). Rentals of cars, cottages, cabin cruisers, and horse-drawn caravans can also be made through the office.

Italy. Many of Italy's medieval and Renaissance castles and patrician villas have been converted into elegant hotels and restaurants. You can also stay in former palaces; in converted convents, cloisters, and monasteries; and in historic town houses and country villas once owned by Italian aristocrats. The Italian Government Travel Office can provide information on hotels of special interest.

Luxembourg. Travelers in Luxembourg find enjoyable country hotels in the Ardennes, in Little Switzerland, and along the Moselle. Many are family operated. Some are relatively elegant; others are quite informal. For an illustrated hotel directory, contact the Luxembourg National Tourist Office.

Netherlands. You can sleep under the roof of a country castle, stroll through its gardens or woods, and dine by candlelight amid antiques.

In the countryside you'll find many small, cozy, typically Dutch hotels. Usually varying in size from 8 to 20 rooms, they range from family hotels to country houses.

Dutch hotels have set up the Netherlands Reservation Centre (NRC), P.O. Box 404, 2260 AK Leidschendam to arrange hotel reservations throughout the country. For information, contact the Netherlands Board of Tourism.

Portugal. Castles, palaces, monasteries, and other historic buildings in all parts of the country have been converted to *pousadas* by the Portuguese Tourist Organization; other pousadas have been specially built. You'll find these inns in towns, mountain areas, and in the countryside. To maintain a welcoming atmosphere, most are relatively small. They are furnished in Portuguese style, and you'll usually find local foods and wines on the menu. For information on pousadas, contact the Portuguese National Tourist Office.

Scandinavia. You'll find an engaging informality and hospitality when you stay in country hotels in Scandinavia. Many enjoy scenic settings overlooking lakes, fjords, and other waterways.

Tucked away in Denmark's rolling green hills and farmlands are many charming country inns, ranging from simple-but-comfortable to luxurious. When you spend the night in a Danish *kro*, you may be staying in a cheery roadside guest house that is hundreds of years old.

In Norway, Sweden, and Finland, you'll find a number of mountain chalets, inns, and lakeside hotels where guests enjoy accommodations on a pension basis. In Norway and Sweden, fjord hotels and manor houses serve much the same purpose as Danish country inns. Situated in scenic locations, they have a distinctly Scandinavian character and charm. Skåne, Sweden's southernmost province, has its own unique inns, built by royal command during the 17th and 18th centuries. For detailed information, write to the appropriate government tourist office.

Spain. Many historic buildings in all parts of the country have been converted into government-operated *paradores* (see page 108), renowned for atmospheric settings, warm hospitality, and regional menus. Other historic buildings have been converted into luxury hotels. For information on hotels of unusual interest, contact the National Tourist Office of Spain.

Switzerland. Some of Switzerland's historic hotels are situated in parklike grounds; others enjoy a dramatic site edging a lake or dominating a town from a wooded slope.

Country inns abound in Switzerland. Most are relatively small, simple, immaculate, and family run. A few are luxuriously appointed; others have baths down the hall. Some inns offer regional food specialties. For information on historic hotels or country inns, contact the Swiss National Tourist Office.

Yugoslavia. Between the 13th and 16th centuries, feudal noblemen and monks built fortified castles and monasteries in Northern Croatia and Southern Slovenia to protect themselves against invading Turks. Some

of these strongholds have been converted into hotels, providing guests with old world settings and modern conveniences. For information, contact the Yugoslav National Tourist Office.

Farm & home visits

Instead of sightseeing as a tourist, why not pause in your travels and live with a European family for a few days as a paying guest? A farm vacation is a healthy and relaxing change of pace, a chance to get acquainted and share ideas with people of another culture, and a great way to beat the high cost of traveling. Farm holidays are especially popular for families traveling with children.

You can stay on a farm in Belgium, Britain, France, Germany, Ireland, Switzerland, and in the Scandinavian countries. Write to the appropriate government tourist office for information. Rural families in other countries also accept paying guests, but sometimes you can't find out about them until you're on the scene.

You can also make arrangements through one of the organizations that coordinate home-based holidays in Europe. Visitors become paying house guests—staying not only with families in rural areas, but also in towns and villages.

Usually you'll stay in rooms in the farmhouse and take your meals with the family. You'll enjoy a warm welcome, a clean room with a comfortable bed, and delicious hearty food—but you may have to share the bathroom with the family. Most farms take only a few guests at a time in order to preserve the family atmosphere. Some farms offer a separate cottage with cooking facilities so you can come and go as you please.

Unless you can communicate easily in the local language, make sure that at least one member of the host family speaks English. A foreign language phrase book and dictionary will help you communicate your basic needs, but it's pleasant to be able to exchange ideas more fully. Pick an area where you have access to transportation and several nearby destinations.

Bed-and-breakfast accommodations

Budget travelers have popularized the economy of bed-and-breakfast accommodations, but these lodgings have more to offer. If you enjoy the informality of home stays, you'll appreciate the friendly atmosphere that is an integral part of a well-run operation. You'll spot "bed-and-breakfast" and "zimmer frei" signs that welcome you to inquire.

You'll have your own room, usually with a sink, but often you must share the bathroom with other guests. Each morning, guests gather for a hearty, home-cooked breakfast, then branch out for independent excursions or travel.

Entire books and directories are devoted to dwellings offering bed-and-breakfast accommodations. You'll come across traveler-recommended lodgings in your readings and during your travels. You can make arrangements in advance or book accommodations on the spot.

Cottages, chalets, cabins

Do as the Europeans do: Rent a house or cottage, a chalet or cabin, in an area that appeals to you, and use it as your base for day trips to nearby attractions. An increasingly popular idea with experienced travelers, short-term rentals offer a chance to become part of the community.

You'll find vacation cottages, mountain chalets, and even log cabins available for rent by the week, with accommodations ranging from luxurious to rustic. Some, such as many in Ireland and Scandinavia, may be clustered in a popular vacation area—by the sea, on a lake, or in the mountains. In eight Greek villages, traditional dwellings have been restored and converted into guest houses with modern amenities (see page 132). Visitors in France can rent country cottages (*gîtes ruraux*). For more information on alternative accommodations, contact the government tourist office for the country in which you wish to stay.

Mountain huts, campgrounds

If you're a serious hiker, you may want to investigate the mountain huts that serve hikers, mountaineers, and skiers along high-country trails. Most are operated by Alpine or Scandinavian hiking or mountaineering associations in areas where no other shelter exists. Contact the appropriate government tourist offices for information.

Tourist offices can also provide general information on campgrounds and youth hostels.

FOOD & DRINK

Any traveler who ventures beyond Europe's major cities quickly learns of the interesting variety in foods and preparation methods. These change not only from country to country but also within different regions.

To penetrate a region's culinary mysteries, you must look at its geographical location and the cultural origins of its people. Each country traditionally borrows ideas and methods from its neighbors, from other nations who governed it, or from its colonies.

Regional dishes primarily reflect the products of the land. In one region you'll find an abundance of cream and butter; in another, an emphasis on hearty servings of meat and game; in a third, a spareness in cooking typical of the land itself. Seasonal foods and local wines add flair to regional menus.

Do your homework

If you want to make a self-guided food tour—or at least locate some restaurants where you'll enjoy both the food and the atmosphere—jot down appealing ones you discover in your reading. You'll find restaurant suggestions in all price categories. Ask well-traveled friends with similar tastes for recommendations.

Do a little homework to minimize the trauma when you first confront a handwritten menu in a foreign language without English subtitles. Read about a country's cuisine so you'll recognize some of the national or regional food specialties.

On the scene, ask tourist officials or your hotel concierge for suggestions. Be as specific as possible about the kind of restaurant you want—price range, location, lively or quiet ambience, and type of cuisine.

Check out local specialties

Most European restaurants post the menu outside, so you can figure out the daily specials before you even open the door. Regional wines usually pair well with the food of the same region.

If you're looking for good value, consider the menu of the day (also called the *Tagesmenu*, *menu du jour*, *menu del giorno*, or tourist menu). It is usually a 3-course meal that you can order at a clearly stated price with no extra costs except beverage.

Unless you're fluent in the local language, you'll find no substitute for a good pocket-size menu translator. It can ease the problem of deciphering menus and give you confidence to try new dishes.

Snacking on street food

Europeans believe food and the outdoors go together—in open-air markets, picnicking and other *al fresco* dining, and in food stalls located on many city street corners.

Your food sampling need not be confined to restaurants. Sidewalk snacks are popular with locals-on-the-run and offer more new food experiences for you. Food stalls and carts can also be found at festivals and street fairs.

Sausages are a favorite snack in countries with a Germanic heritage. No morning visit to Munich's outdoor Viktualienmarkt is complete without a *Weisswurst* or two, eaten with fingers at a stand-up sausage stand. Viennese often stop at a *Wurstelstand* before an evening at the opera. In Scandinavian cities, you can buy hot tasty sausages at sidewalk *Polser* stands.

Want a quick sandwich? In the Netherlands, find the nearest *broodjeswinkel*, where a soft roll is heaped with your choice of meat, fish, or salad fillings. In Germany, ask for a *Wurstsemmel* or a *Schinkensemmel* (sausage or sliced ham on a roll).

The English snack on fish and chips. Belgians enjoy their *frites*, deep-fried potatoes wrapped in paper that are sold at strategic street corners. The Dutch like raw herring, popped into the mouth and eaten with chopped raw onions.

Another Belgian favorite is *gaufres* (waffles), baked in cast-iron molds and eaten warm. Ice cream lovers find interesting flavors but varying quality.

Autumn is ushered in by the sidewalk chestnut vendors, who tempt passers-by with hot sweet chestnuts freshly roasted on small portable stoves.

Plan a picnic

Europeans enjoy eating outdoors at every opportunity. You'll see them having lunch along country roads, beside streams in the forest, or on mountain benches with a view of snowy peaks.

For travelers, a picnic provides a delightful break. Pause in your journey or sightseeing and relax outdoors. Picnics can save time if you're driving, and they allow you to avoid a large midday meal.

Selecting a spot for your picnic can be as simple as pulling off the road beneath a tree or spreading your meal on a handy bench. Memorable picnics result when a dramatic setting enhances good food and good company.

Shopping for your picnic. Buying the makings of your lunch can be part of your eating adventure.

Often you'll go from shop to shop, buying crusty rolls or a long thin loaf of bread at the bakery, meats and cheese at another store, fruit in an outdoor market, cookies or tarts in a pastry shop, a bottle of wine in a wine store. Add a bit of elegance with slices of pâté, or individual quiches or pastries. Friendly European shopkeepers are accustomed to selling foods in small portions, even single pieces or slices.

In the cities, most large department stores have a food market and delicatessen section that offers a cosmopolitan selection of hot dishes and cold foods that you can purchase in single-serving containers. They also carry an ample selection of cheese, bread, fruit, wine, and sweets.

Your picnic kit. If you plan to picnic often, bring along minimum picnic supplies from home: a corkscrew, a small serrated knife, plastic glasses, foil-packed towelettes.

You may want to include a small cutting board, miniature salt and pepper shakers, paper plates and napkins, and plastic forks and spoons. In Europe you can purchase tubes of mayonnaise, mustard, and catsup that need no refrigeration. A net or string bag is handy for carrying small purchases.

Traditions linger on

Allow time in your travels to pause and join residents in enjoying some of these long-standing traditions.

Coffee houses. A Viennese coffee house is a haven of peace where you're welcome to relax as long as you like—catching up with newspapers, conversing with friends, writing letters, enjoying coffee and pastries, or watching passers-by. You'll see habitués settling in for hours. The coffee house becomes a retreat, an office, or a drawing room. Some people even have mail sent to their

coffee houses and take their telephone calls there.

Lunch in a pub. Some of the jolliest places in Britain are the pubs, which provide food, refreshment, and sometimes entertainment and shelter for travelers. Most pubs serve simple lunches at the bar or in a separate room. Try the ploughman's lunch—a plate of hearty bread, Cheddar cheese, sliced tomatoes, and a couple of pickled onions—washed down with a pint of "bitter" beer or local ale.

Hours are strictly controlled by law. Generally, pubs are open between 11 A.M. and 10:30 P.M., but they close for 2½ or 3 hours in the afternoon (shorter hours on Sunday). Women and couples use the "saloon" or "lounge bar;" the "public bar" is traditionally a men-only preserve.

Teatime. The British take genteel pleasure in their tea, which is accompanied with marvelous breads, scones, crumpets, cakes, and dainty sandwiches. "Cream teas," with clotted cream and jam spread atop scones, are popular in Devon and Cornwall.

When you visit a Viennese *Konditorei* (confectioner's shop), you'll face a mouth-watering array of tortes, strudels, and other delectable pastries. Ordering coffee is a science in itself.

Café sitting. When the first sunny days of spring arrive, Europeans move outside. Sidewalk cafes provide one of the best places for Europe's favorite spectator sport: people-watching. Late afternoon is a pleasant time, when you can relax after the day's activities before dinner.

Tapa-sampling. Meal hours are much later in Spain than in other Western countries; the usual dinner hour is 10 P.M., though in Madrid and the south it may be even later.

If you find it difficult to last until mealtime, find a café and select from a variety of tempting hot and cold snacks called *tapas*. You can stave off hunger or make a miniature meal on the tiny hors d'oeuvres—from prawns and meatballs to fried mushrooms, cheese, open-faced sandwiches, and slices of sausage. Pair your food with beer or a glass of red or white wine or sherry.

Tapas are displayed and served at *tascas* or *mesones*, traditional Spanish bars. Patrons ease up to the counter and choose from the array. Later they'll stop at another bar to repeat the procedure.

Sherry & port sampling. In Jerez de la Frontera, Spain's sherry capital, visitors are welcomed at bodegas (cellars) to sample different sherries. Most bodegas are open to visitors Monday through Saturday in the late-morning and early-afternoon hours; they are closed on Sundays and holidays.

Oporto is the home of Portugal's famous port wine. On weekdays you can visit the wine lodges in the city's

Vila Nova de Gaia quarter to sample port and learn how it is made.

New wine. The first new wine of the season is cause for celebration in the vineyard suburbs around Vienna. A branch of greenery hanging over the door of the local *Heuriger* (wine garden) announces to passersby that the new white wine is being served inside.

In France, the arrival of the year's new Beaujolais wine in mid-November is likewise a cause for festivity in Paris and in good restaurants throughout the country.

Sweet tooth specials. If dessert is your favorite part of the meal, you'll find a grand array of pastries, cakes, fruit tarts, and other confections. Window-shop the bakeries and pastry shops. Chocolate candy reaches heavenly heights in Belgium, Holland and Switzerland.

TRAVELING WITH A SPECIAL FOCUS

If you're seeking new travel experiences, plan part of your European holiday with a special focus. It adds depth and purpose—and unexpected pleasure—to your trip. You can concentrate on a country's culture or language, or try a new sport or skill. Or mold your itinerary around one of your hobbies—such as art appreciation, food and wine, gardening, or unusual railroads. Outdoor-oriented travelers can participate in a wide range of active vacations.

Senior travelers may wish to contact the appropriate government tourist offices to learn of any special values in transportation, hotels, and sightseeing fees. Eligibility and concessions vary by country.

Most countries issue an annual calendar of events that lists the dates of folk festivals, theater and opera performances, sports events, trade fairs, and other events.

Study vacations

An increasing number of travelers use their time abroad as a learning opportunity, taking language classes or delving into a country's culture.

Many U.S. colleges and universities sponsor "study abroad" programs for travelers as well as full-time students. Among topics you can study are history, geography, fine arts, drama, music, literature, and archaeology.

You can also learn about national social programs, industries, and agriculture. Travelers take courses on topics ranging from music to wood-carving and painting. Government tourist offices can provide information on courses offered for English-speaking visitors.

Many large museums, zoological societies, and similar organizations offer trips that allow you to participate in an archaeological dig, study a region's unusual plants and animals, or learn about a nation's cultural heritage.

Outdoor holidays

If you thrive in the outdoors, why not enjoy your favorite sport in a new environment? Perhaps fishing is your idea of fun; if so, you'll find some of the world's best trout and salmon waters in Scotland and Ireland. You could investigate mountain streams in Austria and Yugoslavia, or enjoy a trout-fishing holiday in Germany's Black Forest.

If you're happiest astride a horse, you might consider a pony-trekking holiday in Iceland or Ireland, or a leisurely trip in a horse-drawn caravan (see page 131). Government tourist offices can also provide information on riding instruction and equestrian holidays.

Traveling golfers can play the historic courses of Scotland (see page 16), where golf was born centuries ago, or seek out top courses in other countries.

If you prefer to spend your days on the water, you can enjoy sailing, cruising, canoeing, kayaking, and river rafting excursions. Boating holidays are a popular way to see the countryside, whether you cruise rivers and canals as a passenger or rent your own boat.

Skin divers can explore in the clear waters off the coast and islands of Yugoslavia, Greece, and Italy.

Hiking. European hikers revel in a network of long-distance footpaths that provide access to some of

Europe's unspoiled countryside. Some routes wend through relatively flat country, and others traverse hilly and mountainous areas. Britain has several lengthy trails, including the Pennine Way, along England's rugged backbone to the Scottish border; and Offa's Dyke Path, which follows the England-Wales border between the Bristol Channel and the Irish Sea. Scandinavian long-distance trails include routes along the mountainous border between Norway and Sweden, and a footpath across Lapland. Many mountainous trails wend through the Alps.

On some routes, hikers stop at trail huts spaced a day's hike apart. You may wish to join a national or regional hiking group to obtain special member privileges. In more populated areas, walkers stay overnight in village inns, pensions, or private homes; on some group excursions, you can arrange to walk unencumbered, while a van transports the luggage.

You may prefer to insert short day hikes into your travels. From many urban areas, you can board a bus or train—or a cable car, mountain railway, or chair lift—and from its terminus follow well-marked trails across the hills or through rural countryside. Hikers and walkers can follow canalside towpaths, amble beside placid lakes, stroll above the sea, trek across lonely moors, or roam forested slopes and lush valleys. You may see villagers mowing hay, gathering grapes, making cheese, or hanging up the family laundry against a backdrop of wooded hills or snowy mountains. Frequently, though, you'll have only a few inquisitive cows or a couple of sheep for company.

City walks. In cities, it can be satisfying to focus your energy on a particular district or pursue your favorite interest or hobby. You can visit literary or artistic haunts, ancient pubs or churches, or an area with special historic ambience. City tourist offices can suggest routes or guided walking tours, or you can plot your own route with a guidebook and a good map.

London visitors might follow the footsteps of Sherlock Holmes or seek out the churches of Christopher Wren. In Paris, good city walks include the aristocratic Marais district, the historic islands in the Seine River,

and the northwest slopes of Montmartre, where you still can discover streets reminiscent of an Utrillo painting.

Cycling trips. Almost anywhere north of the Alps, you can rent bicycles and roam over paved, traffic-free roads where cycling is still a joy. Government tourist offices and local information centers can tell you where bicycles can be rented and suggest scenic routes.

You can rent a bike for an afternoon cycling excursion, or pedal with friends for a few days on a prearranged itinerary, stopping at comfortable hotels along the route. Dedicated cyclists often spend their entire holiday touring by two-wheeler.

In Holland, Denmark, and other countries, you can obtain package trips where you cycle with friends at your own pace on a preplanned itinerary. Bike rental, accommodations, and meals are arranged in advance. Trips range in length from a 3-day weekend to about 2 weeks, but most last about a week or 10 days.

Throughout northern Europe, you'll see cyclists everywhere—in large parks, along canal towpaths, pedaling from castle to castle, along scenic backroads, on island routes. In Holland, cyclists enjoy a network of bicycle paths that link villages and towns, and signposted routes lead cyclists through scenic areas.

Mountaineering. In the Alpine countries, mountaineering schools offer instruction and expeditions for both novice and experienced climbers. You can hire your own guide or join a group whose climbing skills approximate your own. Write to the appropriate government tourist office for a list of resorts where mountaineering schools are available.

Winter sports. Skiers have a choice of downhill or cross-country excursions. Famous Alpine resorts garner most of the publicity, but there are many excellent lesser-known winter sports centers with correspondingly lower rates. Your travel agent can provide information on ski packages.

In Norway, Sweden, and Finland, Nordic skiing is popular, and skiers enjoy cross-country trails in many areas. Winter sports resorts are generally casual; many skiers go ski touring from hut to hut.

Germany alone has more than 300 winter sports resorts in the Bavarian Alps and in wooded mountainous districts, such as the Harz Mountains, the Black Forest, and the Bavarian Forest. In Switzerland and Austria, cross-country skiers find many good trails.

Spain's Sierra Nevada range near Granada attracts skiers who spend the morning on the slopes and the afternoon swimming and sunbathing along the nearby Costa del Sol. Other skiers head for ski areas in the Pyrenees Mountains.

If you want to enjoy other winter sports, Alpine resorts have ice-skating rinks, ski jumps, bobsled and toboggan runs, and facilities for curling, ice hockey, ice boating, and *skijoring* (skiers towed by horse or vehicle). Nonskiers enjoy rides in horse-drawn sleighs and cable cars, snow hiking, and après-ski activity.

Hobbies & interests

If you plan your journey around a favorite hobby or interest, it adds enjoyment and may lead you to other like-minded travelers.

You can enjoy trips on steam trains and paddle-wheel steamboats, explore Roman ruins, tour historic castles and houses, make brass rubbings, visit the *ateliers* of famous painters, go cave exploring, attend music festivals, visit war museums, join a photography tour, or go hang gliding or ballooning.

You can travel independently, or join a special-interest tour. Your travel agent can usually provide suggestions. You often can learn of special-interest classes and tours in publications that cater to that specific interest.

Architecture. If you enjoy variations in architecture, take a look at Dublin's elegant Georgian squares, the handsome canal houses along Amsterdam's waterways, or the old quarters of Swiss towns, such as Lucerne and Berne.

Discover the essence of Barcelona as you wander along the Ramblas, an everchanging parade and open-air marketplace. For a personal look at the ruins of ancient Rome, take a Sunday morning walk on Palatine Hill.

Or you might focus your attention on bridges—taking a close look at structures as different as the Pont du Gard in southern France; Swiss wooden bridges across Lucerne's Reuss River; and the world's first iron bridge, built in Britain's Severn Valley in the 1770s.

If you're intrigued by windmills, you'll find plenty in Holland, of course. Examples can also be found in Denmark, Sweden, and in other areas where wind is harnessed to power machinery.

Art, antiques & books. Travelers with a special interest in certain artists or sculptors can seek out museums specializing in their work. Often you can visit their homes or studios. Some museums focus on the work of

a single artist. You can also visit the homes of many writers and see the countryside that inspired their work.

If Impressionism or modern art appeals strongly to your artistic sense, you can find specialized art museums that concentrate on particular schools of painting. In cities, art galleries offer an intriguing look at current offerings.

Travelers with a specialized interest—such as posters, botanical prints, old maps or nautical charts, lithographs, or etchings depicting early scenes—delight in seeking out specialized shops that stock these items. Often you can thumb through boxes of unframed art.

Collectors will delight in the antique shops and antiquarian and secondhand bookstores, where you can find an intriguing array. England's bookstores are a special joy; you'll discover handsomely printed volumes on your favorite topic. It's also fun to browse in sidewalk stalls.

If you're planning to ship bulky or heavy items, check with the shop owner before making your purchase. Often the shop can arrange shipping; if you must arrange packing and shipping on your own, however, it can be a complicated and time-consuming process.

Cave touring. Caves riddle Belgian's wooded Ardennes plateau, stretching east of the Meuse River. Best known of the Belgian caves is the cavern at Han-sur-Lesse, southeast of Dinant, where you tour an underground labyrinth by train. In Holland's Limburg province, caverns near Maastricht and Valkenburg sheltered inhabitants from bombing raids and served as a hiding place for valuable art during World War II.

In France, caves pierce the Massif Central in the heart of the country. Among caves you can visit is the Gouffre de Padirac, northeast of Rocamadour, where you descend into the wide, deep chasm by elevator and stairways and explore the underground galleries by boat. In France and Spain you can see prehistoric art in underground caverns.

Greece has more than 5,000 caves, and some of the best have been opened to the public. In the Alpine countries, ice caves offer a different underground perspective. If you are interested in cave tours or spelunking excursions, contact the

appropriate government tourist office to learn what is available.

Folklore. You'll find folk festivals listed in a country's calendar of events. Often local people will wear regional dress and traditional foods will be served. Visitors can often join in celebrations, such as Midsummer in Scandinavia, Oktoberfest in Munich, and many local events.

Various folklore entertainments scheduled for tourists usually include a meal followed by music, dancing, or dramatic entertainment. Some are relatively formal, but others are quite casual.

Food & wine. To learn more about a country's foods and wines, sign up for a series of regional cooking classes abroad. Some cooking classes are demonstration only; others encourage students to participate and eat the results later. Some classes are given in English, or translated into English for the students; others are given only in the local language.

Or you might join a wine-tasting or restaurant tour focusing on the foods and wines of a particular region. As a member of such a group, you may have opportunities to meet winemakers or chefs and to sample specialties of the house.

You can also plan your own restaurant and wine-sampling tour with the aid of reliable guidebooks, such as Michelin or Gault-Milleau. You can spot your travels with stops at highly rated restaurants and country inns. Reading at home will direct you to restaurants with imaginative chefs and to regional food specialties.

You'll find public food markets throughout Europe. They're colorful and fun to explore, and they offer fascinating insights into how the local people shop.

Occasionally, you can time your visit with a local festival that highlights the region's asparagus, strawberries, onions, sausage, or another local product. Many wine festivals are held in vineyard areas, and Munich's Oktoberfest draws huge crowds each September. If you'd like to include special events in your journey, ask for a calendar of events when you write for information.

Gardening. Home gardeners can obtain new ideas at outstanding demonstration and estate gardens. In

Britain, for example, you'll find publications listing many public and private gardens that are open to visitors. We've listed a few on page 8.

Floral events are scheduled throughout the year, but spring and early summer offer prime viewing in display gardens. Sometimes signposted tours guide travelers through blossom and flower districts.

At Holland's Keukenhof Gardens, you can note the bulbs and color arrangements that you particularly like. You'll also find ideas at Copenhagen's Tivoli Gardens and other public parks. Take along a notebook and camera to record combinations that appeal to you. To learn more about how commercial flowers are sold and processed for international markets, you can visit a Dutch flower auction.

If you're interested both in gardening and in art, consider a visit to Claude Monet's garden at Giverny, west of Paris (see page 28). To see Alpine plants, visit one of the Alpine gardens. There's one at Valnontey, south of Aosta, Italy (see page 95) and another in Switzerland, above Interlaken at Schynige Platte.

Flower markets bloom with color year-round; you may want to purchase a bouquet at a sidewalk stall to brighten your hotel room.

Industry on display. For a fresh perspective, include an industrial tour or two in your travels. You can learn how beer is brewed, how cheese is made, or how your favorite car is assembled. Fascinating museums also focus on industries; government tourist offices can alert you to specialized attractions.

In Britain, for example, you can learn about the beginning of the Industrial Revolution in the Severn Valley, visit the Staffordshire potteries near Stoke-on-Trent to see how china is made, learn about canal barges at the Waterways Museum at Stoke Bruerne in the Midlands, and follow the Whisky Trail (see page 17) through Scotland's Spey Valley.

Several German car makers conduct factory tours. You can see how valuable glassware is made at factories in Ireland, Sweden, and Denmark. Several leading breweries offer regular plant tours. To pursue a special interest, contact the appropriate government tourist office for the best way to proceed.

Markets. Open-air markets offer a special way to enjoy a country and its people. More fun than visiting monuments and museums, sampling Europe's outdoor markets offers a colorful, noisy, fragrant, good-humored view of a city.

Nearly every city and large town has at least one market, its origin going back centuries to when farmers brought surplus produce to the city to sell. Markets may operate nearly every day in large cities. But in most towns, market day comes once or twice a week—occasions when the happy atmosphere of a local fair prevails.

The most frequently found markets are those selling produce, but you'll find other fascinating varieties as well: flowers and plants, foods, live birds and farm animals, fish, stamps, antiques, clothing, flea markets, craft bazaars, and seasonal food specialties.

In a number of German and Austrian towns, the opening of the Christmas market signals the start of the holiday season.

Music, theater, opera. In most European capitals the primary theater, symphony, and opera season begins in autumn and runs through winter and into spring. Many special music festivals are held in the summer.

To learn about scheduled events and how to obtain tickets, contact the appropriate government tourist office. If you arrive without tickets, consult your hotel concierge about ticket availability.

Open-air museums. In many European countries, open-air folk villages preserve the architecture and life style of an earlier time. Many museum towns are rural, but some recreate town life of a century or two ago. A few depict structures of prehistoric times.

Most open-air museums welcome visitors only from April or May to September or October, but a few stay open year-round. Tourist offices can provide information about dates and hours of operation.

Visit a folk museum, and you may see farm buildings complete with animals, thatched cottages or sod-roofed log cabins, and timbered brick houses or plank-sided dwell-

ings. Shops often announce their businesses with interesting wooden or wrought iron signs. Buildings may be furnished in period style.

Sometimes (especially in summer or on weekends) you can watch costumed artisans working at the old-time crafts; some museums have adjoining craft shops. In summer, costumed entertainers occasionally perform folk songs and dances.

A few touring suggestions: Weekends are busy days, when many local folks visit; however, the museum towns have more vitality when people are present. Try to go on a sunny day. Obtain a guidebook and map at the entrance, and check to see if any special events (craft demonstrations, music, dancing) are scheduled. Try to get an overview first with a guided tour or a ride around the grounds; then you can go back to see the buildings you want to inspect more closely.

Railroads. If you have a passion for riding the rails, you'll find some delightful narrow-gauge railways and steam trains in Europe.

Britain has dozens of steam trains that operate in all parts of the country. Switzerland and Austria both have a number of narrow-gauge railways that you can ride. You can also take a Swiss cog-wheel mountain railway from Brienz up to the Brienzer Rothorn (page 81) for a panoramic view of the Bernese Alps. Government tourist offices can provide information on unusual train excursions.

Other ideas. Your experiences can be as varied as your imagination allows. You could visit city zoos or war museums, seek out the Roman heritage in various countries, make rubbings in historic churches or cemeteries, or just dedicate yourself to sampling the beer or chocolate in every country you visit.

SHOPPING FOR CRAFTS

One of the most enjoyable mementos of your European journey may be a distinctive handcrafted article, perhaps purchased from the person who made it. You can choose handmade objects for the home, clothing, jewelry, toys, or intricate Christmas ornaments and carvings.

You'll find handcrafted pottery and ceramics, glassware, wood carvings, lace and embroidery, jewelry and filigree work, carpets, handwoven textiles, metalwork, woven straw and wickerwork, basketry, and leatherwork.

Starting the search

To learn more about a country's crafts, and possibly visit a workshop or two, where do you start?

Government tourist offices can often direct you to permanent design centers, craft centers, and rural cooperatives where you can see excellent examples of regional work. In your travel reading, jot down regions noted for specific crafts.

In Britain and Ireland, you can purchase comprehensive guidebooks at tourist information centers that list regional workshops and retail outlets.

Design & craft centers

In some countries, government sponsored handicraft stores offer regional work in provincial capitals and tourist centers. Look for *Heimatwerk* shops in Austria and Switzerland, *Artespaña* stores in Spain, and *Narodna Radinost* shops in Yugoslavia.

During your British travels, look for craft displays at National Trust shops (on the sites of many NT properties). You'll find quality crafts for sale in shops like Craftcentre Cymru, which has regional outlets throughout Wales. In Ireland, stop at government-sponsored Kilkenny Design Workshops. You can watch demonstrations of traditional Dutch crafts at the Holland Handicraft Centre, located between Hoorn and Enkhuizen.

Workshop visits

Some of the most satisfying—and economical—craft shopping is done on the scene, direct from the artist. Local tourist offices can direct you to workshops that welcome visitors. Roadside signs also alert you to rural artisans and country crafts shops.

You can watch glass blowers work in sites as diverse as tiny Wolfach, deep in Germany's Black Forest; the French Riviera hill town of Biot; and the Norwegian fortress town of Fredrikstad, south of Oslo.

Wood furniture is still painted by hand in the Dutch village of Hindeloopen. Wood-carvers fashion intricate figures in mountain valleys throughout Europe.

Good cooks take special pleasure selecting French copper cookware in the Normandy town of Villedieu-les-Poêles, where it has been made for several hundred years.

If you don't have luggage space for your purchases, inquire about shipping *before* you buy. Most shops do not have packing and shipping facilities.

Classes & tours

If you're interested in expanding your craft skills, consider studying with an English-speaking artisan or joining a craft-oriented tour with workshop sessions. Hobby magazines may be helpful in directing you to craft-oriented classes and tours.

SUNDAY IN THE CITY

On Sunday, a city shows a different face. Stores are closed, theaters and many restaurants are dark, and traffic diminishes. For one day each week, the city pauses—and allows you to see its residents at play.

Earlier in the week, inquire at the local tourist office if any special weekend events are scheduled in the city or nearby areas. Perhaps you'll discover a local wine festival, a folklore celebration, a sports event, or a riverside band concert that you'd like to attend.

Many persons enjoy visiting Europe's churches to admire the lofty architecture and stained-glass windows. Sunday services add pageantry and music.

Explore the city

With the aid of a good guidebook, plan your own walk through an interesting or historic section of the city. Or join an organized group walk; in London, these often begin at Underground stations and encompass sights on a general theme, such as historic pubs.

Sunday is the week's busiest day at many museums, so plan to arrive early. In addition to superb art exhibits, you'll discover many special-interest museums.

Visit the park. Europe's city parks are a delight. Weekend afternoons, you'll see entire families relaxing—children sailing toy boats on ponds or watching Punch and Judy shows, young men in striped jerseys playing soccer, couples strolling along tidy gravel paths through beds of blooming flowers. You may want to go cycling or rent a rowboat. You can also pause to enjoy a band concert, relax in an outdoor café, or just sit on a bench and watch the people flow by.

Go to the zoo. Another great place for Sunday people-watching is the city zoo, where families are both entertained and educated by the world's animals and birds.

Prowl in the market. Sunday shoppers head for city flea markets, where they browse amid colorful stalls of antiques and other used merchandise. Hucksters shout their wares over the noisy throngs.

Take an excursion

No visit to a large city is complete without a look at nearby attractions. The city tourist information office can provide destination suggestions and advice on how to get there using public transportation.

Walk in the woods. Join city families for a Sunday walk in the forest. Plan ahead and purchase picnic supplies. Often you'll find wooded areas within the city itself, or you can head for the suburbs.

Board a boat. Most large European cities are built along the coast or bordering a major inland waterway. For fresh perspectives of the city, take a sightseeing cruise—on the harbor, lake, river, fjord, or canal.

On some trips you can disembark at your destination and return on a later boat.

SEEKING FAMILY TIES

Many travelers combine European travel with a bit of amateur genealogy when they visit the land from which their ancestors emigrated. Searching for family ties in "the old country" can be personally fulfilling and add pleasure to your holiday, as you learn more about your family origins and gain a new sense of identity.

Even if you don't add a new limb to your family tree, the effort provides an opportunity to make new friends who will try to help you find your cousins or trace your ancestors.

Your search may lead to out-of-the-way hamlets. Perhaps you'll walk the same narrow old streets to the house where your great-great-grandparents lived a century or more ago. In the parish cemetery, weathered tombstones may provide a tangible link with the past.

Before you depart on a roots-finding trip, write to the appropriate tourist information office to learn exactly what facts and records will be most helpful in your search and how best to proceed.

Try to learn in advance the town or region of your family's origin; their birth dates; name of their parish church; what they did for a living (tenant farmer, laborer, servant, fisherman); and when the family migrated to the New World and where they settled.

Ask older relatives and longtime family friends for precise information about deceased family members, and keep a separate record of pertinent dates and facts for each ancestor you learn about. Examine written family records, including Bibles, birth and marriage certificates, correspondence, documents, diaries, photograph albums, and scrapbooks.

Your local library or historical society can direct you to a variety of sources and give you suggestions on how to proceed in your genealogical research.

The search can be a diverting challenge, leading to interesting places you'd otherwise have missed. When you know your family's hometown or region of origin, check with the local tourist office or town authorities to learn where records are kept. Registrars in vital statistics offices maintain records of births, marriages, and deaths. In some countries, church registers go back for centuries and are a vital source of family information.

On-the-spot research is far from dull. Discovering an original handwritten record penned by a contemporary of your great-grandfather may give you a special thrill. And each time you discover a new clue, your sense of excitement renews the urge for further research.

WINTER VISITS

When the summer crowds depart, Europe settles back to relax and enjoy itself. Travelers in the off-season find a different holiday experience on the Continent.

During the mellow days of autumn, woods turn from green to gold. Harvest and wine festivals dot the calendar. A new arts season begins in autumn, featuring an impressive array of concerts, opera, ballet, and drama in the major cities.

Winter visitors enjoy numerous folk celebrations, fairs, and markets —but these are events geared to residents rather than tourists. In the mountains, snow signals the beginning of another ski season.

In the winter months, you'll find faster and more cheerful service, less waiting in line, and time to relax and enjoy surroundings.

Winter is the festive time. If you're planning a visit during the holidays, you'll find Christmas markets in Germany and Austria; carol singing around the tall Christmas tree in London's Trafalgar Square; and torchlight processions in southern France. Zurich brings out its bright red Fairy-Tale Tram.

In many countries, the pre-Lenten Carnival (or Fasching) season is a time of great revelry. At fancy-dress balls, costumed processions, and outdoor dancing, participants kick up their heels in celebration.

Great outbursts of religious fervor and splendor mark the Holy Week celebrations in Spain. In Greece, Easter is the year's most important holiday.

You'll also find colorful festivities to bid good-bye to winter and greet spring. Farming traditions to ensure a good crop are preserved in some rural areas. In Spain, springtime is a joyous season with fairs and pilgrimages. In many German and Austrian villages, maypoles are decorated with greenery and ribbons on May 1, and villagers join in dancing and merrymaking.

INDEX

Sunset
Proof-of-Purchase
ISBN 0-376-06174-X

PHOTO CREDITS

Inga Aistrup/National Travel Association of Denmark: 54. **Dave Bartruff:** 112, 114, 122 top right. **Morton Beebe/Image Bank:** 26 bottom left, 104, 121. **Jon Brenneis:** 15, 44, 101, 109, 119. **Kathleen N. Brenzel:** 115. **Jack Cannon:** 26 center left and bottom right, 93, 97. **Ron Carlson:** 62. **Ken Cooperrider:** 102 center left. **Betty Crowell:** 52, 78 bottom, 126. **David Falconer:** 71. **Richard Fish:** 34. **Shirley Maas Fockler:** 55. **Cornelia Fogle:** 20 center left, 40 bottom, 42, 50 bottom left and bottom center, 68 top right, 74. **Lee Foster:** 40 top, 45. **Fremdenverkehrsverbad Hallstatt:** 84 top. **Jon Gardey:** 25, 122 bottom right. **F. Grehan/Image Bank:** 80. **Richard Gross:** 90 top right. **Keith Gunnar:** 70. **Bruce Hayes:** 68 bottom left, 84 bottom left and bottom center, 89. **Dave G. Houser:** 1, 18, 20 top left, 23, 30, 65, 86, 110 center, 113, 124, 125. **Kess Photo:** 10, 90 center left. **Russell Lamb:** 2, 33, 37, 47, 68 top left, 77, 102 right and bottom left. **L. Linkhart:** 122 bottom left. **Milt & Joan Mann:** 48. **Steve W. Marley:** 22. **Ruth Mason:** 110 top. **Mary Ord:** 6 left. **Tim Ord:** 8 top. **Karen Stafford Rantzman:** 90 bottom. **Richard Rowan:** 66. **William Rubenstein:** 72. **John Running:** 95. **David Ryan:** 57. **Claire Rydell:** 116 center and bottom left. **Ron Sanford:** 6 center right, 17, 19, 20 top right, 29, 38, 50 top, 58, 78 top right, 107, 110 bottom, 116 bottom center, back cover. **Ted Streshinsky:** 98. **Swiss National Tourist Office:** 78 top left, 83. **Darrow M. Watt:** 6 top right, 12, 50 right, 61. **Nikolay Zurek:** 40 center.